MARRIAGE AND THE MORAL IMAGINATION

This fresh and engaging book opens up new terrain in the exploration of marriage and kinship. While anthropologists and sociologists have often interpreted marriage, and kinship more broadly, in conservative terms, Carsten highlights their transformative possibilities. The book argues that marriage is a close encounter with difference on the most intimate scale, carrying the seeds of social transformation alongside the trappings of conformity. Grounded in rich ethnography and the author's many decades of familiarity with Malaysia, it asks a central question: What does marriage do, and how? Exploring the implications of the everyday imaginative labour of marriage for kinship relations and wider politics, this work offers an important and highly original contribution to anthropology, family and kinship studies, sociology and Southeast Asian studies.

JANET CARSTEN is Emeritus Professor of Social and Cultural Anthropology at the University of Edinburgh. Her work focuses on the anthropology of kinship, encompassing domesticity, the house, bodily substance, migration and memory. She is the author of *After Kinship* (2004) and *Blood Work: Life and Laboratories in Penang* (2019).

NEW DEPARTURES IN ANTHROPOLOGY

New Departures in Anthropology is a book series that focuses on emerging themes in social and cultural anthropology. With original perspectives and syntheses, authors introduce new areas of inquiry in anthropology, explore developments that cross disciplinary boundaries, and weigh in on current debates. Every book illustrates theoretical issues with ethnographic material drawn from current research or classic studies, as well as from literature, memoirs, and other genres of reportage. The aim of the series is to produce books that are accessible enough to be used by college students and instructors, but will also stimulate, provoke and inform anthropologists at all stages of their careers. Written clearly and concisely, books in the series are designed equally for advanced students and a broader range of readers, inside and outside academic anthropology, who want to be brought up to date on the most exciting developments in the discipline.

Series Editorial Board

Michael Lambek, University of Toronto
Laura Bear, London School of Economics and Political Science
Naveeda Khan, Johns Hopkins University

Marriage and the Moral Imagination

JANET CARSTEN
University of Edinburgh

Shaftesbury Road, Cambridge CB2 8EA, United Kingdom

One Liberty Plaza, 20th Floor, New York, NY 10006, USA

477 Williamstown Road, Port Melbourne, VIC 3207, Australia

314–321, 3rd Floor, Plot 3, Splendor Forum, Jasola District Centre, New Delhi – 110025, India

103 Penang Road, #05–06/07, Visioncrest Commercial, Singapore 238467

Cambridge University Press is part of Cambridge University Press & Assessment, a department of the University of Cambridge.

We share the University's mission to contribute to society through the pursuit of education, learning and research at the highest international levels of excellence.

www.cambridge.org
Information on this title: www.cambridge.org/9781009601023

DOI: 10.1017/9781009601030

© Janet Carsten 2026

This publication is in copyright. Subject to statutory exception and to the provisions of relevant collective licensing agreements, no reproduction of any part may take place without the written permission of Cambridge University Press & Assessment.

When citing this work, please include a reference to the DOI 10.1017/9781009601030

First published 2026

Cover credit: Keystone-France via Getty Images

A catalogue record for this publication is available from the British Library

Library of Congress Cataloging-in-Publication Data
NAMES: Carsten, Janet author
TITLE: Marriage and the moral imagination / Janet Carsten, University of Edinburgh.
DESCRIPTION: Cambridge, United Kingdom ; New York, NY : Cambridge University Press, 2026. | Series: New departures in anthropology | Includes bibliographical references and index.
IDENTIFIERS: LCCN 2025024729 (print) | LCCN 2025024730 (ebook) | ISBN 9781009601047 hardback | ISBN 9781009601030 ebook
SUBJECTS: LCSH: Marriage – Social aspects | Marriage – Moral and ethical aspects
CLASSIFICATION: LCC HQ515 .C38 2026 (print) | LCC HQ515 (ebook)
LC record available at https://lccn.loc.gov/2025024729
LC ebook record available at https://lccn.loc.gov/2025024730

ISBN 978-1-009-60104-7 Hardback
ISBN 978-1-009-60102-3 Paperback

Cambridge University Press & Assessment has no responsibility for the persistence or accuracy of URLs for external or third-party internet websites referred to in this publication and does not guarantee that any content on such websites is, or will remain, accurate or appropriate.

For EU product safety concerns, contact us at Calle de José Abascal, 56, 1°, 28003 Madrid, Spain, or email eugpsr@cambridge.org

For Jonathan and Jessica

Contents

Acknowledgements		*page* viii
	Introduction: Marriage and the Moral Imagination	1
1	Anthropological Engagements: Fieldwork, Marriage, Malaysia and Penang	29
2	Marriage and Gender in the Political Moment	54
3	Marriage over the Generations	91
4	Marriage in the Flux of Self-Fashioning	119
5	Negotiating Difference in Marriage: Conjugality and 'Mixing'	144
6	Those Who Leave and Those Who Stay: Marital Uncertainties Narrated through Time	178
7	Imagining Conjugal Futures: The Personal and the Political	208
	Conclusion	241
Bibliography		255
Index		271

Acknowledgements

Works of anthropology rest on many kinds of collaboration and support. This is especially true when they are not only the product of recent research but also the outcome of long-term engagements with particular places, institutions and people – as is the case here. I am acutely aware of the debts accrued over many years to teachers, colleagues, research participants, students, friends and family, not all of whom are named here, who have made this book possible. Remaining flaws, of which I am all too conscious, are mine alone.

The research and much of the writing for this book were funded by a European Research Council (ERC) Advanced Grant under the European Union's Horizon 2020 Research and Innovation programme, grant agreement No. 695285 AGATM ERC-2015-AdG, held at the University of Edinburgh from 2017 to 2022. It is a pleasure to acknowledge this funding here. The work was uniquely shaped by its development as a collaborative project, 'A Global Anthropology of Transforming Marriage' (AGATM), for which I was Principal Investigator. It was conceived as a multi-stranded programme carried out by different researchers in five very different contexts. Concurrently with my own project on marriage and 'middle-classification' in Penang, Malaysia, Hsiao-Chiao Chiu worked on marriage under different political and economic regimes over the twentieth century in Taiwan and China; Siobhan Magee researched religious and legal contestations over marriage in Virginia in the US;

Acknowledgements

Eirini Papadaki examined marriage under conditions of economic austerity in Athens, Greece; Koreen Reece worked on marriage in the context of the HIV/AIDS crisis in Botswana. The design, implementation and analysis of themes from our work were carried out in close conversation. Being able to visit the different research sites and discuss our work together over a period of five years – and still ongoing – established an extraordinarily rich discussion that has informed and nourished the insights developed here. I am more grateful than I can say to Hsiao-Chiao Chiu, Siobhan Magee, Eirini Papadaki and Koreen Reece for their intellectual inspiration as well as their warmth and enthusiasm.

The collaborative nature of the research encouraged me to take a broad perspective on the personal, familial and political import of marriage beyond what is specific to Malaysia or Penang. Members of the Advisory Committee of AGATM – Ammara Maqsood, Sidharthan Maunaguru, John McInnes, Susan McKinnon, Perveez Mody and David Sabean – generously gave their support and comments on our work at different stages – I thank them all. I am very grateful to all the participants at a workshop on 'Marriage in Past, Present, and Future Tense: Biography, Intimacy, and Transformation', held at the University of Edinburgh in September 2019, for their insightful and constructive comments and suggestions. I thank Alex Edmonds and Toby Kelly for their comments on drafts of the grant application and Sarah Walker for help with collecting bibliographic materials as the project was getting under way.

In Penang, I owe an enormous debt to all those who helped with the research, especially to those who agreed to be interviewed, and who are anonymised in the chapters that follow. Telling me their own and their family stories constituted extraordinary gestures of trust, which I hope I have not betrayed here. I am extremely grateful to Professor Dr Nor Hafizah Selamat for providing local sponsorship for the research, and to her and Professor Dato' Dr Noraida Endut for facilitating affiliation in the form of an Honorary Professorship at KANITA at Universiti Sains Malaysia as well as for their advice and support. Khoo Salma Nasution

Acknowledgements

and Abdur-Razzaq Lubis provided their unique knowledge of Penang, helpful advice, contacts and hospitable support throughout my research. Professor Dato' Dr Wazir Jahan Begum Karim and Professor Dato' Dr Mohd Razha Rashid have been there from the beginning of my engagement with Malaysia in the 1980s, generously offering stimulation, advice, conversation, brilliant hospitality and the blessings of long friendship to me and to my family during many visits to Penang.

I am very grateful to the Economic Planning Unit (EPU) of the Prime Minister's Department of the government of Malaysia and the State Government of Penang for permission to carry out the research. I thank members of staff at the Women's Centre for Change, the Penang Institute, the Penang Heritage Trust, the Penang Women's Development Corporation, Sisters in Islam, lawyers in Penang and others who generously gave their time for discussion, suggested contacts and provided background information. In Penang and Kuala Lumpur, Dr Yeoh Seng Guan gave his generous encouragement and advice. I thank Professor Shanthi Tambiah and Dr Rusaslina Idrus at University of Malaya for their advice and hospitality. For occasional assistance with the research in Penang at different times, I thank Mazidah Musa and Praveena Balakrishnan. Gwynn Jenkins has been a special friend as well as a knowledgeable source of advice during research trips to Penang and since; Rebecca Duckett-Wilkinson was a wonderful and generous landlady; Gareth Richards has been an extraordinarily skilled and erudite interlocutor. I am deeply grateful to all of them for their friendship.

Papers and talks based on material in this book have been given at seminars and invited lectures at the University of Cambridge, the London School of Economics, University of Malaya and Universiti Sains Malaysia. I am very grateful to audiences and participants at all these events for their suggestions, questions and comments. An earlier version of Chapter 4 was previously published under the title 'Marriage and self-fashioning in Penang, Malaysia: transformations of the intimate and the political', in Carsten, J., Chiu, H-C., Magee, S., Papadaki, E. and Reece,

Acknowledgements

K.M. (eds) 2021, *Marriage in Past, Present and Future Tense*, London: UCL Press. I am grateful for permission to use this material here.

Earlier drafts of chapters were written under the special conditions of the COVID-19 pandemic; later ones were revised in sometimes anxious times. I owe huge thanks to my Edinburgh friends, Sue Fyvel, Fran Wasoff and Lorraine Waterhouse for cups of tea, lunches, walks and encouragement throughout. Colleagues and students in Social Anthropology at the University of Edinburgh have been unfailingly supportive and constructive at every stage of research and writing.

I am very grateful to the editors of the New Departures in Anthropology series, and especially to Michael Lambek, for encouragement and support as well as for comments on an earlier version of the chapters. David Repetto at CUP expertly steered this volume through to publication together with Anna Hubbard, Sari Wastell, Hemapriya Eswanth and Anjali Kumari. I am grateful to Sarah Veeck for indexing.

Finally, I thank Jessica Spencer and Jonathan Spencer who have lived with the research and writing of this book since the beginning in Edinburgh and in Penang. Jessica brought her unique blend of wise counsel, humour, incisive intelligence and loving support to every stage. Jonathan's guidance and editorial advice have helped shape this work, as has the long conversation about novels and films that we began together more than thirty years ago. The moral imagination of marriage has been a joint project, and he has been its unwavering, generous and rock-like centre.

Introduction

Marriage and the Moral Imagination

What does it mean to marry or not to marry, to become or to be married, to stay married – or not – over many years? How do women and men reflect on these different states and experiences? On the one hand, so ubiquitous, much-discussed and apparently conventional as to seem hardly worth new exploration, on the other, fraught with contradictions and paradox – what are we to make of contemporary marriage? In spite of widespread anxiety about the demise of the modern family, exemplified in rising divorce and non-marriage rates as well as falling fertility levels, marriage nevertheless remains popular. Moralistic talk about marriage and the family is not confined to Western contexts but occurs in many parts of the world, including Malaysia, from where the ethnography in this book is drawn, and other Asian countries. Notwithstanding such concerns, weddings continue to be a central life course ritual (and major expense) for many people around the world – as witnessed during the COVID-19 pandemic when the impossibility of celebrating marriages publicly was the subject of bitter disappointment. Marriage, in short, has not gone away either as an institution or as a subject of literary, cinematic, social, personal or familial interest. It remains an abiding public and private concern, as well as a central relationship in many people's lives. This is one starting point for this book.

In the sociological and anthropological imagination, marriage often seems to encapsulate many unspoken assumptions. But what are we

Marriage and the Moral Imagination

really talking about when we talk about marriage? How are marriages located in a particular place and at a particular historical moment? Embodying conservatism, continuity and conventionality, marriage may seem devoid of obvious interest for those focused on political crises and change in the contemporary world. Indeed, recent anthropology of kinship and relatedness has often left it to one side in favour of more obviously contemporary concerns, such as assisted reproduction, technology, LGBTQ activism or migration. A second starting point, then, is that much of what we, as social scientists, think we know about marriage is built on assumption rather than close scrutiny. It might yet be possible to consider this seemingly too-familiar institution in new ways.

One under-examined assumption is that marriage *reacts to* rather than initiating or constructing change. We assume that marriage, as a conservative institution, changes in the face of external pressure rather than itself generating wider change. In this view, political crises, technological developments, health or activism captivate anthropological interest as apparent sources and indicators of social transformation. Kinship and marriage (merely) respond to such forces. In this book, I show how marriage, rather than simply reproducing what was there before, is itself a site of creativity and innovation.

But how does marriage produce or reflect continuity or rupture between generations and the connections and disjunctions between personal, familial and wider social and political settings? To answer this question requires a close-grained scrutiny of marital experiences – something that anthropologists of relatedness are well-placed to provide. The kinds of innovation and creativity that I consider here are small-scale, occurring in intimate or familial realms and difficult to discern. But over time, they have incremental effects that travel beyond individual relationships to families and communities, and to wider publics and polities. Indeed, I argue that marriage may be a potent source of political transformation. This is not of course to say that the experiences which generate these shifts are inherently positive. On the contrary, it may well be the case that negative experiences, for example, of abusive or violent relations, have a greater potential to generate changes in perception and values about how relationships ought to be conducted than positive ones. There are examples of these in the chapters that follow.

This brings me to a third starting point for this book. Perhaps the most obvious sign of a deep shift in values regarding marital and other personal relations in many (but not all) parts of the world is the acceptance and legal institution of same-sex marriage. This profound change, which not many would have predicted even a few decades ago (see, for example, Borneman 1996, 1997), can hardly be attributed to a single cause.[1] It is implausible to suggest that it has come about simply through the enforcement of a political or legal statute. Instead, we need to account for the alterations to moral values that have made such a major transformation to a seemingly normative institution widely desirable and achievable. And at the same time we should consider other, parallel shifts in values concerning personal and gendered relations that suggest patterns to how change occurs. But there are parts of the world where same-sex marriage is deeply resisted or the subject of bitter contestation – Malaysia, from where the ethnography in this book is drawn, among them. I suggest that we need to explore the realm of personal and familial relations anthropologically to better understand these institutionalised and often highly polarised processes – without omitting negative experiences as part of this story.

Marriage, as Chapters 3–7 of this book show, is the site of much moral and imaginative labour as conjugal partners and members of their respective families grapple with its everyday relational problems. Indeed, it might be considered unique as an institution in the way that it draws 'others' into a close realm of intimacy. Because it brings together

---

[1] Part of Borneman's argument was that anthropologists were overly preoccupied with marriage because of its normativity, paying it too much attention, and devoting too little to other – and less normative – relations of care (see also Blackwood 2005; Carsten et al. 2021, 8–9).

spouses and their relatives, who may have more or less familiarity with each other, from backgrounds that may be more or less similar, marriage requires planning and consideration of different priorities and points of view – as the often fraught arrangements for weddings attest. But after the rituals have been completed, on a more everyday level, this moral and imaginative work continues – albeit with more or less positive outcomes, and often with considerable gendered imbalance – as conjugal partners accommodate (or not) to each other, making compromises or holding their ground at different times and on different issues, and sometimes subject to abuse or threat. This everyday, ordinary and ongoing, moral labour, which is closely linked to the way marriage requires accommodating others in the intimate zones of familial life, is not generally hidden from view – on the contrary, it is the subject of much consideration and reflection. Contrary to the impression given by some of the recent literature on the anthropology of ethics (as discussed later in this chapter), moral labour does not centre only on heroic figures grappling on their own with ethical conundrums, but with people who are thoroughly embedded in relationality. And yet the implications of this ethical and imaginative work for marriage – and for kinship relations more broadly – have hardly been considered by those concerned with the anthropology of kinship and relatedness.

To grasp the nature and import of this moral and imaginative labour requires exploring how people consider and reflect on their own marital experiences and those of others they know comparatively through time – a terrain perhaps more often inhabited by novelists and filmmakers than anthropologists. It requires a close familiarity with protagonists and the contexts in which they live. In this book, that context is Penang, Malaysia, a place I have been familiar with for more than forty years. I take up this long engagement – my own, more personal starting point – alongside the unexpected parallels between marriage and anthropology in Chapter 1. Penang, as I explain there, has many special attributes. One of these is its unusually diverse demographic composition and cultural

Introduction

heritage. This ethnic, linguistic, religious and cultural diversity makes it a particularly apt location for a study of marriage that focuses on the ethical and imaginative work that marriage entails. Marriage across lines of religious, ethnic or class differences requires explicit imaginative and moral labour. Such boundary-crossing and its concomitant ethical and imaginative work can hardly be ignored in Penang. But the moral dilemmas confronted by the protagonists of this book – of whether to diverge from parental paths, or how closely to follow conventions, of grappling with uncertainty, insecurity and infidelity, whether to stay with or leave a marriage, whether to transgress social boundaries of religion or ethnicity or to come out to parents – are not particular to Penang. Readers will be familiar with many of them from their own lives. In this way, though strongly anchored in particular personal biographies and social contexts, the arguments of this book are broad and general.

Continuity and Difference in Marriage

The accounts of two women in Penang – I will call them Lydia and Haryath – about their own and other marriages in their families have stayed with me through the writing of this book. Lydia was of mixed Chinese-Malaysian and British background; Haryath came from a Sikh family. Both were in their mid-fifties and well-placed to reflect forward and backward in time. In different ways, their narratives touched on many of the themes of this book, and I return to their stories again in the Conclusion to draw together these intertwining themes. Each of them spoke to me about marriages in different generations of their families to explore both continuities and contrasts with their own. Their reflections underlined how considering and experiencing a marriage is a process of comparative evaluation with other similar or dissimilar relations over time. For Haryath, a sister's unhappy marriage, which had ended in divorce, was evoked as a negative example of what to avoid. Lydia was more eloquent about the continuities in her family and about marriage as a creative partnership involving family and work. But here too a negative example – in this case of her maternal grandmother's troubled relations with her in-laws in the early part of the twentieth century – seemed to exert a powerful hold on her own marital imaginary. Explicitly in Haryath's case, and more implicitly in Lydia's, both accounts evoked a tension in marriage between convention and nonconformity. In many respects, the marriage of each of them could be seen as in keeping with the norms of their respective families and communities. But Haryath spoke eloquently of 'breaking the rules' and 'running red lights' in her marriage, and Lydia's artistic and creative endeavours, as well as her mixed background, had laid a trajectory of less conventional possibilities within marriage as what she called 'a working partnership'. There is an implication here that conventions and rules implicitly carry their own potential disruptions, which we will meet again in Chapter 6.

The productive potential of comparative reflection about marriage over time and generations is at the heart of this book, as is the tension between the conventionality that marriage appears to embody and the possibility of doing things differently within it. It is the significance of these entwined and seemingly muted processes, which together express the continuity and change of marriage, that I explore in this work. The accounts of marriage to which I listened in Penang convey the trajectories of families through time. Talking about marriage, as Lydia's and Haryath's narratives made plain, involves reflecting on family life, often over several generations. These reflections were mainly, initially at least, elicited in response to my questions, but the enthusiasm and expansiveness of responses underlined how my enquiries resonated with the concerns of those I spoke to and interviewed. Respondents talked of matters to which they had clearly already given thought, and which they seemed to enjoy relating. Their narrations encompassed judgements about how things were done in the past, and how differently – or similarly – they are done today, or might be done in the future. This evocation of the past,

Introduction

present and future – the multiple temporalities of marriage (Carsten et al. 2021; Maqsood 2024, 68) – articulates and contributes to the continuity of kinship. Processes of kinship are at least partly about ensuring the persistence of families and property (Bourdieu 2008, Chapter 1), even if this aim may not necessarily be successful. In this way, they have reproduction in the broadest sense at their core.

Continuity in kinship rests on a balance between reproducing sameness – which, at the limits, would create stasis – and producing difference – which, at the limits, would be the antithesis of continuity. Marriage has a crucial place here in the reproduction of families, balanced as it is between these two poles.[2] In the accounts of marriage that are articulated in this book, there is a tension between sameness and difference, a tension more commonly articulated in the anthropological literature as between endogamy and exogamy (see, for example, Carsten 1997, Chapter 7). If marriage necessarily introduces new and different elements into the zone of the close family, too much difference poses a threat to the values and integrity of existing family life and sometimes wider communities, while too little difference may pose other challenges – of boredom, sameness, stultification or, at the extreme, connotations of incest (Lévi-Strauss 1969 [1949]). Striking the 'right' balance (Clark-Decès 2014) of difference and sameness, often expressed in idioms of complementarity, marriage carries with it possibilities of transformation – personal, familial and political – alongside what may be experienced as the comfort and assurance of continuity. What we often see as 'continuity' in kinship thus inevitably encapsulates change. Marriage has a crucial role in the reproduction of difference, which is a requirement for both change and continuity. The moral and imaginative labour of marriage is thus partly about finding the right balance of continuity and difference that makes change bearable and sustainable over time, and sometimes over generations. As

---

[2] See also Bourdieu (2008, 12) on marriage as continuity.

Marriage and the Moral Imagination

Ammara Maqsood writes, 'Marriage is one such intimate site where difference does not collapse but becomes a means through which people relate to one another, evaluate their relationships, and make sense of their lives' (Maqsood 2024, 60). Time may enhance the possibilities for changes to endure and to ripple out from one marriage to others. In the stories of individual marriages and families recounted by Lydia and Haryath and others in this book, we can observe how these somewhat abstract considerations are experienced and expressed by individuals in the most immediate, emotionally salient and visceral ways. They are at the heart of many people's everyday and intimate experiences of life, both their difficulties and what they most value. Lydia's evocation of the vicissitudes of her grandmother's life or Haryath's more veiled allusions to her sister made clear that kinship continuity can be lived as violence and threat rather than offering the comfort of familiarity. Conjugal relations may provide negative models of what to avoid rather than the stuff of emulation.

The recurring touchstone of creativity that was present in Lydia's account (in her own marriage as well as that of her parents) gave pause for thought. Creativity and a working partnership were at the heart of Lydia's marital story, as was the case for many others without necessarily being so clearly articulated. In her narrative, marriage emerged as an encounter with difference that occurs on the smallest and most intimate scale but contributes to, and is part of, larger historical change. The marriage of Lydia's parents in the 1950s had incorporated and was lived alongside the geopolitical shifts of the Cold War in the form of the 'Malayan Emergency', which had brought Lydia's father to Malaya from England on his compulsory military service at the very end of the colonial era. Building a life there after his army service, his encounter with Lydia's mother, from a Chinese and working-class background, led to a marriage that at least partly encapsulated a rejection of some of the forms of colonial and immediate post-colonial relations, which embargoed marriage across 'racial' lines.

Introduction

Marriage, as I argue here, is a close encounter with difference on the most intimate scale that carries with it the seeds of social transformation as much as the trappings of conformity. These contradictory qualities are amplified through the deceptively obvious dual nature of marriage as at once a private, intimate relation and a public one. Both transformation and conformity matter, and they co-produce each other just as the private and public aspects of marriage do. But partly because anthropologists and sociologists often interpret marriage – and indeed kinship – largely in conservative terms, I have tended in this book to emphasise the transformative possibilities of marriage. While marriage is the focus of this study, it should be clear that the argument pertains to kinship relations more generally – partly because of the centrality of marriage to kinship, but also because the generative qualities of ethical imagination that I describe apply to relatedness more broadly. Rejecting assumptions that prioritise the state as the driver of political change, and the separation of the domains of kinship and politics on which this model rests (see Carsten 2004; McKinnon and Cannell 2013b; Thelen and Alber 2018), I explore how familial worlds can, sometimes, imperceptibly and gradually, engender social transformation.

The Anthropology of Marriage: A Short Prelude

Since anthropology's nineteenth-century beginnings, marriage has held a central place because of the way it brings together economy, law, property, religion and kinship. Rather than providing an exhaustive account of the extensive literature here, I pick out some key points relevant for the discussion that follows (see also Carsten et al. 2021, 6–13). Nineteenth-century social theorists, such as Henry Maine, Lewis Henry Morgan, John Stuart Mill and Friedrich Engels, concerned with the late Victorian 'woman question' or 'marriage question' – a set of debates about women's rights, property and divorce – saw marriage as a political institution rather than an individual one. Their discussions, cast in evolutionary terms, were part of the British and North American societies in which they lived. These discussions can be considered too as part of the backdrop to some of the classic mid-twentieth-century anthropological studies of marriage, which were explicitly articulated against this evolutionary framing, but continued to consider marriage as a central social institution, and were concerned primarily with its political and economic importance (see, for example, Evans-Pritchard 1951; Fortes 1949; Lévi-Strauss 1969; Radcliffe-Brown and Forde 1950). The protagonists in anthropological debates at the time argued fiercely about the primacy of principles of 'descent' versus 'alliance' (in other words, relations between different generations of kin as opposed to those between groups that were connected through prescribed marital alliances). Today, these differences seem in many ways less significant than what they held in common – a firm understanding of marriage as a social institution that concerned groups rather than individuals and a close attention to formal rules governing choice of spouse in societies where marriage took place between related groups.

To a considerable extent, mid-twentieth-century anthropological scholarship on marriage ignored the implications of marriage for gender relations as well as the more intimate aspects of relationality. Not surprisingly perhaps, the rise of feminist anthropology in the later part of the twentieth century coincided with a shift away from consideration of the structural aspects of marriage and kinship in anthropology to a study of gender relations. What has been termed 'the new kinship studies' was built on the insights of feminist scholarship concerning the denaturalisation of gender, procreation, bodily substance, blood and ideas about nature (see, for example, Carsten 2004; Franklin 1997; Franklin and McKinnon 2001; Strathern 1992; C. Thompson 2005). Much of this work, however, focused on processes of reproduction and birth rather than on what earlier generations of anthropologists would have considered core institutions of kinship, such as marriage (Carsten 2004; Lambek 2011).

Introduction

In more recent studies of marriage and the family, it has become conventional to view marriage as an affective relation of egalitarian intimacy based on love and to see a shift from obligation to choice in conjugal relations as a fundamental attribute of modern subjectivity (Giddens 1992). The increasing emphasis on affective relations between individuals, a shift *From duty to desire* as Jane Collier (2020) has aptly termed it, is one important aspect of these changes (see also Abeyasekera 2021; Cole and Thomas 2009; Hirsch and Wardlow 2006; Jamieson 1998; Padilla et al. 2007; Peletz 2023). The proliferating literature has illuminated how love and intimacy intersect with other contemporary dynamics, including migration, transnational marriage, capitalism and consumption, changing gender relations and values of equality (see Andrikopoulos and Duyvendak 2020; Boellstorff 2007; Brettell 2017; Charsley 2012; Charsley and Shaw 2006; Constable 2003; 2010; 2015; Yan 2003). Anthropologists and other social scientists have recently also turned their attention to increasing rates of delayed marriage or non-marriage that correlate with other kinds of shifts, including increased education and changing patterns of employment, especially for women (Davidson and Hannaford 2023; Inhorn and Smith-Hefner 2020; Jones 2005). These newer patterns are apparent in the ethnography in Chapters 2–7.

While anthropologists and sociologists have focused on love and intimacy, whether in the context of marriage or not, this scrutiny paradoxically sharpens our understanding of what Perveez Mody (2022) has termed the 'politics of love'. As she concludes in her perceptive survey of the recent literature on love and intimacy,

Contrary to the assumption that modernization makes intimacy or love less political as it becomes more individual, the ethnographies that I have surveyed show that, if anything, love becomes more political in post-traditional settings. (Mody 2022, 281)

This crucial insight, that the apparent 'privatisation' of intimacy and its lack of political import under modernity are illusory, brings us back to the institutional and legal framing of love, its surveillance and legitimation and hence to marriage – broadly defined to include the changing definitions of what is or is not permissible in a given context.

In the narratives that I draw on in this book, love is sometimes in tension with familial ties, but protagonists are quite unlikely to ignore the latter. Partly because many of those I spoke to could be viewed as coming from families whose members have lived 'modern lives' in urban Penang for several generations (see Barker, Harms and Lindquist 2014; Lewis 2016) and yet were also thoroughly immersed in the obligations of family life, I examine the implications of these seemingly contradictory pulls. This requires an attentiveness to the relations between marriage, generation and historical transformation, but in a more modulated sense than the sharp dichotomy suggested by theories of modernity (see McKinnon and Cannell 2013a).

For anthropologists and sociologists who have been keen to pay attention to the relation between rules and actual practice, as well as to generations and change, and to marriage as a 'juridical field', the work of Pierre Bourdieu (1977; 1987; 2008) has provided a generative theoretical touchstone over several decades. His influence is clear in several important studies that consider the changing economic, legal and property considerations of marriage and its affective registers (see Clark-Decès 2014, 58–59; Collier 2020, 12, 24; Peletz 2020b, 49, 97–100). Isabelle Clark-Decès's work on Tamil marriage is an outstanding example of how a restudy of a classic anthropological case of preferential close kin marriage (so-called 'Dravidian kinship') can illuminate the changing nature and the lived reality of marriage practices. Her work, showing the subtle implications of this type of marriage for status, and for affective ties, while still attending to its formal rules, bridges continuity and change in terms of both its subject matter and its anthropological approach. Such scholarship has provided stimulation for the present study, but I have also started from somewhat different and broader questions – as outlined earlier – and I have incorporated different kinds of material,

Introduction

including the work of historians, as well as keeping in mind the insights provided by literature and film.

Marriage as Ethical Work in/on Time

Considering the recent anthropological literature on changes to marriage practices, I have found particular inspiration in the work of Perveez Mody (2008) on love marriages in Delhi and Asha Abeyasekera (2021) on 'self-choice' marriages in middle-class Colombo. Both authors show the considerable capacities of families to absorb transgressive marriages and demonstrate the degree to which their protagonists assign importance to, and are embedded in, familial relations. In this way, they provide powerful critiques of a stark binary of arrangement versus choice. Abeyasekera's approach – in particular, her foregrounding of narratives, life histories and intergenerational accounts – bears many similarities with this book. There is in addition a thematic overlap with her work in terms of marriage, morality and modernity, but there are also differences of analytic terms, emphasis and focus. I am less explicitly concerned with the relations between individual agency, modernity and the production of gendered selfhood in my analysis. Instead, I bring together imagination and the ethical or moral to underline more strongly how judgements are not necessarily foreclosed in advance by pre-given moral scripts but may be generative and flexible.[3] Further, I focus more on experiences of being married than on choices about whom to marry. These divergencies arise partly from the questions we are asking (as well as discussion of the causal weight to ascribe to narrative, see Chapter 1). While Abeyasekera 'use[s] the lens of marriage to capture in miniature social transformation in Sri Lanka from the early twentieth century to the present' (Abeyasekera 2021, 177), in this book, the central question is

---

[3] Here and elsewhere in this book, following Mattingly (2014, 5) and others, I use the terms moral and ethical interchangeably.

Marriage and the Moral Imagination

'what does marriage do, and how?'. In this way, the resulting studies may be seen as complementary.

The accounts of Lydia and Haryath, as of many others in this book, illuminate how considering a particular marriage is intertwined with comparative judgements and assessments of other marriages – those of parents, grandparents and siblings or of children, nieces and nephews, for example. As I discuss later, and as was evident in Lydia and Haryath's stories, when people consider their own marriages, or those of relatives or consociates, they exercise 'ethical imagination' (Rumsey 2010, 117)[4] as they explore how intimate relations should be lived in comparison to other marriages, past and present, with which they are familiar. I argue that this is a creative process resting on the consideration of possible alternative, different ways to live rather than simply based on the imposition of pre-given moral rules. Ethical imagination encapsulates possibilities for change (even if these are sometimes masked as continuity). By ethical or moral I do not mean of course that decisions and judgements necessarily entail *being* ethical in the sense of contributing to some larger, notional good. Rather, this implies surveying the possible and exercising judgements in everyday ways and situations to take what may seem the *least bad* option available and to try to avoid obvious pitfalls and unhappiness. Thus, Haryath had wished to avoid the unhappiness and violence in her sister's marriage, which had ended in divorce, while Lydia's mother sought to escape the intensely difficult family circumstances of her upbringing in which her own widowed mother had lived under the authority of her in-laws. Sometimes, as in this case, people take radical, transformative steps to marry beyond the bounds of community or convention, or they may avoid marriage altogether.

---

[4] See also Julie Livingston (2005) who has productively used the notion of 'moral imagination' to examine how debility and bodily suffering are envisioned in Botswana through the mobilisation of history and collective memory. As she notes, imagination is a requirement for empathy (Livingston 2005, 19).

Introduction

Kinship in the stories examined here enables journeys across generations, constituting, in effect, a kind of time travel (see Carsten 2019b; Shryock 2013). Crucially, however, kinship provides not just a mode of transport backwards and forwards through time enabled by intergenerational relations; it is also the relational and emotional content that motivates reflection, relative judgements and decisions. It is in this sense that considering marriage occurs in past, present and future tense (Carsten et al. 2021). There are other noteworthy aspects of this temporal process. First, such judgements are relative: They encompass views about what may be better or worse conjugal relations, and they merge and distinguish subjective experience with what may seem to be more objective stances. As Ammara Maqsood (2024, 70) notes, 'the work of time' – with all its uncertainties – is crucial to the evaluative interpretation of events and relations, and to the negotiation and absorption of difference. The consideration of past, present and future relationships thus enfolds and generates ethical judgements and visions.

I see this study as a contribution to the anthropology of ethics because of the myriad ways in which envisioning a marriage and experiencing conjugality in everyday life require accommodating – or not – to the life of another. For many people, such accommodations and compromises (or their absence) impact the lives of a spouse's close relatives as well as their own family members. Making small or larger compromises, confronting, overriding or ignoring the preferences, wishes or everyday habits of a spouse requires ethical judgements and decisions even if these are not articulated or explicit. As I have indicated, 'ethical' is used here in the broadest sense, which may or may not carry moral overtones as instilled in explicit rules and obligations (Lambek 2010a); what may be better for me may or may not also be better for my spouse and vice versa.[5]

---

[5] Notably, Lambek highlights the role of judgements 'as the fulcrum of everyday ethics' (2010a, 26). His discussion productively illuminates the entanglements of judgements with temporality (Lambek 2010c, 42–58).

Marriage and the Moral Imagination

Sometimes, but not always, reflections about relationships may explicitly take into account the expectations, preferences or visions of others, such as family or a wider community or society more broadly. The dual nature of marriage as at once an intimate relation and a public one permits – and even dictates – sometimes imperceptible transitions between different registers of the ethical, intimate and political. This was evident in the criticisms of many I spoke to, including Haryath, of increasing materialism and the proclivity for large, showy weddings among young people.

Engaging with the anthropology of ethics has brought me into conversation with the work of Veena Das and Michael Lambek, first, because of the attention they pay to everyday life, and their understanding of the ethical or moral, not as constituting a separate domain of existence, but as threaded through ordinary life. This sense, captured in what Michael Lambek (2010b) has called 'ordinary ethics', has been central to the work of Veena Das (2007; 2010; 2018a; 2018b; 2020). My engagement with the insights of this scholarship through the prism of marriage (rather than through violence, its threat and its aftermath, or lives lived in extreme poverty, as in Das's work) is woven through this book. Kinship relations, as has been emphasised by James Faubion (2001) and Robert McKinley (2001), are an obvious arena for moral or ethical consideration, partly because of the altruism and consideration of close others that expectations and ideologies of kinship demand. For most people, kinship as it is lived and imagined is a realm of the everyday that is suffused with ethics. Here Cheryl Mattingly's (2014) evocation of the 'moral laboratories' in which African American parents in Los Angeles reach decisions about what may be best for their children against a backdrop of heavy constraints is apt.[6]

A further point that I take from the work of Veena Das is that, because of its embeddedness in ordinary life, ethical work may be inconspicuous, unarticulated and difficult to discern. Marital relations are frequently alluded to or discussed in Lambek's and Das's considerations

---

[6] See also Mattingly (2014, 25–27) on the generativity of the everyday.

Introduction

of ordinary ethics and are central, for example, in Das's discussion of the coming into being of a Hindu-Muslim marriage (Das 2020, Chapter 5). She pays close attention here to the 'minute shifts in actions and dispositions … in which to inhabit the everyday' (2020, 170) on the part of a couple and their families, and to how these small changes have their histories and their sequelae that are part of 'engaging the life of the other'. The ethical (and temporal) work of marriage, embedded as it is in 'everyday' or 'ordinary' life, may be, following Veena Das, (2018a; 2020), difficult to track – not because it is purposefully hidden from view, but on the contrary, because it often occurs in mundane, sometimes unspoken or insignificant gestures, acts or contexts. Das alludes to how domestic relations, marriage, neighbourly ties and the taken for granted, repetitive and habitual, are zones 'in which the life of the other is engaged' (2020, 15–16).[7] Notably, the meanings of words, actions, gestures and objects here may emerge or shift, taking on different forms, as they are reflected upon by the protagonists and by the ethnographer over many years (Das 2020, Chapter 4). Such inconspicuous shifts (rather than abstract moral judgements), she suggests, potentially hold the seeds of alternative possibilities in relations of care that move beyond the confines of given categorical imperatives and communal boundaries (2020, 169–71). The pertinence of these insights for the experiences of marriage I discuss is evident in Chapter 3 and in Chapter 5 where I consider 'mixed marriages' in Penang, as well as in the final chapter, which focuses on how more public or activist stances may sometimes arise out of marital experiences.

What is clear from the accounts of marriage presented in this book is the centrality of relationality to ordinary ethics. As Webb Keane

---

[7] Importantly, for Das (2020, 117), this conceptualisation brings to the fore the voices and actions of women in a life together: 'habits, routines, repetitions, and their undercurrents that are continuously addressed and contained through such work as that of minor repairs – the way that women darn tears in garments with the delicate placing of one thread on another' (2020, 131).

emphasises, 'People don't live moral life in the abstract, they live it within specific circumstances and social relations' (2024, 11–12). This is in marked contrast to an anthropology of ethics which often seems to centre on a lone and heroic self-grappling to achieve ethical outcomes (see, for example, Laidlaw 2002). Here Jarrett Zigon's call for a 'relational ethics' (2021) appears initially promising, but I have found his work less helpful than might be expected for understanding the moral labour of marriage. Zigon (2021, 390) proposes a relational ethics based on a phenomenological view of language and seems to misrecognise not only the importance of relations in the writings of Das and Lambek but also to ignore the emphasis they place on habitual actions and practices.

It is worth noting that marriage encompasses ethical work that, as well as being implicit and ongoing, embedded in the relational practices of a marriage, can also at times emerge in explicit and performative forms – for example, at a 'vital conjuncture' (Johnson-Hanks 2002), such as deciding whom to marry or what kind of wedding to hold. The productive tension between these aspects of the ethical work of marriage, encompassing varied attitudes to sameness and difference, the public and the private, conformity and change, are part of what enables us, analytically, to tease out the transformative potentialities of marriage.[8] Ethical work may be directed simultaneously or separately at an expansion of relational personhood for the individual, at enhancement of familial relations and status, and towards broader communal concerns. In fact, these different aims and spheres, rather than being necessarily contradictory, may be mobilised to enable each other. Ammara Maqsood's (2021) exposition of how middle-class women in Pakistan navigate the constraints of patriarchal authority within the existing norms of joint families to negotiate new marital possibilities is a case in point. Here expanding the possibilities of 'love as understanding' enables women to 'use the very kin connections and family arrangements that otherwise inhibit them

---

[8] I am grateful to Koreen Reece for working through these insights.

Introduction

from imagining and building toward a new future' (Maqsood 2021, 94). Importantly, such expansions of zones of possibility come about, not by means of direct challenges to authority but through 'traditional' practices; nevertheless, she suggests, they reflect 'a sense of hope and transformative desire' (Maqsood 2021, 102).

Imagination

In focusing on the importance of imagination in marriage, I have taken inspiration from the work of Phyllis Rose (2020 [1984]) on five Victorian literary marriages.[9] Through a feminist lens, Rose analyses marriage 'as imaginative projections and arrangements of power' (Rose 2020, 16). While both power and imagination are fundamental to understanding marriage, the latter route has been less travelled by anthropologists. The ordinary ethics of marriage, as I highlight here, require imaginative work from their participants.[10] Inhabiting a marriage, as well as considering it in prospect or retrospect, requires placing a spouse, their relationships and histories, needs and preferences, alongside one's own. The other may be given shorter or longer shrift, but the demands of conjugality are not simply or straightforwardly a habitus grown up with. As we begin to discern in Chapter 3, the degree to which a parental marriage provides a conjugal model in the next generation is partial and contingent; adjustments to and departures from it are possible. Conjugality is thus an intimate and long-term encounter with the new that is, at least to some degree, a subject of reflection, judgement and planning.

[9] I am very grateful to Siobhan Magee for calling my attention to this book.
[10] Elsewhere Elana Buch (2018) and Julia Kowalski (2024) have used the term 'moral imagination' to analyse the kinship contexts of elder care in the US and family counselling in north India, respectively. Buch uses this term to capture 'the dynamic ways people play with, work on, and adapt their ways of thinking about what "should be" through ongoing engagements with one another over time' (Buch 2018, 15). She shows how bodily practices, memory and storytelling are part of this morally inflected process.

Marriage and the Moral Imagination

Notably, the imaginative demands of marriage is a topic familiar from the works of countless novelists and filmmakers – indeed one might say this has long been their particular terrain. From the novels of Jane Austen to the films of Pedro Almodóvar (to suggest just two from a seemingly limitless list of authors and film directors), the imaginative qualities demanded of familial and marital relations (though not necessarily met), and the variable and uncertain capacities of protagonists, are at the heart of such stories. Phyllis Rose includes the unconventional marital relations of George Eliot and of Charles Dickens, two of the most celebrated English nineteenth-century novelists, in her study of Victorian marriage, and I return to George Eliot in Chapter 7. The interiority of protagonists, their internal narratives and shifts of subjective perspective between different characters no doubt lend themselves particularly well to literary and cinematic genres. Nevertheless, it does seem surprising that imaginative aspects of relationality should be so rarely discussed in anthropological accounts.

My interest in experiences of marriage over time concerns not just objective changes or a focus on choices about whom to marry but also qualities of reflection, in other words, how people assess marriage and conjugality, and the judgements they make at the time, as well as retrospectively and prospectively. This connects with the temporality of marriage discussed earlier, a temporality that Cheryl Mattingly underlines for 'projects of care' more broadly. Such temporality leads Mattingly 'to insist that there is an inherent narrativity to ethical practice and its self-constituting nature' (Mattingly 2014, 19). This, however, is not to suggest that such narratives necessarily provide coherence or order. Rather, for Mattingly,

narrative provides a useful approach for investigating projects of moral becoming riddled by uncertain possibilities and informed by pluralistic moral values, concerns and communities. (Mattingly 2014, 20)

Here Mattingly is concerned with what she refers to as the 'narrative re-envisioning' through which new ethical possibilities are imagined 'in and through participation in social worlds' (Mattingly 2014, 20). Drawing on the work of Alasdair MacIntyre (2013) and Charles Taylor (1989), she specifically points to the role of narrative in actions, and to the entanglements of the ethical with the political in what she terms 'moral laboratories' (Mattingly 2014, 17–25). This line of her argument is thus helpful in linking together the role of moral imagination in marriage with the narrative accounts which I present in the chapters that follow. It differs somewhat from the approach of Asha Abeyasekera who, drawing particularly on the work of Jerome Bruner (1987; 1990), and Elinor Ochs and Lisa Capps (1996; 2001), argues that the narrative accounts of marriage she collected are part of a process of ordering and settling life events. By providing opportunities for reflection and resolving and clarifying discrepancies between different expectations or between expectations and actual outcomes, Abeyasekera argues, narratives about marriage construct meanings and make order, and this is not just an individual process but a collective one involving the audience (Abeyasekera 2021, 22, 26, 153). Without ignoring this important ordering quality of narrative accounts, I want also to draw attention to their open-endedness and contribution to social transformation. Imagination, I suggest, is a key aspect of narrative.

The material I present in this book can be taken as a contribution to discussions about the role of narrative in the production of new or changing ethical imaginaries. Narrating accounts, whether to family members, consociates, social researchers or others, can be one expression of transformation, but, crucially, such narrations take place alongside, before or after actions and events that are their subject. In other words, they both express and contribute to transformative processes, but they are not the only way transformation occurs. In Chapter 7, I show how experiences of marriage may, directly or indirectly, lead to a trajectory of social activism in the field of gender relations with the explicit aim of bringing about communal or political change. Here we gain some sense of the complexity of possible trajectories of change.

Marriage and the Moral Imagination

The significance of imaginative capacities for kinship is of course not restricted to marital relations alone. In a quite different context, Rayna Rapp and Faye Ginsburg have explored how parenting children with disabilities in the US brings about an expansion of kinship horizons for parents and 'widen[s] the space of possibility in which relations can be imagined and resources claimed' (Rapp and Ginsburg 2001, 537). Here it is the immediate intimacy of encounters with difference that stimulates such imaginative work; the effects of this, however, are not necessarily limited to intimate familial zones but may produce new cultural forms that 'create new social landscapes' (Rapp and Ginsburg 2001, 551). The connections Rapp and Ginsburg draw between kinship and social activism provide insights into how familial kinship may generate political change. For those I interviewed and spoke to in Penang, considering intergenerational marital experiences in their own families meant, above all, reflecting on gender relations between wives and husbands. Here the most marked and most commented-upon change over two or three generations has been the increasing tendency of women to enter tertiary education before marriage and after marriage to continue to work outside the home. This theme was present in Lydia's and Haryath's larger narratives – both had achieved tertiary education and both worked outside the home after marriage. It reflects wider patterns in Malaysia and beyond that were generally perceived as fundamentally altering the dynamics of conjugal relations. Women whose mothers worked, or who themselves work – in contrast to their mothers or grandmothers – were described as more independent, more autonomous and having more equal relations with their husbands. Although there were some variations, this was broadly the case across all ethnicities and religions. This fundamental shift, and the way it was spoken about by women and men, indicates too the expansion of imaginative horizons entailed for women about their own life course as well as those of their female forebears. But it prompted men too to imaginatively reconsider their ideals and expectations of women and wives in the past, present and future as they articulated these to me in conversations and interviews.

Imagination does not, however, always imply an expansion of possibilities, and there are limits and constraints to the potential for transformation. One area of possible change that is highly controversial in Malaysia, as in other parts of the world, is LGBTQ rights – an anathema to more conservative Muslims (for whom it has the capacity to galvanise anti-Western attitudes), but more acceptable in some form to many young, urban, middle-class liberals. This fracture, which starkly contrasts with radical changes in the acceptance of same-sex relations in Europe and North America, opens up questions about the political possibilities of intimate relations, or their perceived capacities for change. In Chapter 7, I consider the trajectories of women for whom marriage has provided an ambivalent template for gender relations, some of whom have remained or become unmarried. I connect their experiences with different kinds of community service as well as activism in women's rights and LGBTQ contexts. Here the direct impact of family relations has propelled some women to devote time and energy to the service of wider improvement of marital and gender relations. Putting these ethnographic stories side by side with insights about ordinary ethics, imagination and time illuminates how political change may be generated through (sometimes negative) conjugal and familial experience. As Mattingly (2014, 24) has argued, 'the ethical here is intimately intertwined with the political'.

The Chapters

The architecture of the chapters that follow is thematic, emerging 'organically' from my ethnographic encounters rather than predicated on pre-scripted sociological frames. While the detailed narratives are drawn from Penang, the debates and concerns are framed more widely to capture experiences of marriage beyond the narrow circumstances of the ethnography. In Chapter 1 I introduce a perhaps unexpected analogy between marriage and anthropology as encounters with difference, highlighting the transformative potential of both. Research on marriage in Penang drew me back to my first fieldwork on kinship and domestic relations in a fishing village on the island of Langkawi beginning in 1980. Reflecting on this long anthropological engagement with Malaysia, I trace some of the profound changes that have occurred there over the past decades. Recent fieldwork in urban Penang provides food for considering the very different contexts of research then and now and the concomitants of a long-term anthropological commitment.

In Chapter 2, to set the scene in urban Penang at the time of the research, I take up public discourses about marriage and gender relations – looking at newspaper accounts, public events, debates, exhibitions and theatrical productions in Penang's capital, George Town. Bringing these together with interviews with lawyers in Penang, I show how discussions about what are perceived by many as 'dysfunctional relations' or deviations from ideal patterns, including child marriage, polygamy, the conversion of minors to Islam, divorce and LGBTQ rights, have the capacity to expand and take on a vibrant life of their own at moments of national tension. Dense and cross-cutting connections between ethnicity, religion and law in Malaysia, as in other parts of the world, intensify the porosity of each of these domains. The recapitulation of contestations around child marriage, for example, on the eve of Malaysian Independence and in 2018, suggests how marriage and gender relations can not only metaphorically stand for the nation but also vividly express and constitute national fractures and divisions over time. Such stories thus condense ethical and political concerns and contestations at times of radical change.

In Chapter 3, we take a closer look at the intimate world of the family through an intergenerational lens. Education and work outside the home are understood by many women to have fundamentally altered the dynamics of conjugality over several decades. Variations

Introduction

in individual life courses, availability of resources, education and ethnic or religious backgrounds partly shape trajectories of life and marriage. Exploring continuity and change between generations, we see how marriage encapsulates both possibilities, enabling radical departures from conventional norms under the guise of conformity as well as the replication of past patterns. Here, the binary of 'arrangement' versus 'choice' constitutes, simultaneously, a reference point and a somewhat misleading way to calibrate transformation – as anthropologists of South Asia have shown (Abeyasekera 2021; Donner 2016; Fuller and Narasimhan 2008; Osella 2012; Parry 2020, Chapter 11). Beyond this, we see how marriages mark time, and are a means to tell and reflect upon family histories. Efforts to change the course of events or escape cycles of misfortune may be rare and difficult to achieve. Reflecting on differences and change across generations engages qualities of moral imagination, and is part of making history.

A comparison of the trajectories of two women from different generations, ethnic and religious backgrounds is the subject of Chapter 4. Both were to a considerable degree 'self-made' women, and the question raised in this chapter is, how is marriage relevant to their success? As elsewhere in this book, the stories that these women tell are replete with ethical judgements and reflections on their own and their parents' marriages as well as those about others. Part of what is of interest here is the intriguingly tangential significance of marriage. Apparently a necessary part of a normative life course even in an unconventional scenario, marriage here takes forms that are at once accepted and 'transgressive'. Both women had married foreign husbands; in one case, this ended in divorce; in the other, what seemed a successful partnership has endured. We see how marriage allows the expansion of convention but, paradoxically, also reinforces social norms. Indeed, at the boundaries of difference and what is acceptable, marriage has the capacity – as the work of Perveez Mody (2008) in India has shown – to be re-enfolded into what is normative through its conventionality.

Marriage and the Moral Imagination

It can hold a promise of transformation for individuals, families and wider communities and nations.

Chapter 5 takes forward the exploration of difference through an examination of what are locally perceived as 'mixed' marriages. Of course, difference can be calibrated in many registers – for example, those of age, wealth, class, familial background, religion, language, 'race' and ethnicity. The cultural and ethnic diversity of Penang offers unusual scope for marrying outside familiar boundaries. In this chapter, I consider which sorts of difference are most salient, which boundaries are more permeable and which are easier to bridge. 'Malayness' and Islam have a historically privileged legal status in Malaysia, and marrying a Muslim legally requires a non-Muslim spouse to convert. The bodily, culinary, religious and legal concomitants of this conversion are likely to impact close family members – especially the parents and siblings of a non-Muslim partner (see Kessler 1992, 139). At the extreme end of a range of possibilities, 'mixed' couples encountering or expecting opposition from their families sometimes elope to marry. But after marriage, a long process of accommodation and absorption is likely to occur. Experiences of 'mixed' marriage and the negotiation of difference, which is part of marriage everywhere, offer a perspective on other changes in Malaysia over several decades. More broadly, it also provides a way to understand how intimate worlds may generate wider social transformation.

Although many people marry in order to provide a secure future, there are no guarantees this will be assured. In Chapter 6, we look at forms of marital uncertainty occurring at different stages of married life. A central question here is what does uncertainty produce? The chapter focuses partly on Malay protagonists, and on two particularly fragile moments in Malay marriage: during betrothal and, counter-intuitively, much later on, after several decades when one might expect marriages to be highly stable. The former was a pattern with which I was familiar from earlier research. But some older Malay women spoke to me of a more recently emerging trend – for husbands of many years to marry

Introduction

a younger woman polygamously. Meanwhile, other non-Malay couples have adopted unconventional living arrangements or have taken unusual paths to suit their particular circumstances. In considering how different kinds of marital uncertainty play out, the significance of expectations about marriage and the registers of temporality through which they are calibrated and recalibrated are illuminated. The force of unanticipated events stimulates the reflection of protagonists and their consociates – as readers may recognise from their own experiences – reformulating ideas of what is appropriate or acceptable behaviour, and precipitating new ethical stances.

The final chapter returns us to an examination of the import of marriage at the interface between intimate, personal lives and wider political transformation. Highlighting the experiences of those who have remained unmarried beyond the usual marrying age, I build on discussions of ethical imagination from earlier in the book by exploring submerged connections between non-marriage and activism. The multiple temporalities in which reflecting on marriage occurs (here by those who remain unmarried) reveal how such judgements constitute imaginative and political work. Involvement in gender-related activism is a possible trajectory for those concerned about women's or LGBTQ rights. The potential fractures between conservative Islam and the more liberal attitudes of urban, middle-class, youthful Malaysians constitute a zone of contention – but also, for some, a suggestive field for imaginative reflection about their own situation, about the marriage of their parents or those of siblings or friends. In these fissures, transformative standpoints and visions may carry the seeds of wider political change.

Neither Lydia nor Haryath, whose accounts I have briefly referred to, and who will reappear towards the end of this book, were political activists. Nevertheless, as older women, both were highly engaged in community life. In one sense 'ordinary', in that neither had achieved exceptional fame or status, one could equally well say both were remarkable in the way that many life stories, when examined closely, reveal extraordinary conjunctures, qualities and talents, resilience or tenacity. Both women showed a disposition to reflect on their own marriage and those of others through time and generations. This exercise of relational and moral imagination is at once completely ordinary and also, through the possibilities it engenders to create and absorb change, transformative. It is at the heart of marriage as an intimate and deeply political relation. It is also, as I argue in Chapter 1, at the heart of doing anthropology.

ONE

Anthropological Engagements

Fieldwork, Marriage, Malaysia and Penang

In the Introduction, I suggested that marriage can be seen as an encounter with difference and that it has in this respect some parallels with anthropology – an analogy that I return to at various points in this book. At its most ambitious, anthropology carries the hope of political transformation through fieldwork encounters and pedagogical experience. But how do we do anthropology now, at the political conjuncture in which we find ourselves – in the aftermath of a global pandemic and in the face of a climate emergency and persistent or worsening inequalities? What constitutes 'a possible anthropology' (Pandian 2019) for our times? These questions seem particularly fraught as the discipline confronts old issues of representation and appropriation in new ways. With a radical vision, but burdened by its problematic history, anthropology often seems all too caught up in its own contradictions and knots.

This chapter introduces Malaysia and Penang where the research for this book was conducted. While much of the content of the main chapters is drawn from interviews and conversations about marriage in Penang, as I emphasised in the Introduction, the arguments that are derived from this material are broader and more general. The specificity of the material requires some knowledge of the local cultural context. This tension between a grounding in local context and broader generalisation is at the heart of most anthropology. Considering the possibilities and impossibilities of doing anthropology now, while conducting research on one of its oldest and most well-worn themes, has also prompted me to review my own trajectory over several decades.[1] Investigating marriage in contemporary urban Malaysia drew me back to my first fieldwork when I worked on kinship and marriage on the island of Langkawi in rural Malaysia in the early 1980s. Reflections on doing anthropology over time are woven through this chapter, and those that follow, to illuminate both processes of marriage and research.

The chapter is divided into three sections. In the first, after a brief outline of the ethnic complexity of Malaysia through the lens of my research visits since the 1980s, I indicate some of the profound changes that have taken place there over the last forty years. The cultural, religious, ethnic and linguistic hybridity that are prominent features of Malaysian life create particular tensions, which fieldworkers must learn to navigate. This hybridity is a particularly dominant feature of Penang through its location and trading history. The second section focuses on Penang and its diverse population, again through the lens of my own encounters with it over four decades. In the third section, I describe how the research for this book was undertaken between 2017 and 2022, considering the place of narratives as well as salient differences between this and my earlier fieldwork. Periods spent in Penang were a particular pleasure and allowed me to expand and consolidate earlier connections. But these forays were abruptly curtailed by the COVID-19 global pandemic in 2020, and I turned instead to writing – a process that underlined the separations as well as the connections out of which this book has emerged.

Marriage in Malaysia and Fieldwork (Part 1)

Some of the most visceral memories from my first fieldwork in Malaysia are of attending village wedding feasts. After a long and complex set of ritual exchanges between the bride's family and the groom's, in which

---

[1] For comparison, see Peletz (2023) who also reflects on forty years of fieldwork in Malaysia.

1 Anthropological Engagements

villagers had to draw on ritual experts, each other and occasionally the resident anthropologist, to confirm the proper order and manner of doing things, two feasts were held, one in the bride's house and one in the groom's, some days apart from each other. While I enjoyed participating in the betrothal rituals and exchanges, the wedding feasts, *kenduri kahwin*, which were the ritual highpoint of nuptial celebrations, were often something of a trial. These were mass occasions that involved many hundreds of guests – the whole village or representatives from each house, as well as others who had travelled from further afield – and they were highly formalised. The food, which was communally prepared and cooked outside over the previous day and night, was meatier, richer and heavier than everyday food. It was usually eaten quickly with men and women fed in separate areas of a house that had become exceptionally hot and crowded. Meanwhile, the bride and groom were required to sit in state, *bersanding*, on a raised and decorated wedding dais. Everyone wore their best formal attire with tight-fitting Malay costumes in synthetic fabrics contributing to the general feeling of heat and discomfort. It was some way into my fieldwork that I discovered with relief that others too often found these occasions tiring and the food less satisfying than its everyday equivalent. Nevertheless, it was quite clear that these were the central ritual occasions of Malay village life. They brought together an entire community and re-inscribed idioms of everyday cooking, commensality and domesticity in differently gendered terms.

Betrothals, weddings, spouse selection and the general tenor of relations between wives and husbands were core topics of my research on Malay kinship in the early 1980s (Carsten 1997, Chapter 7). But this is not a book about Malay kinship, or even Malay marriage – although my account of marriage focuses on marriage *in* Malaysia, and more specifically, in Penang (see later).[2] The difference is crucial as Malays are

---

[2] For perceptive and thorough accounts of changes to Malay marriage and divorce practices in recent decades and their gendered correlates in the context of an expanded

31

only one of several ethnicities making up the population of Malaysia, and ethnicity (often locally articulated as 'race') exerts a powerful social force in Malaysia. The main demographic groups, as defined in government policies, censuses and on Malaysian identity cards, are 'Malay', 'Chinese', 'Indian' and 'Other'. These categories, notoriously, conflate 'race' with ethnicity in official and public discourses. They have a long history going back to British colonial policies and to colonial census categories (see Carsten 2019a, 18–20).[3] In fact, each of these broad delineations comprises further, smaller communities, which define themselves with reference to particular histories, religious affiliations, cultures and languages.[4] Ethnic identities in practice are less tidy and more overlapping than simple categorisations imply; they conflate diverse regional and other backgrounds and histories of migration and intermarriage (see, for example, Carsten 1995; Kahn 2006; Kessler 1992; King 2021a). It is indicative that both Lydia and Haryath, whose accounts I referred to in the Introduction, spoke of the mixed languages of their upbringing – in one case Hokkien, Bahasa Malaysia (Malay) and English, and in the other, Punjabi and English. Marriage is highly salient within and across communal boundaries since it may be both the source of, and a disruption to, reproduction and continuity of these

---

Islamic bureaucracy and heightened emphasis on patriarchal Muslim values, see Maznah Mohamad (2020, Chapter 6) and Michael Peletz (2020b).

[3] There is a very extensive critical literature on discourses and usages of 'race' in Malaysia (usually rendered as *bangsa* or *keturunan* in Bahasa Malaysia) and its overlaps with ethnicity, religion, nationality, language and culture (see, for example, Hirschman 1986; 1987; Holst 2012; Leow 2016, 189; Manickam 2015, 98–111; Milner and Ting 2018; Milner 2008; Shamsul 1996; Shamsul and Athi 2014). For a recent compendium that sets out new paradigms for the analysis of agency and identity in Malaysia through different empirical case studies, see King et al. (2021).

[4] The novelist Tash Aw writes eloquently from his personal experience of the distinctions between different diasporic Chinese language communities in Malaysia – Hokkien, Cantonese, Teochew and Hakka – with their different temple associations and clans in his family memoir, *Strangers on a Pier* (2021, Chapter 5). The categories 'Indian' or 'Malay' likewise obscure heterogeneous historic, geographic, linguistic and cultural affiliations.

groups. This is one reason that Malaysia – and especially Penang – is a particularly rich and illuminating place to study marriage and to draw conclusions about its generativity.

The ethnic complexity of Malaysia is reflected in its legal systems and marital codes, which, although modified since, are partly derived from colonial policies and legal enactments. Muslim marriage in Malaysia as well as other 'customary' and religious matters for Muslims are governed by *syariah* law, and regulated through *syariah* courts at state level.[5] This applies to all Malays (who are by definition Muslim) and those Indians and others who are also Muslim. All non-Muslim marriages are governed by civil family law, which is regulated by the federal judicial system. Legal adjustments to civil marriage can only be made through civil law changes and by act of parliament.

Religion and ethnicity in Malaysia cross-cut each other and, except in the Malay case, are not coterminous. Malays are defined on the basis of religion, language, custom and their claims to indigeneity or '*Bumiputera*' status, which carries significant political privilege.[6] In many urban contexts, contemporary Malaysians of different ethnicities and religions work and live cheek by jowl – as I describe later for Penang. This does not, however, preclude aspects of domestic and religious lives being more separated from people's working environments and from members of different communities. Taking account of processes of urbanisation and middle-classification in Malaysia, particularly over the

[5] For simplicity, I have used the conventional Malaysian spelling, 'syariah', in this book, rather than 'sharia'. On the changing historical relation between the state and Islam in Malaysia, see, for example, Maznah (2010a; 2010b; 2020); Maznah et al. (2009); Ahmad Fauzi and Zawawi Ibrahim (2017).

[6] Those defined as indigenous to Malaysia, that is, Malays (who are by definition Muslim) and the indigenous groups of Sabah and Sarawak (whether Muslim or non-Muslim), hold Bumiputera status. On the fracturing of both national Malaysian and Malay visions of identity, and the simultaneous recourse to discourses of identity invoking language, religion, history and tradition, see Kahn (1992); Kahn and Loh (1992); Kessler (1992); King (2021); Leow (2016). For a case study showing the complexities of these processes of contestation in Penang, see Goh (2018).

Marriage and the Moral Imagination

last thirty to forty years (Abdul Rahman 2018; Goh 2002; 2018; Kahn and Loh 1992), the ethnography in this book focuses on middle-class urban marriage in Penang. Rather than concentrate on a single ethnic group as, historically, much anthropological and wider social scientific work in Malaysia has done (King 2021a, 38; Yeoh 2019), I consider marriage more broadly among and across different communities. This approach has advantages and disadvantages. Placing marriage rather than ethnicity in the foreground allows consideration of how it intersects with ethnicity while avoiding the essentialising and reifying pitfalls of taking ethnicity as a primary frame (see Carsten 2019a, 22–23). It also takes account of the profound changes that have taken place in Malaysia over this period, which have resulted in many Malaysians having greater familiarity with members of other ethnic groups than did their forbears. Undoubtedly, however, there is a loss here too in terms of ethnographic skills and depth. While I can claim some competency in Bahasa (Malay), and have a background in scholarship on Malay culture, I am less well-equipped with respect to Chinese-Malaysian or Indian-Malaysian histories, cultures and languages. Some implications of this for carrying out research are discussed later.

In the Malaysia of the early 1980s, whose population was less urban, things were somewhat different from today. At that time, a high proportion of the Malay population was based in rural paddy-farming and/or fishing villages. A focus on Malay kinship and marriage, personhood and gender seemed an obvious project for fieldwork in a rural setting (Carsten 1997). Many villagers on the island of Langkawi, where I carried out research, could be shown to have had recent ancestors who had come to the island from the mainland or elsewhere in the region in the late nineteenth and early twentieth centuries, often escaping warfare or poverty. Marriages were arranged by parents of the bride and groom; the couple, ideally, would be 'close' (*dekat*) in terms of a similarity of background, incomes, neighbourhood and religiosity. Although they might know each other's families, the betrothed

1 Anthropological Engagements

pair were not supposed to have had personal contact before marrying. In this bilateral and loosely endogamous kinship universe, those who married were often also genealogically related as second or third cousins. Historically, one could see marriage in a demographically mobile and fluid Malay world as part of a process of integrating Malay people of different geographic origins and backgrounds and producing similarity, largely conceived in terms of siblingship (Carsten 1995; 1997, Chapter 7).[7] These were the terms in which I came to understand Malay marriage in Langkawi.

Alongside learning about Malay kinship in Langkawi in the early 1980s, I also underwent my own transformation as a neophyte fieldworker. I lived as a foster daughter (*anak angkat*) in a village house with a Malay family where the more intense aspects of hospitality – in the forms of strong encouragement to take on many aspects of Malay life appropriate for young women (including food, dress, name, bodily comportment and participation in labour) – could sometimes seem overpowering. Eventually, I came to see this as part of a wider history of incorporation that enabled migrant incomers to Langkawi (and to other rural destinations) to settle into new locations. Undoubtedly, and in common with many other cultures, hospitality had a coercive edge, and this was challenging as an experience of fieldwork, but it also afforded a privileged opportunity to learn about Malay culture from the 'inside' of a family and village community (see Carsten 1997, 5–9, 275–80).

My early anthropological encounter with difference was in many ways transformative. To understand how this was internalised, it should be situated in its particular era. For graduate students in anthropology at the London School of Economics setting out on their studies in the late

---

[7] Although the category 'Malay' carries strong associations of local origins and national identity, anthropologists and historians have shown how it in fact enfolds a history of regional demographic mobility and diversity (see Carsten 1995; Kahn 2006; Milner 2008; Thompson 2003; 2007).

Marriage and the Moral Imagination

1970s, it seemed crucial – and perhaps all too simple – to refigure anthropology through the prisms of anti-colonial struggles, second-wave feminism and structural Marxism. In this intense political atmosphere, we thought out how to conduct fieldwork 'from below' and (generally with some less certainty) how to write up the results. Rejection of the colonial vestiges of anthropology and a concern to avoid earlier ways of working with interpreters, servants or other colonial trappings shaped how many in this generation of anthropological fieldworkers conducted research. Today, the idea that this was merely a matter of intention or a change of attitudes seems uncomfortably naïve as we confront again, and attempt to recognise, the persistent corrosive effects of colonial encounters – in anthropology, in educational institutions and in the political contexts in which we live. But this may serve to situate how I embraced the closeness of my fieldwork encounter in the 1980s as well as why it could at times seem overpowering. I take up other aspects of doing research in Malaysia later.

Much has changed in Malaysia and in anthropology since those years. Part of what is different in Malaysia, as already mentioned, relates to the shift from rural to urban living over recent decades. It now seems less timely in terms of contemporary social processes to study villages in Malaysia. Beyond this, while villages in the 1980s were often very largely mono-ethnic with populations that were predominantly or exclusively Malay, this is not the case for Malaysian cities (see, for example, Yeoh 2014a; 2014b). As I have indicated, studying urban life in Malaysia can in this way also constitute an invitation to consider social processes across and between its different ethnic communities. Linked to demographic shifts and alongside increased ethnic interaction, anecdotally, many of those I spoke to mentioned an increase in what they referred to as 'mixed' marriages (see Chapter 5).

Important changes affecting marriage in Malaysia have occurred over the last forty years or so and were frequently discussed by those I spoke to in Penang. As in other parts of the world, there has been a

1 Anthropological Engagements

very marked rise in women's education and participation in the workforce, in line with trends in many other developed or developing nations (Jamilah 1994; Jones, Hull and Maznah 2015; tan beng hui and Ng 2014). Marriages tend to occur later, and marital partners are usually 'self-chosen' rather than arranged.[8] Older women, particularly, often spoke to me about the differences between marriage in their parents' and their own or their children's generations in terms of the more equal marital relations fostered by women working outside the home and a decline in patriarchal attitudes.

These changes have been accompanied by the partial co-opting of rights-based ideals of gender equality into public policy and governmental rhetoric – whatever the realities such rhetoric may obscure. Connected to this, a flourishing middle-class feminist movement and civil society activist groups were established (Ng, Maznah and tan 2006). In apparent contradiction to these trends, the same period has seen the institutionalisation, bureaucratisation and standardisation of a more conservative, patriarchal Islam and its co-option in legal and governmental procedures and policies, as Maznah Mohamad (2010a; 2010b; 2020), Norani Othman (Norani 2005; Norani, Puthucheary and Kessler 2008) and Michael Peletz (2002; 2020b; 2023), among others, have documented. These authors have detailed the impact such changes have had on Muslim family law and gender relations for

---

[8] For overviews of demographic trends in marriage and divorce in Malaysia over recent decades, see Jones (2021); Jones and Tey (2021); Tey (2015; 2021), and for trends in Southeast Asia more broadly, see, for example, Jones (2007; 2009); Jones, Hull and Maznah 2015; Yeung (2022); Yeung and Jones (2024). These trends include urbanisation, rising education and age at marriage, a decrease in the spousal age and education gap, falling fertility, an increase in dual-income households and a rise in inter-ethnic marriage. Their effects on life experiences and conjugal relations are matters of discussion and reflection as is clear throughout this book. The Muslim divorce rate in Malaysia has historically been much higher than that of non-Muslims, but patterns of divorce have also changed with divorce rates increasing for all ethnicities after a sharp decline for Muslims in the final decades of the twentieth century (see Jones 2021; Chapter 6 this volume).

Malays and other Muslims.⁹ Arguably, this expansion of conservative Islam also impacts the non-Muslim, non-Malay population (even though they do not come under the same legal jurisdictions) and gives rise to increasing concerns among non-Muslims about their own position, interethnic relations and the future trajectory of Malaysian society more generally (see, for example, Baxstrom 2008; Nonini 2015; Peletz 2020b, 8, 183–86, 188–91; Willford 2006; 2014a).

The tensions between these two sharply distinct processes with their sources in different roots of Malaysian society are profound. As Michael Peletz has acutely observed, they result in apparently contradictory trends that are often difficult to disentangle:

Progressive developments in Malaysia's *sharia* judiciary with respect to (Malay/Muslim) women ... have gone hand in hand both with a punitive turn in the juridical field as a whole and with acute polarization among the nation's ethnic and religious groups. (Peletz 2020b, 221)

Such tensions are expressed too, I suggest, in the prominence of concerns about 'anomalous', dysfunctional or aberrant forms of marriage and intimate relations in public and academic discourse, including domestic violence, child marriage and polygamy – as we will see in Chapter 2 (see also Maznah 2020; Peletz 2020a; 2023b). I sometimes found it difficult to reconcile these anxieties with the assertiveness of the Malay women I recalled from the 1980s, and with the general tenor

---

⁹ This literature tends to focus on formal and legal contexts, which no doubt also affect more everyday perceptions and practices (see Maznah 2015). But see also Karim (2021) for a discussion of the intersection of Malay kinship norms and recent shifts in Islamic ideas in Malaysia. She emphasises the persistent importance of economic productivity and autonomy for Malay (and other southeast Asian) Muslim women as a core value of *adat* (custom) and as part of gender complementarity and 'an ideology of bilateralism in synchronicity with practical Islam' (2021, 106). Karim notes that '*adat* rules of marriage, equal inheritance, matrilocal residence, and equal preference for daughters and sons continue to be practised in everyday life' (2021, 110).

1 Anthropological Engagements

of marital relations I had encountered in Langkawi, which did not, in the cases I knew, seem to be markedly patriarchal but was founded on a relatively equal basis, especially as spouses became older and more familiar with each other. My understanding of older, rural patterns of Malay kinship and gender relations thus caused me to puzzle over some of the public discourse about dysfunctional aspects of domestic relations, as well as the comments of some of the younger Malay women I interviewed in Penang who spoke about the 'patriarchal' attitudes of their fathers or previous generations, implying these were derived from earlier and now outmoded stances. Scholars have shown how, in the past, gender complementarity rather than hierarchy was emphasised in Malay kinship (as elsewhere in the region) while age and generation were more marked principles of differentiation than gender (Carsten 1997; Karim 1995; 1992; 2021; Ong and Peletz 1995; Peletz 2009).[10]

In line with this gendered complementarity, Malay polygamy (polygyny) was extremely rare in both village and urban contexts.[11] But the push towards a more conservative Islam in recent decades has encouraged a more patriarchal tendency in gender relations for at least some Malays, producing tensions not just within Malay kinship but in Malaysian

---

[10] In this respect, there is a distinction between the bilateral (or cognatic) principles of Malay kinship and the patrilineal basis of Chinese and Indian kinship, the former possibly being more amenable to complementary or less patriarchal regimes of authority than the latter – but this is not necessarily a straightforward association.

[11] Malay polygyny (or polygamy) was noted to occur infrequently in ethnographies from the mid- and later twentieth centuries (Carsten 1997; Djamour 1965, 82–87; Firth 1966, 48). This was partly a matter of wealth but also of women's reluctance to enter polygynous unions. That attitudes and practices have at least partly shifted is clear from recent studies (Nurul Muda 2021a; 2021b; Zeitzen 2018). Although now a more visible part of the Malay middle-class cultural repertoire, polygyny requires financial resources for men and is not generally widespread – partly because, as Karim (2021, 121) argues, the Islamic requirement for equal treatment is difficult to achieve. On the changing application of legislation restricting men's access to polygyny, see, for example, Maznah (2010a; 2020, 198–202); Norani et al. (2005, 91); Peletz (2020b, 220, 251 n.2).

Marriage and the Moral Imagination

society more broadly.[12] This theme runs through the following chapters, which show marriage as a productive lens for understanding the intersection of familial and personal life with wider politics.

Penang Now and Then

If everyday experience seen through the prism of moral imagination over time is a productive way to understand the larger significance of marriage and conjugality, as I argued in the Introduction, something similar holds true for anthropology. The process of fieldwork, assimilating new experiences and ways of doing things and becoming close to people with whom one has previously had no connection, requires imaginative empathy and time, as does marriage. But, like intimate relations, anthropology could be regarded as susceptible to what Laurent Berlant (2011) has termed 'cruel optimism'. Researchers in anthropology – and perhaps most especially graduate students whose expectations are prone to be particularly high – are often intensely aware of the limitations of their fieldwork – of not meeting their own unrealistic standards. My 1980s' fieldwork in rural Malaysia provided a lesson in the precarious balance between ethical engagement and retaining one's own inner moorings. But it also gave me a background and context in which to locate experiences of marriage in Malaysia some forty years later. The connecting thread that drew the research for this book forward was urban Penang.

How to explain the strong attachments to particular places that, sedimented in layers of memory, creep up on one over many years? Lodged in the senses, smells, sights and sounds, in food and friendships and in visceral and emotional processes, these bonds seem so dense as to be

---

[12] See also Thambiah (2012, 157) on how urbanism, an expansion of the middle class, an increased emphasis on conservative Islamic principles and Malaysian state policies have together resulted in an increase in the frequency of polygyny. Thambiah (2012, 155) notes that this has gone together with an expansion of women's educational achievements and economic independence.

1 Anthropological Engagements

impossible to unpick. My first encounter with urban Penang was in June 1980 when, quite new to Malaysia, I arrived there on the train from Kuala Lumpur and then the ferry from Butterworth that landed in the heart of Penang's state capital, George Town, at Weld Quay. Greeted by a baffling cacophony of sounds and demands for custom in multiple languages, I made my way to what was then a somewhat decayed and crumbling but still rather grand Eastern and Oriental (E & O) Hotel, where I stayed for a couple of nights before decamping to the considerably simpler and more affordable guest house of Universiti Sains Malaysia some miles out of the city.

Over the following four months, I had an unanticipated opportunity to get to know Penang as I made the most of having to kick my heels while waiting to sort out research permits to begin fieldwork. During that period, affiliated with the university and generously given an office there, I worked on improving my Malay and reading historical and social science literature on Malaysia. Perhaps more importantly over the long term, I made friends through the School of Comparative Social Sciences, then a vibrant centre of local and foreign researchers, including historians, anthropologists and sociologists. There was plenty of warm and convivial hospitality and some of the friendships made then have endured to this day. After a few weeks at the university guest house, I found a small room to rent in a house within walking distance from the university, shared with other expatriate lodgers working as lecturers and presided over by its hospitable, widowed Chinese owner.

Undoubtedly, my love affair with Penang took hold in those first months and is rooted in friendships from that period. I was helped in getting to know the island by several people who took me round, showing me local sites or were happy to have me along as they carried out their own research. The island was greener then, with exceptionally beautiful landscape, reasonably clear roads and without the major highways, dense traffic and ubiquitous high-rise developments it has today. There were numerous crumbling and rapidly decaying colonial-era

Marriage and the Moral Imagination

mansions, some rented by people I knew, many of which have since been demolished and replaced by brutalist skyscrapers. Social occasions inevitably involved food – cooked in the different styles and cuisines for which Penang is justly famous. Although in this period I got to know George Town only slightly, within quite a short time I felt at home in the university-centred world in which I was situated. This was perhaps both a blessing and a hindrance for fieldwork in Langkawi. Until I left Malaysia in April 1982, I kept a room in Penang and returned there once a month or so for some days to recoup and recharge my batteries. This was always a source of pleasure and anticipation, so much so that I often found it hard to leave again for the village.

In this somewhat schizophrenic existence, the difficulties of my life in Malaysia – of loneliness, of living under the close surveillance and supervision of a warm Malay family and their neighbours – became associated with the village, while the more enjoyable parts generally happened in Penang. In actuality, things were not quite this simple, but I did sometimes wish I might have been doing fieldwork in Penang rather than in a Malay village. It was late 1988 before I returned again to Penang and Langkawi for further fieldwork over four months, to some extent replicating the peripatetic pattern I had established earlier. After this, there was a gap of more than ten years while I established an academic career, wrote up the Malaysian research, took up a new project in the UK and attended to family responsibilities of motherhood and elderly parents. In the interim, I began slowly to think about what new projects might be possible.

Seeking a way to reconnect with Malaysia that might take account of the vast changes that had occurred there in terms of urbanisation and development in the intervening years, I considered the possibility of working in urban Penang. Research on kinship and relatedness had led me to focus on ideas about blood, and I formulated plans for working in medical contexts. Given my earlier familiarity and contacts, Penang, with its well-resourced medical infrastructure and multiple hospitals, seemed

1 Anthropological Engagements

feasible. But beyond this, the island's unusually diverse population and cultural make-up within Malaysia suggested a particularly interesting context for such a study. Long-established communities of Malays, Chinese, Indians and others, with their multiple sub-communities and religious affiliations deriving partly from Penang's colonial and trading history (Yeoh et al. 2009), precipitated a productive set of questions about blood with its plethora of medical, ethnic, religious and kinship resonances.

After a brief refamiliarisation visit in the late 1990s, in the early 2000s I made a number of short exploratory trips to Penang. These eventually led to a sustained period of fieldwork based in two hospitals in 2008 and several shorter fieldwork trips over the following years (see Carsten 2019a). Over a ten-year period, I thus became more familiar with George Town and its diverse population. I learned too about doing fieldwork in a different way – urban and less immersive, but with more autonomy. I extended earlier connections, contacts and friendships, adding new qualities of attachment to a place that seemed somehow to have become layered into my existence.

Penang now is very different from when I first encountered it in 1980. The total population of the state grew from 960,600 in 1980 to 1,740,200 in 2020.[13] The administrative state of Penang (Negeri Pulau Pinang) includes the island of Penang (Pulau Pinang) and Seberang Perai (formerly Province Wellesley), the area adjacent to it on the mainland. Seberang Perai has seen a very great population influx in recent decades and major urbanisation, expansion and development of its two cities, Seberang Perai (formerly Butterworth) and Bukit Mertajam. The island of Penang, where the research for this book was conducted, has been

---

[13] These figures are taken from the Penang Institute website: https://penanginstitute.org/resources/key-penang-statistics/visualisations-of-key-indicators/penang-population-and-demographics/ Accessed 13th Feb 2024. Source: Department of Statistics Malaysia. The Malaysian government census is undertaken every ten years, and these figures are from the census for 1980 and 2020.

transformed too by high-rise developments, brutalist housing schemes, bridges to the mainland, traffic problems, shopping malls, land reclamation projects and other developments that have had a severe impact on its ecology and environment.[14] But for many Penangites, in spite of these problems, the island retains some of its charms, and these undoubtedly have to do with its people and its history. Those I spoke to in the course of researching this book often spoke warmly of their particular attachment to Penang and its multi-generational depth.

These attachments arise at least partly from Penang's atypicality in Malaysia as well as its island landscape and ecology. Established as a British colony for the East India Company by Francis Light in 1786, it became a Crown Colony together with Melaka and Singapore as part of the Straits Settlements in 1867 until the Japanese invasion and occupation of Malaya in 1941. After the Second World War, Penang became part of the Malayan Union in 1946 until Malaysia gained independence in 1957. Penang's historical importance as an entrepôt trading centre from the late eighteenth century meant that it attracted migrants from both the local region and much further afield, including China, the Arabian Peninsula, India, Ceylon (Sri Lanka) and elsewhere. These migratory flows have left their strong imprint in the architecture and places of worship of George Town's historic centre, and the unusual diversity of the languages, religions, cultures, schools and culinary traditions of Penang (see Bonney 1971; Khoo 2007; Tan 2009; Yeoh et al. 2009). This has increasingly made it an attractive tourist destination for both domestic and international travellers. The island of Penang is probably the most demographically diverse part of Malaysia, with a vibrant and historic concentration of non-Muslim Straits Chinese. Historically, it was also a regional centre of Islamic education and an embarkation point for the Hajj (Tagliacozzo 2013;

---

[14] See Jenkins (2008; 2019) on building development and the promotion of high-rise urban modernity as well as the contestations over urban space in Penang.

Tan 2009, 12–13). The statistics for the population of Penang state by ethnic group in 1980 and 2020[15] are:

	Chinese	Bumiputera	Indian	Other
1980	526,100	312,800	110,400	11,500
2020	718,400	715,900	155,500	10,100

The diversity of Penang's population is part of what makes it an unusually interesting place to study marriage. While some of the migrant communities mentioned earlier have remained distinct, intermarriage in the nineteenth and early twentieth centuries, for example, between Chinese men and local Malay women, or between Indian Muslims and Malays, resulted in distinctive hybrid communities – Baba-Nyonya or Peranakan in the former case and Jawi Peranakan in the latter – with their own cultural traditions. Tim Harper and Sunil Amrith (2012) stress the importance of cities, and especially port cities, as 'sites of interaction' in Asia. Importantly, they note that these were also sites 'where people could lose some of their ethnic definition' through 'pseudonym, fleeting encounters and subterfuge' (2012, 254). While the positive connotations of these regional and global cultural encounters might seem obvious, Kirsty Walker (2012) traces the tensions and difficulties of cosmopolitanism and cultural contact in the more intimate realm of Eurasian family histories and marriages in colonial Penang – as well as its pervasive distinctions of class, race and status.

Cultural hybridity was also central to the impression Penang made on me as a neophyte fieldworker carrying out research in the apparently more monocultural context of rural Malaysia in the 1980s. In that unexpectedly intense and sometimes overpowering first encounter with the

---

[15] These figures are taken from the Penang Institute website: https://statistics.penanginstitute.org/dashboards/social/pop.html (accessed 26th June 2025). Population estimates given here are based on censuses conducted in 1980 and 2020. Source: Department of Statistics Malaysia.

Marriage and the Moral Imagination

Malay world, Penang provided an intellectual base as well as a refuge, a space and relations that offered scope and stimulus to engage imaginatively with difference in a less monocultural register than afforded by village life. With the stimulation of local and foreign academics I met there and plenty of enjoyable sociality, I was drawn to discover more about Penang's history and sociology, and this expanded the scope of my attempts at everyday ethical evaluation and empathy. The effects of this vividly experienced process have remained with me over the ensuing decades. If a close encounter with difference is central to what marriage – as well as anthropology – is about, then, as this book illustrates, Penang affords a privileged view of how such difference is met and absorbed over time for spouses, families and communities.

Fieldwork/Marriage-Work

The focus of this book is what might be termed 'ordinary' or 'everyday' marriage, broadly defined, rather than particular categories, ethnicities or exceptional cases. Over the course of four visits to Penang and ten months between 2017 and 2019, as well as a follow-up visit in 2022, I talked to and interviewed middle-class people of different backgrounds in Penang to explore trends and patterns in marriage emerging over the last fifty to sixty years. The premise in carrying out the research was that marriage condenses kinship practice and history, encompassing personal, affective, familial, political, legal and religious facets – and that these might often be hard to distinguish or separate.

Carried out under the auspices of a European Research Council Advanced Grant, the work was one strand of a larger collaborative project in five very different locations. Although the contexts for the other strands – in Taiwan, the US, Greece and Botswana – were divergent, they all concerned marriage and had the theme of transformation at their core. Planning, fieldwork and writing were undertaken in ongoing conversation with the researchers for these projects, Hsiao-Chiao

1 Anthropological Engagements

Chiu, Siobhan Magee, Eirini Papadaki and Koreen Reece, and with their unfolding work in each of these locations, which I also visited in between carrying out research in Penang. Thus, as well as being urban-based and building on friendships and connections I had made over many years in Penang, this work was undertaken on a collaborative basis, quite different from my first rural fieldwork in Malaysia in the 1980s. The arguments in this book have been forged through the rich conversations that collaboration encouraged, and with comparative themes, convergences and disparities firmly in mind (see Carsten et al. 2021).

During stays in Penang, I rented a studio flat in the old part of George Town, which allowed me to get to many destinations on foot as I engaged in various kinds of 'marital activities'. I followed public events, including discussion panels, exhibitions and film screenings in Penang that had a bearing on marriage and gender relations more broadly, and I talked to and interviewed lawyers and activists and followed media accounts that were relevant for this research. Accompanied by different friends, I went to wedding shops in the neighbourhood and further afield to look at wedding clothes and paraphernalia and, similarly accompanied, to local flea markets to search out old photographs of weddings and other items associated with marriage. I talked to wedding planners and photographers to whom I had been forwarded by people I knew or whom I came across incidentally during the research. I visited wedding venues and spoke to their staff, and, if invited, I attended weddings. Some of these events and activities, which provided a rich background to more intimate interviews and conversations, are discussed in Chapter 2.

It was not weddings, however, that were the intended focus for this research. Perhaps my earlier, overintense, experience of Malay weddings, referred to earlier, had left its mark in shaping new interests. These centred on experiences of marriage over time rather than the process of becoming married or marital negotiations. But there are obvious difficulties in accessing such experiences as part of urban fieldwork (see Carsten 2012). The core part of the ethnography discussed in Chapters 3 to 7

Marriage and the Moral Imagination

is drawn from interviews and conversations with middle-class, urban Penangites of different backgrounds, ethnicities, genders and ages (from their twenties to their eighties) about their own experiences of marriage. I also asked participants about their childhood and their parents' marriage, and where relevant, the marriages of adult children. Sometimes these interviews also included reflections on the marriages of grandparents or siblings and more general discussions. Often, as was the case in Lydia's interview, which I referred to in the Introduction, they involved looking together at family photographs or wedding albums. Perhaps it is not surprising that, in many ways, these conversations tracked personal lives, families and generations. They were often strongly located in Penang and reflected its twentieth-century history and economy. And they told of significant social changes over many decades and several generations, which are threaded through the narratives.

The central place of narratives in the depictions of marriage in this book, which I discussed in the Introduction in terms of its connections to temporality and to imaginative and ethical aspects of relationality, thus partly reflects the process of research. Use of narrative accounts also raises questions about the interpretation and arrangement of such material, about memory and about difficulties of verification. The stories of marriages I present were elicited at least in part in response to questions that I asked or prompts from me – although these were loosely framed and depended on the age, generation, marital and personal experience, gender and background of interviewees. Interviews usually began with some general questions about childhood and background and moved on to questions about parents' marriage. Accounts might include discussion of the marriages of siblings, grandparents or adult offspring depending on the experience of interviewees and the direction their reflections took. In this way, they resembled life history interviews with an important intergenerational component in that the story of one's parents', one's own and one's children's marriages also tracks a life course and a family history – a correspondence noted by

1 Anthropological Engagements

Asha Abeyesekara (2021, 22–24), whose research on middle-class marriage in Sri Lanka was carried out in a broadly similar way. The degree of engagement and depth of responses strongly suggested that narrations articulated ongoing processes of reflection on the part of interviewees. But however much I suggest that the themes and content of discussions arose as it were 'naturally' and spontaneously in interviews and conversations with research participants and directly reflect their concerns, it is clear that the arrangement and selection of material in this book are mine. The presentation adheres to narrative conventions of anthropology and other Western literary genres.[16]

While interview material has pride of place in the accounts given here, it has been complemented and considered in the light of a much longer experience of Malaysia and Penang. The interviews took place alongside many informal conversations and sociable meetings with old and newer friends. Narrative accounts were considered against a backdrop of what I had come to know about marriage and people's lives in Malaysia over many years. At times, zones of intimacy collided when conversations about my research bled into unanticipated revelations from friends about their own marriage or their family. Although such material has not been directly quoted, it would be impossible to discount these conversations or their contribution to my developing reflections, and they too inform this work. In this respect, 'fieldwork' (or marriage-work) has stretched over a rather long period of familiarity and friendship. The analogy I drew at the beginning of this chapter between marriage and anthropology as encounters with difference thus encompasses the temporal qualities of these engagements. In anthropology, as in a marriage, what initially seems new and strange gradually, over the years, becomes

---

[16] In an important critique of the use of narratives in anthropological accounts of crisis with particular reference to the AIDS 'crisis' in Botswana, Koreen Reece (2023) draws on her long-term, close and immersive fieldwork with one family to show the distorting effects of uncritically applying such conventions and ignoring local genres of telling or not telling.

familiar. Malay conjugal relations have formal qualities that are likened to siblingship, and, over time, spouses are likely to become more 'sibling-like' in qualitative aspects of their everyday intimacy. Anthropological encounters, likewise, when thickened over many years of familiarity, lose their tenor of strangeness, taking more strongly the form of friendship or kinship.

As I have indicated through the course of this chapter, my 1980s fieldwork in Langkawi was helpful in situating the material on Malay marriage that I gathered in Penang, giving me a grounding in earlier Malay practices of betrothal, marriage rituals, conjugality and divorce, and for highlighting changes that had occurred in the intervening years. I was much less familiar with non-Muslim, Indian-Malaysian or Chinese-Malaysian marriage cultures and also lacked language skills in Hokkien, Mandarin, Tamil and other local languages that would have been helpful. All the interviews drawn on in this book took place in English, in which, as is generally the case for middle-class Malaysians (many of whom are multi-lingual), participants were fluent. For many, English was either their first language or one of the main languages of their daily lives.[17] Many but not all had, like Lydia and Haryath, been educated partly or wholly in English-medium schools or universities; some had grown up in English-speaking or bilingual families; many used English as well as other languages in their workplaces and everyday lives. Malay participants and others often peppered their accounts with Malay terms, and my familiarity with these contributed to my capacity to contextualise their references. To recruit interviewees, I drew on a network of friendships and contacts built up over many years in local universities, heritage contexts, hospitals, arts and activist circles, where people I knew

---

[17] For an account of Malaysia's linguistic hybridity, see Rachel Leow's groundbreaking historical study, *Taming Babel* (2016). On the pervasiveness of English and its capacity to express a 'transethnic Malaysian identity', see Mandal (2001, 160). Both Leow's discussion and that of Mandal are particularly pertinent to the consideration of 'mixed marriages' in Chapter 5.

1 Anthropological Engagements

helpfully forwarded my requests to those they thought might be willing to talk to me. In all, I formally interviewed about forty-five people about their own marriages, their families and lives or about marriage more generally. In several cases, I had one or more follow-up conversations with these participants, and I had many more informal conversations about marriage with friends or acquaintances whom I did not formally interview. I endeavoured to interview participants of different ages, ethnicities, religions, occupations and backgrounds. About two-thirds of those I interviewed were women, one-third were men.

The particular local context and its historical contours are central to any anthropological analysis. Events in Malaysia during research shaped this work in unforeseen ways. As discussed in Chapter 2, general elections in 2018 resulted in the toppling of the political coalition Barisan Nasional, dominated by the United Malays National Organisation (UMNO), which had ruled the country since independence from British colonial rule in 1957. This result was the culmination of widespread disgust at numerous long-running corruption scandals under the regime of the ruling prime minister, Najib Razak. A new government composed of a coalition of parties, Pakatan Harapan, led by veteran politician and former Prime Minister Mahathir Mohamad (who had resigned from his position as leader of UMNO in 2016), was formed. The extraordinary electoral upturn was part of an unprecedented and short-lived period of optimism among what had previously been opposition parties, activists and many in the general population. Seemingly unconnected to marriage, the election result nevertheless formed a context for the conversations about marriage and the atmosphere of change which I encountered in Penang. As I describe in Chapter 2, the unusually lively and outspoken cultural ambience in George Town, as well as the subjects of debate and public commentary, suggested the salience of connections between the 'political' and the 'domestic' and raised questions about how political change might be fostered or generated within families.

Marriage and the Moral Imagination

By 2020, things were looking considerably darker on the Malaysian and global stages. The elected government that had been formed in Malaysia in 2018 fell in February 2020 in another extraordinary and long-running political crisis when several parties joined forces to oust the Pakatan Harapan coalition and form a new government under Muhyiddin Yassin. Although in some sense unprecedented in that the elections of 2018 had been the first time the Barisan Nasional had been defeated since Independence, the manner in which the new government was toppled – through deals in which elected MPs 'crossed the floor', changing their allegiance and joining what had been opposition parties – seemed depressingly familiar in Malaysian politics. I followed these disheartening events from a distance and sporadically, distracted by another kind of crisis. I had planned a research visit to Penang between February and April 2020 to carry out follow-up interviews and further work on those who had remained unmarried but cancelled this at short notice as the swiftly developing COVID-19 pandemic took hold in Europe and seemed likely to engulf Southeast Asia. In the event, it was Europe that was engulfed, while Southeast Asian nations on the whole successfully held off COVID-19 until 2021 by adopting measures learned during the SARS outbreaks of 2003.

During the main initial period of writing, research was on hold and visits to Penang were suspended until 2022. Lockdowns proved conducive to writing – at least for some – but the fieldwork on which this book is based was abruptly curtailed. This was a further lesson in the always contingent and necessarily incomplete nature of anthropological research (another aspect of its 'cruel optimism'), which resonates with its topics of enquiry. The separations wrought by the pandemic provided space to reflect on qualities of deeply internalised but interrupted connections, established over more than four decades, to a place and people that I had previously encountered only through written texts.

Anthropology, I have suggested, can be likened to marriage as an encounter with difference and in the demands it makes from participants of imagination and empathy – qualities that may deepen and change with time and with increased familiarity, or may be left unmet. Marital shocks are often quietly and imperceptibly absorbed, but they may also lead to ruptures, as we learn in Chapters 6 and 7, precipitating new and unanticipated transformations of relations. Anthropological connections, like marital ones, are liable to suffer from unpredicted events and uncertainties – as was all too vividly instantiated during the COVID pandemic. These may sometimes stimulate new modes of engagement, different ways of reflecting on or presenting material and new forms of connection.

TWO

Marriage and Gender in the Political Moment

This chapter is concerned with the political salience of marriage and with public discourse. Because the religious and legal connotations of marriage are central to it as a public institution, issues to do with marriage are not contained within any one sphere. In fact, they force us to question the way that social scientists have divided their subject matter between the supposedly separable domains of economics, politics, kinship and religion. The historical emergence of 'modernity', as conventionally understood, apparently requires the separation of politics (its purification) from kinship or religion. But, as Sylvia Yanagisako and Carol Delaney (1995) and Susan McKinnon and Fenella Cannell (2013a) have convincingly argued, this 'domaining effect' is an artefact of modernity rather than a portrayal of lived experience. In other words, by analysing social worlds in such terms, and thus reifying these domains, social scientists have actually reproduced an ideology of modernity that rests on their separation. Marriage could be a paradigmatic example. As we see in this chapter, far from being 'simply' a kinship institution, marriage is also simultaneously a legal, religious, political and economic one.

The fact that marriage is inherently multifaceted means that public controversy about any particular aspect of it is liable to have effects that are not confined to a single area of social life but may ricochet between them. In this way, as we see in this chapter, marriage can be something of a political lightning rod, attracting and refracting contentious issues and

2 Marriage and Gender in the Political Moment

sensitivities, which often emerge particularly sharply at times of heightened political change or tension. It follows from the 'uncontainability' of marriage as a public institution that, although sexuality is certainly not confined to marriage, marriage may come to stand for sexuality or gender relations – and vice versa – in public discourse. Issues about LGBTQ rights or domestic abuse often ineluctably segue into, or arise from, discussions about marriage. In this chapter, I consider controversies about marriage but also those that concerned gender and sexuality more broadly, as they emerged in public discourse during my research.

While the focus of this chapter is on events and debates in Penang and Malaysia, where law, religion and ethnicity are deeply entangled and are seldom possible to keep apart, the multifaceted characteristic of marriage as an institution is not particular to Malaysia. In Lynchburg, Virginia, in the southern US – to take just one example – where another strand of the project investigating transformations of marriage was undertaken (see Chapter 1), personal, legal and religious aspects of marriage were impossible to prize apart and also central to wider public debates. Siobhan Magee writes:

> Marriage was not only a matter of personal pleasure, but something people 'believed in': a spiritual-cum-political conviction held by people who said they 'weren't political' (were not interested in electoral politics), the backbone of happy and 'healthy' communities and the source of 'secure and stable' children who would grow up to nurture their own covetable marriages and righteous communities. (Magee 2021, 54)

Notoriously, enslaved people were legally barred from marriage. In the long aftermath of slavery, interracial marriage was outlawed in Virginia until the Supreme Court ruling in the case of *Loving v. Virginia* in 1967 that the ban on interracial marriage violated the Fourteenth Amendment of the US Constitution (see Cashin 2017). As Magee (2025) makes clear, the history of marriage in Lynchburg is in fact interwoven with histories of race and legal, political and religious exclusion in Virginia.

Marriage and the Moral Imagination

Contemporary public debates, for example, on same-sex partnerships, marital equality or the politics of race were enmeshed with each other and with wider discussions about marriage, religion and morality.

***

There was an unusual vibrancy in the air and an openness to discussions in public and private forums when I visited Penang from July to September 2018. The atmosphere was a marked contrast to the generally pessimistic and low-key mood about the forthcoming elections during a previous research visit earlier in the same year. After the elections of May 2018, expectations were high – no doubt overly so – that real political change might be forthcoming. As one lawyer told me, she was for the first time really proud to be a Malaysian and, as a mark of this, was sending out her assistants for a flag to put out on Merdeka Day (National Day) on 31 August. In the newspapers and at public meetings and events organised as part of the annual George Town Festival, there was forthright and often outspoken debate around various topical issues.

It seemed surprising that many of these issues concerned gender and marriage. A shocking child marriage case involving an eleven-year-old Thai girl and a Kelantanese man in his forties received widespread negative commentary in the media and triggered more general debate about child marriage and agitation for reform (see also Peletz 2023). A long-running case of disputed child custody following a formerly Hindu husband's conversion to Islam was likewise the topic of general debate about the implications of religious conversion for marriage and custody rights. LGBTQ rights were the subject of public debate in the aftermath of comments by a government minister criticising an exhibition in Penang featuring photographs of public personalities, some of whom were civil society activists. The comments, and the subsequent removal of photographs of two gay rights activists by the organisers in response to the minister's demand, were followed by a spate of self-imposed 'sympathetic removals' by other personalities featured in the exhibition.

2 Marriage and Gender in the Political Moment

In this chapter, I trace some of the ways that marriage, sexuality and gender relations more broadly came to the fore in public discourse and cultural events in Penang and elsewhere in Malaysia in 2018–19. How does marriage come to be politically salient? To begin to answer this question, we need to situate marriage in unfolding national and local events and in a broader picture of what was happening at the time of research. Drawing on newspaper reports and interviews with lawyers, as well as cultural performances and debates that took place in Penang during the annual George Town Festival of July–August 2018, I consider the contemporary political resonances of marriage and gender relations in the public culture of Penang, and more widely in Malaysia. A central question of this book is how are marriage and wider political transformation connected? There is no simple or straightforward answer. By showing the myriad and often nonobvious links between discussion of overtly political matters and points of tension in gendered relations at a critical juncture of political change, this chapter draws some possible threads of connection. I return to these links from a different perspective in Chapter 7, after first exploring more personal and familial aspects of experiences of marital relationships.

As outlined in Chapter 1, 2018–19 was a unique period in Malaysian politics. The fall of the government coalition, after more than fifty years of uninterrupted post-Independence rule, in the elections of May 2018 inspired a new and unusual spirit of political optimism. This was particularly palpable in Penang, a long-time centre of political opposition, and especially in activist and intellectual circles. On the face of it, gender and marriage seemed of rather peripheral pertinence to these momentous events. Nevertheless, and perhaps surprisingly, they figured prominently in public discourse and media reports in the period following the elections.

While one might construe some of the issues referred to in this chapter as expressing the widespread conservatism of Malaysian attitudes on issues of gender and marriage, the tone of exchanges at meetings and in the media instead suggested an openness to perceptions about political possibilities and a new forthrightness about what might be publicly articulated. The fact that concerns about gender relations and marriage figured prominently also intimated that something about the extraordinary political moment might make the research about marriage on which I had embarked unexpectedly timely. The critical nature of public commentary and the impetus for legislative reform show how the linkages between private, personal lives, family issues and legal and political matters were more densely entangled than might be assumed. I wondered whether the visibility of dysfunctional marriage and familial life in media accounts, and also as a topic of academic interest – in the forms of child marriage, polygamy, domestic violence, incest and sexual abuse – might in some respects be misleading. Likewise struck by the heightened tone of public discourse about anomalous cases of gendered relations in the same period in Malaysia, Michael Peletz has framed this in terms of 'moral panic' (Peletz 2023, 202), which he analyses in the context of contested ideas about masculinity and ambivalence and anxieties surrounding a shift towards ideals of companionate marriage. Here I consider discourse about these concerns ethnographically to probe *why* they figured so prominently in public exchanges at this time and what this tells us about how marriage and gender relations are situated in wider politics. Crucial though these issues are for public awareness and government policy, one might gain the erroneous impression that in Malaysia, as compared to other countries, such problems are unusually prevalent or intractable.

A focus on public culture thus provides both a backdrop and an introduction to the more intimate familial stories presented in Chapters 3–7. It also serves as one kind of entry to the city of George Town where many of those stories are situated, to its urban flavours and cultural life. That this cultural life is particular within Malaysia partly because of Penang's long history of ethnic and religious diversity is a point taken forward from Chapter 1. This also means that, for its diverse inhabitants, there are many different 'versions' of Penang that one might highlight, and

2 Marriage and Gender in the Political Moment

it would be impossible to even attempt to do these justice here. The account I give is inherently partial and selective. Although I describe scenarios that were on the face of it separate and disconnected from each other, their effects rippled out into the wider zeitgeist, and debates about them bled into one another in suggestive ways. Placing them side by side allows us to consider how these events participated in, and were expressions of, the same political moment.

Notably, much of the discourse reproduced in this chapter makes reference to law or legal reform. The dense connections between marriage and gender relations with politics and religion that are refracted through public discourse have particular salience in Malaysia because of its dual legal systems, civil and Islamic, noted in Chapter 1.[1] This means that law and legal reform can be especially charged and contested along religious and ethnic lines. Lawyers who work on family cases and divorce have particular experience and knowledge of the ways in which law comes to matter and how it inserts itself into conjugal lives. This too is part of the public culture of marriage, and I include excerpts from interviews with lawyers towards the end of this chapter. But I begin with an exhibition that, curiously enough, came to be defined by absent images. While these did not concern marriage as such, they did arouse concerns about sexuality and wider public morality.

Viewing Gender, Exhibiting Absence

I had been aware of the 'Stripes and Stokes' exhibition of portraits by Malaysian photographer Mooreyameen Mohamad on the ground floor of Penang's major cultural auditorium, Dewan Sri Pinang, for some time before I went to see it. A high-profile event of the George Town Festival in 2018, and displayed in one of George Town's most imposing

[1] For a clear account of the recent history of the expansion of jurisdiction of the Syariah Courts in Malaysia in relation to prominent contested cases of Muslim-non-Muslim family disputes see Maznah et al. (2009).

municipal spaces, the exhibition showed twenty-eight portraits of prominent Malaysians each draped in the Malaysian flag. Something about the patriotic imagery did not make me hurry to see it. It was at another event, a panel discussion that was part of a series of 'Tanjung Talks',[2] billed as 'Sisters under the Skin' – focusing on 'What does it mean to be a Malay woman?' that my interest was piqued.

The speakers were Marina Mahathir, a well-known journalist, activist and daughter of Malaysia's then (and longest-serving) Prime Minister, Mahathir Mohamad; Regina Ibrahim, a trans activist; and Siti Kasim, a lawyer and civil rights activist. The members of the panel spoke about their own backgrounds and gendered experiences, reflecting on the ethnic and religious framing of these. Malay Muslims, one of them said, came under syariah law in terms of family matters. This meant that (Malay and other Muslim) trans women were under syariah law. This was 'both a silencing and a privilege'. Another speaker mentioned the controversy that had surrounded the 'Stripes and Strokes' exhibition – there had been newspaper reports about the demand from government minister Datuk Dr Mujahid Yusof to remove photos of LGBT activists Nisha Ayub and Pang Khee Teik featured in the exhibition (the latter apparently holding a small rainbow flag). The minister was quoted in a newspaper report as stating that this was not a matter of their personal orientation but 'to comply with the government's policy of no promotion of LGBT culture'. He was further cited as stating:

'We do not interfere in their personal life but as the government, our concern is whether there is any breach of law or any promotion of the culture'. ('Portraits of LGBT activists taken down', *Star*, 9 August 2018).

Coming from a representative of the newly installed reformist government, this seemed to many liberal observers a retrograde move.

---

[2] 'Tanjung' (literally, cape or promontory in Malay) is a common way of referring to the island of Penang or to George Town its capital.

2 Marriage and Gender in the Political Moment

Mentioning what she called the 'flag issue' – that the photos were about patriotism and not about promoting LGBTQ rights – a panel speaker questioned why there was such a gap between Malay and non-Malay thinking. 'It's different from twenty to thirty years ago', she said. This was all about politics, the panel agreed, and politics should not be mixed with religion. There had been an intrusion of religious views into an art exhibition. 'We need to take back the space to stop politicians using religion against us [women]. Using religion is the number one enemy in Malaysia', a speaker proclaimed. But, she noted, when people had been indoctrinated since they were small children, it was difficult to change things. There were further comments about the difficulty of separating religion from politics in Malaysia and about the erosion of women's rights since the 1980s.

There followed a general discussion in which members of the audience posed questions to the panel. The topics ranged broadly around religion and politics with gender issues providing a kind of touchstone. One member of the audience spoke of the difficulty she had encountered, as a Malay woman, of going unveiled; another brought up gender-based violence; and another mentioned a child marriage case that had figured largely in the press, which I discuss further later in this chapter. These were familiar issues on the Malaysian gender-based activism horizon. But the debate around trans issues and religion was unusually forthright, and the references to the exhibition, which ran through the conversation, were particular to the immediate context.

I visited the 'Stripes and Strokes' exhibition on the following day. By then, it was several days since the image that had been found objectionable by Dr Mujahid had been removed. His comments were in turn received with ridicule in more liberal circles. The exhibition sponsor, Datuk Vinod Sekhar, a prominent businessman (whose portrait was also featured in the exhibition), social activists and others made supportive statements to the press. Following the first removal, twelve out of twenty-eight further photos had been removed in solidarity, at the request of their subjects – including those of two of the speakers from the panel event I had attended the day before, Marina Mahathir and Siti Kassim. This had the strange effect of creating an exhibition in which the gaps, together with simple labels added by the organisers showing whose portrait had been withdrawn (in the form, 'Datin Paduka Marina Mahathir was here' or 'Siti Kasim was here' together with another placard eulogising Siti Kasim), were as eye-catching as the images.

Reaction to what was widely seen as an act of censorship continued to ricochet out over the following days with calls for anti-discrimination policies, which Dr Mujahid Yusof was pressured to address:

On Friday Dr Mujahid said the Government would consider introducing anti-discrimination policies to protect 'vulnerable' trans-gender group [sic] but admitted more understanding on the issue was needed.[3]

Mooreyam, the photographer, was reported to have received offers from several private galleries to host an uncensored version of the exhibition:

'I am against the censorship but this incident has sparked some important conversations about our nationhood and as Malaysians' he said, urging the people to visit and support the exhibition.[4]

There was a feeling that, in the short term at least, the minister's intervention had seriously backfired.

The public discussion I had attended highlighted the dense and historically configured entanglements of religion, ethnicity and politics in Malaysia that were noted in Chapter 1, which make it almost impossible to talk about one of these topics without implicating the others (see also Carsten 2019a, 19–20). It also illuminated how gendered experiences could simultaneously be a proxy or an entry point for discussing

---

[3] 'Vinod Shekar: 'Let's hear it for the LGBTs', *Star*, 12 August 2018.
[4] 'Vinod Shekar: 'Let's hear it for the LGBTs', *Star*, 12 August 2018.

religion, politics and ethnicity. Referring to syariah law, which particularly impacts Malay women's marital and inheritance rights, as 'both a silencing and a privilege' registered both the gendered inequalities embedded in syariah law and its protective qualities. We will encounter again these dual aspects in the experiences of Malay women undergoing divorce in Chapters 4 and 6.

The 'Stripes and Strokes' exhibition had apparently been intended as a patriotic visualisation of the plurality of backgrounds, ethnicities, genders, professions and viewpoints of prominent figures making up the Malaysian nation. One could take this as an assertive statement of national pluralism. Clearly, the flag imagery was central both to the messages conveyed and also to the reactions of those who objected to the exhibition. It was the insulting connotations to the nation, which critics perceived in at least two of these images (and/or the views and activities of its subjects), that turned it into a quite different kind of show. The 'exhibition of absences', created through the withdrawal of images, projected another message – one of suppression and also of political solidarity and dissent. Notably, it was the vehement denial of the assertion of LGBTQ rights to be included in the national project that triggered such a bifurcation of messaging. In the attempt at repression, and the ensuing political statement of resistance, materialised in absent images, gender relations seemed visibly to have the power to split the nation. And this echoes the heightened tenor of debates around same-sex marriage equality or the history of race in Virginia that I referred to earlier.

Screening Marriage, Legislating Conversion

The day after the 'Tanjung Talk' on 'Sisters under the Skin' described earlier, I attended another event in the same series, a documentary film screening of 'Diary for Prasana' in the presence of its director, Norhayati Kaprawi. She began her introduction to the film with a statement of solidarity for the LGBT activists whose photos had been removed from the 'Stars and Stripes' exhibition. 'Diary for Prasana' documented a notorious and long-running case of religious conversion and its impact on marriage and child custody arrangements, which had been widely reported in the press. It followed the ten-year search and legal struggle of Indira Gandhi to find and gain custody of her youngest child, Prasana, who had been taken by her husband after he converted to Islam, converted the child to Islam (both without Indira's knowledge), and subsequently filed for divorce. 'Diary for Prasana' had been first screened in November 2017 in Kuala Lumpur. Notably, the case had implications for other similar cases of secret conversions to Islam, particularly on the part of men with divorce in mind.

In the discussion that followed the screening, a panel of three, the film's director, a Penang lawyer and Indira herself, gave comments on the film and answered questions from the audience. In the view of the lawyer, 'a mockery' had been made of the law, which was actually very clear. The case had 'dragged on for 10 years' with different people giving contradictory and confusing interpretations or saying the husband could not be found. The lawyer summarised how, in January 2018, after many years of pursuing her legal rights, Indira had won her case in the Federal Court. The conversion of her children had been nullified, and her children had been ruled to be still Hindu. The police were then instructed to find Indira's husband and Prasana. The police could no longer deny this, the lawyer continued. 'We're pushing the new government for an IDP response', Indira herself commented, 'For the past 10 years they've never met me. Now with the new government?.... I want to see my child'.

The lawyer noted that the civil court was a higher judicial authority than the syariah court and that this principle had not been applied in the legal rulings. More recently, the Malaysian Supreme Court, she said, had decided the conversion of the child was not valid because the children were not there, and their mother had not been heard. Indira's marriage had been registered when it was solemnised in the civil court. Under the

2 Marriage and Gender in the Political Moment

syariah court, non-Muslims did not have rights. But in custody cases, the rule was that the interests of the child are paramount. But these had not been considered. Now the position has been clarified, she said. 'We hope action will be taken' (see also Maznah 2020, 222–23).

The film's director stated that the primary intended audience for the film was Malay. Its purpose was the democratisation of knowledge and information: 'There is a lack of knowledge about the case. Lack of information. That's why freedom of information is important'. She explained that she had previously made a film about wearing the hijab – when it was introduced in Malaysia. 'In the time of our grandparents, women didn't wear it. I hope the younger generation and the current government will give space'.

A member of the audience asked whether there were other cases like that of Indira. The lawyer responded that there were many other cases and that the law for conversion needed to be clarified so that the rights of non-Muslims were protected. The situation where someone could walk away from marriage by the simple act of conversion – at which point a new set of laws and jurisdictions take over – was untenable. It was important to settle problems *before* one partner embraced a new religion. That's where there was a problem. This would require political will, and those concerned needed to push for it: 'We have a new government; there is a lot of hope. Let's push them harder. It needs public pressure. All of us are affected. Lots of families are affected'. The film's director reiterated that 'the law is very clear. If either party is non-Muslim, they have to go to the civil court. The syariah court has no jurisdiction over non-Muslims'. The lawyer then repeated her view that there was nothing wrong with the law: 'The judicial authorities have messed up. The January ruling is clear. Both parents are required in cases of conversion' (see also Maznah 2020, 222–23).

As emerged in the film screening and discussion, both the particular case of Indira Gandhi, and the more general issue of conversion, were long-running and familiar ones that were frequently and widely reported in the Malaysian media. Thus, in July 2018 there were reports in the media of another case, this time involving a Muslim convert mother who had converted her two children to Islam while she and her husband were still in the process of settling a divorce. The two children were aged eight and four in 2015 when they had been converted without the knowledge or consent of their father. The press reported that the lawyer acting for the ex-husband in the case, K. Shanmuga, had argued that the children were too young to understand the meaning of conversion. Furthermore,

> He said even on an interpretation of the Federal Constitution alone, the Federal Court held that the Constitution requires both parents, if both are still alive to consent to the conversion of a child.[5]

The decisive ruling by the Federal Court on 29 January 2018 on the issue of the unilateral conversion of Indira Gandhi's children, reiterating the constitutional requirement for both parents to consent, had been hailed as a landmark decision that would have important implications for other cases as well as 'for the future of multi-ethnic and multi-religious Malaysia' – as one prominent activist and feminist put it.[6] The central point was that in cases of disagreement between civil and syariah law, all legislation needed to comply with the Constitution. For this purpose, the Attorney-General's Chambers announced that a Syariah and Harmonisation of Law division would be established.[7]

In spite of the apparent clarity of the Federal Court's decision and talk of possible amendment of marriage legislation, future disputes were not necessarily ruled out – as was intimated in further commentary. A prominent letter in *The Star* pointed out that, in the original English, Clause 88A of the Federal Constitution, requiring the consent of both parents for the conversion of their children, had been mistranslated in

---

[5] 'Mum converts kids to Islam without dad's consent', *Star*, 13 July 2018.
[6] Zainah Anwar, 'Court verdict shines light on the way forward', *Star*, 4 February 2018.
[7] 'M'sian Bar: All legislation must adhere to Federal Constitution', *Star*, 4 February 2018.

2 Marriage and Gender in the Political Moment

the Malay version, 'which says that only the consent of *"ibu atau bapa"* (mother or father) is required to convert a minor'. There would therefore need to be a correction of the translation of '"ibu atau bapa" to read *ibu-bapa* [parents] in the Malay version of the Constitution'. The same letter also questioned the motivation behind this mistranslation and whether it 'could be construed as contempt of the Federal Court'.[8]

The Federal Court ruling in January 2018 had been widely welcomed in progressive circles. Dr Chandra Muzaffar, a prominent Malaysian human rights activist and Islamic reformist, in a comment piece written in his capacity as Chairman of the Board of Trustees of Yayasan Perpaduan Malaysia, a civil society group promoting cultural diversity, explained that, in prioritising the well-being of the child and the bond between mother and child, the judgement reflected the underlying values of Islam. He also argued that the judgement was in accord with the views of leading Islamic jurists who promoted 'the Islamic public law doctrine of *siyasah shar'iyyah*'. This doctrine, Dr Chandra explained, promoted flexibility in responding to extra-syariah rulings in the interests of good justice and in accordance with the principles of syariah.[9]

The film screening and discussion under the auspices of the George Town Festival that I had attended illuminated once again how easily diverse issues connected with gender inequality, such as veiling, child custody, religious conversion, domestic violence or the suppression of voices promoting gender rights at the 'Stripes and Stokes' exhibition, bled into each other. They also underlined the long-running nature of these issues in Malaysian public discourse. If many perceived the January 2018 judgement in the Federal Court to be long overdue, 2018 as a political moment seemed unusually full of possibilities. As one speaker had said, 'We have a new government; there is a lot of hope'. The suggestion

---

[8] Ravinder Singh, 'Correct Malay translation' *Star*, 3 February 2018, original italics.
[9] 'Court decision resonates with the essence of Islam', Dr Chandra Muzaffar, *Star* 8 February 2018.

that the initiative should be seized without delay, however, also implied a recognition that this opportunity might turn out to be short-lived.

Exposing Rifts: Child Marriage

Through July and August 2018, in the same period as the events described earlier, another high-profile issue concerning marriage erupted in the media. Reports of the marriage, registered in Thailand, of a forty-one-year-old Malay man from the east coast state of Kelantan to an eleven-year-old Thai girl as his third wife had surfaced in June and led to an outpouring of concerned commentary from both Muslim and non-Muslim observers (see Peletz 2023; Nurul Huda 2022). One question was whether the Kelantanese Syariah Court (the body empowered to rule on Muslim marriages in the state) would register the marriage and thus grant it the necessary legal approval in Malaysia. But wider questions about the legal age of marriage were in the foreground of public discourse. The age of legal marriage for non-Muslims, governed by civil marriage law in Malaysia, is eighteen, but, by permission of the Chief Minister of the state, girls can marry from the age of sixteen. For Muslims, marriage comes under the state syariah courts, which deal with personal and family matters for Muslims. Syariah law allows marriage from the age of eighteen for boys and from the age of sixteen for girls, or by permission of the state's Syariah Court, above sixteen for boys and from puberty for girls.[10]

As many commentators and media reports pointed out, however, the issue was not necessarily so clear-cut as this division of jurisdictions implied. The legal age of marriage could be regarded as a matter of public

---

[10] Nurul Huda Mohd. Razif (2022) gives a perceptive analysis of this case, drawing out the economic, legal and cultural pressures among Muslims in Malaysia to marry young. She argues that an ideology of 'masculinist protectionism', articulated in terms of Islam, casts a benevolent aura over marriages between under-age girls and older men, masking more abusive and coercive realities.

2 Marriage and Gender in the Political Moment

concern rather than a personal matter. In this case, parliament could introduce legislation to criminalise child marriage regardless of Islamic law. The new government, which had put raising the legal age of marriage to 18 in its election manifesto, was under sustained pressure to act.[11] Amidst widely voiced disappointment at the prevarication and failure of the Deputy Prime Minister (also the Women, Family and Community Development Minister), Datin Dr Wan Azizah Wan Ismail, to speak out clearly on the matter, the G25 group of eminent Malays urged the government to introduce legislation to make underage marriage a federal crime.[12]

In the event, the state Syariah Court in Kelantan imposed a fine of RM 1,800 (approximately £350) on the husband after he pleaded guilty to marrying an underage child without the consent of the court, and also to polygamy without the required consent of his two other wives. Meanwhile, civil society groups, NGOs, activists, students and other young people launched a hashtag campaign, 'pelajarbukanpengantin' ('schoolnotspouse'), supported by several ministers and MPs. Datuk Dr Muhahid Yusof Rawa, Minister in the Prime Minister's department, announced that the government was proposing to abolish the law allowing Muslim men and women to get married before the legal minimum ages with the permission of the court or other authorities, and that this would pave the way for new laws banning child marriage. 'The ban is not in terms of Syariah law, but just in terms of administration,' Dr Mujahid was reported as saying in an apparent attempt to defuse a delicate issue.[13]

A striking aspect of the particular case that had provoked the public outcry was its extreme nature – the marriage of a forty-one-year-old man to an eleven-year-old girl had disturbing connotations as commentators noted:

---

[11] 'Government needs to get act together on child marriage', Surendra Ananth, *Star*, 14 July 2018.
[12] 'G25: make underage marriage a federal crime', *Star*, 17 July 2018.
[13] 'Govt working to ban child marriages, says minister', *Star* 7 August 2018.

69

Marriage and the Moral Imagination

It's enough to make anyone's stomach churn how a 41-year-old man could take an 11-year-old child as his wife, and later proudly confess that he had wanted to marry her since she was seven.[14]

The same commentary referred to 'paedophilic acts' of the perpetrator, described as 'a rubber tapper' and 'religious teacher'. Furthermore, this writer noted, 'In Malaysia, the furore gets incredibly loud when deliberating the subject of homosexuality' but 'disturbingly silent when it comes to child marriages'. It was not just feminist activists who called for a revision of the law and a raising of the legal age of marriage for Muslims; other less likely candidates, including the Sultan of Selangor, proposed a revision of the legal age of marriage for Muslims in the state of Selangor. This proposal for reform would be enacted through revision of the existing Islamic Family Law (State of Selangor) Enactment 2003 and the Syariah Court Civil Procedure (State of Selangor) Enactment 2003.[15] In other words, it would be introduced through state rather than federal legislation.

The optics of this particular case of 'child marriage' were thus unsettling enough to unite reforming voices from quite different quarters. And like other events concerning marriage and gender relations, it had the capacity to evoke other issues, including polygamy without the consent of previous wives, and homosexuality. But it also instantiated a general perception in Malaysia that Muslims are likely to marry at a younger age than non-Muslims, and more broadly, it had the potential to expose a cleavage between Muslims and non-Muslims with their different juridical authorities. The sensitivity of this, and the political calculation the government was making, was part of what lay behind the latter's failure to speedily institute federal reform.

Like the separate administrative and legal regimes governing marriage and family matters for Muslims and non-Muslims in

---

[14] Wong Chun Wai, 'Baby love no more' *Star*, 22 July 2018.

[15] '"Revise legal age of marriage to 18" Sultan Sharafuddin: Child unions have negative impact on couple's future', Wani Muthiah, *Star*, 4 September 2018.

2 Marriage and Gender in the Political Moment

Malaysia – and the ethnic make-up of the country itself – the issue of child marriage can also be read through a longer colonial history. In fact, the controversy aroused in 2018 had striking resonances with that following a notorious instance of child marriage in Singapore in 1950 on the eve of political independence from colonial rule. In a penetrating analysis, historian Jialin Christina Wu (2017) has placed the public debate surrounding the case of Nadra/'Bertha' Maria Hertogh, who in 1950 was married aged thirteen to Mansoor Adabi, a twenty-two-year-old Kelantanese English teacher in Singapore, in the context of the political events of the time (see also Chee, Jones and Maznah 2009, 2; Hussin 2005).[16] Here I closely follow Wu's presentation of these events and the ensuing larger public debate about child marriage.

The case of Maria Hertogh in the first place involved disputed custody arrangements. Wu (2017) describes how Maria was the daughter of a Dutch-Eurasian Catholic couple and had been born in 1937 in Java in the Dutch East Indies. Following the upheaval of Japanese occupation in 1942 and the internment of her father, she had been brought up by Che Aminah, an educated Malay woman from the Malay state of Terengganu then living in Java. The terms of this arrangement were disputed – the child's mother, Adeline, maintained this had been intended as a stay of a few days' duration, but Che Aminah argued that an adoption had been agreed. Following the internment of her mother, Maria was brought up by Che Aminah as a Malay-speaking Muslim and given the name Nadra. After their release from internment at the end of the war, the Hertoghs returned to the Netherlands and sought to find and be reunited with the child. Che Aminah had by then returned to her home in Terengganu (on the east coast of Malaya) together with the child. Once located, Che Aminah was requested to meet with Dutch authorities in Singapore to negotiate the return of the child. In the

---

[16] I am grateful to Eirini Papadaki for bringing this article to my attention.

course of the negotiations and legal proceedings that ensued in 1950, the thirteen-year-old was (seemingly hastily) married to Mansoor Adabi on 1 August 1950 (Wu 2017, 663).

Following this, there was an outcry in Holland on behalf of the Hertoghs and appeals to the British colonial authorities. In their failure to take action, Wu notes the unfavourable comparisons made in the Dutch press with the long-standing British attempts to prevent the interracial marriage of Serestse Khama, heir to King Khama III of the British Protectorate of Bechuanaland (Botswana), to Ruth Williams, a white British woman, in their efforts to appease the apartheid regime in South Africa (Wu 2017, 664–65). In spite of its potential to garner anti-colonial feeling, there were numerous letters and much public commentary in the English language press in Malaya on the issue of the age of Maria/Nadra with 'one writer ... in the *Straits Times*, appealing for "responsible", "educated", "enlightened" perspectives in view of "modern times" in 1950' (Wu 2017, 665). Significantly, the comments of women's rights activists and letters from concerned citizens in the *Straits Times* at the time indicated that it was the marriage that changed public opinion to support the Hertoghs after initial sympathy for Che Aminah's claims (Wu 2017, 667).

Wu carefully documents the sustained debate in the English-language and Malay press in the subsequent weeks and months about 'child brides' and 'Malaya's marriage laws'. Predictably perhaps, this expressed a cleavage between Muslims and non-Muslims. An article in the *Straits Times* noted that 'all the leading Malay newspapers of the country – *Utusan Melayu* in Singapore, *Majlis* in Kuala Lumpur [Malaya] and *Warta Negara* in Penang [Malaya] have published editorial comment arguing that the marriage should not be interfered with'.[17] Wu notes how the same article placed the issue in the wider context of post-independence marriage reform in India. In doing so, she argues, 'the

---

[17] 'The Child Bride', *Straits Times*, 14 August 1950, p. 6, cited in Wu (2017, 667)

2 Marriage and Gender in the Political Moment

Straits Times underlined Malayan independence as being intertwined with marriage reform' (Wu 2017, 667).[18]

Proposals to raise the legal age of marriage for non-Muslims in Singapore to sixteen were put forward in the midst of the debate. These were fiercely opposed by Muslim authorities as likely 'to widen the gulf of religious difference and constitute the prelude to communal strife', in the words of M.A. Majid, President of the Singapore Muslim Welfare Association, 'and so plunge the future of a nation into the depths of anarchy and disaster'.[19] Towards the close of 1950, Maria Hertogh's case came before the courts in Singapore again. This time, the judge declared the marriage invalid on grounds of her legal domicile (the Netherlands) and that she was not 'in the eyes of this Court a Mohammedan'.[20] Maria was returned to the legal custody of her birth parents and soon after the trial taken by Adeline to the Netherlands. In the aftermath of this judgement and the resulting negative reaction from Muslims, there were several days of public disturbance in Singapore – portrayed, as Wu shows, by commentators in Malaya and elsewhere in terms of rioting and mob violence, and as putting back the cause of national self-determination.

Wu's detailed analysis of these events shows how the issue of marriage took precedence in public discussion over the custody aspects of the Hertogh case. Furthermore,

the debates on child-marriage help to re-envision this historical moment as one in which diverse ethnic and religious communities had a common platform to work out pre-existing ethnic tensions in Malaya through the question of child-marriage reform and its consequences on Malayan self-determination. In hindsight, they also demonstrate the centrality of conjugal concerns within diverse communities of British Malaya. (Wu 2017, 670)

---

[18] Wu also notes, however, that pre-war Chinese opposition to marriage reform in Malaya was articulated in terms of 'cultural traditions' rather than religion (Wu 2017, 667–68).

[19] 'Islam is in Danger', *Malaya Tribune*, 6 September 1950, cited in Wu (2017, 669).

[20] 'Originating Summons No. 248 of 1950', 2 December 1950, cited in Wu (2017, 670).

Marriage and the Moral Imagination

In light of this discussion, it is clear that the debate around child marriage that emerged so strikingly in 2018 did not simply reflect the extraordinary moment of hope and political change in which it occurred. The deeper temporality of this issue illuminates the capacity of marriage, more broadly, both to express and sharpen cleavages between the different religious and ethnic communities of Malaysia and also to unite politically progressive forces. Notably, the two cases made reference to the east coast states of Terengganu and Kelantan – both known in Malaysia as strongholds of conservative Islam with a large rural population base. Contemporary comments at both junctures also referred to polygamy (in the earlier case, as a possible outcome that might detrimentally affect Maria Hertogh in the future). And neither case led immediately to national reform of the legal age of marriage.

The resonances between these two moments – 1950 and 2018 – one, on the eve of Independence, the other following election results that had apparently overturned the existing *status quo* since Independence in 1957, speak to the potential of marriage both to signify the 'modernity' of the nation (as well as of other nations) and the force of resistance to political change. While reaction to the earlier case could clearly be read through the prism of resistance to colonial authority, commentary in 2018 seemed to express a newly achieved cross-ethnic unity against conservative forces in Malaysia and the more liberal values of an expanded urban population – but also the fragile contingency of this alliance.

I referred at the beginning of this chapter to the history of contestations and exclusions surrounding marriage in Virginia in the US and their connections to slavery. The attempts of colonial regimes to regulate marriage and to declare certain kinds of relations across 'racial' lines illegitimate are notorious and manifold (see Stoler 2010). In Botswana, on the eve of Independence, the British colonial authorities mounted a concerted – and ultimately unsuccessful, campaign to block the marriage between Seretse Khama, heir to the Bangwato paramount chiefship, and a British white woman, Ruth Williams. The marriage, strongly opposed

2 Marriage and Gender in the Political Moment

by South Africa because of its potential implications for apartheid policies there, became a focal point of Botswana's struggle for independence (see Williams 2007). British attempts to keep Khama in exile and force him to renounce his chiefship eventually backfired, enabling him to lead Botswana's movement for independence and become its first President. Precisely because marriage is a public institution and a ready symbol of the nation, its control and surveillance are often of paramount importance to the state. This emerges particularly clearly under conditions of colonial rule, when regimes are in question or in times of profound political change.[21]

Performing Gender and Marriage

From time to time during the George Town Festival of 2018 and at other instances during my research in Penang, I attended plays and theatrical events which had marital relations or gender more broadly as their theme. On the same weekend as the 'Tanjung Talks' described in earlier sections of this chapter, I went to a show put on by a prominent Muslim feminist activist NGO, Sisters in Islam. The main theme of the play, 'Broken', was domestic violence. In the lobby area of the venue, staff from feminist activist groups were at desks with leaflets about domestic violence on display. And I recognised some audience members from local feminist activist contexts.

Before the start of the performance, there were warnings about the upsetting nature of the content, and anyone under eighteen in the audience was asked to leave. The central characters of the play were an overtly

---

[21] See, for example, Susan McKinnon's (2013; 2019) account of attempts to bar cousin marriage and polygamous unions in nineteenth century United States. McKinnon shows how such marriages were viewed by legislators – and by contemporary and later anthropologists – as counter to an evolutionary narrative of the emergence of modernity. For studies of the emergence of 'modern marriage' under colonialism in India see Majumdar (2009); Mody (2008).

'religious' Malay Muslim husband, his wife and stepson and the latter's school teacher. The powerful nature of the content featured a rape scene perpetrated by the stepfather on his stepson. At the end of the drama, the latter was rescued from abuse by his school teacher. This disturbing (but also somewhat melodramatic) scenario was clearly designed to be educational. There were a number of young Malay women in the audience. At times when the performance was most distressing, they seemed to be using the leaflets they had picked up in the lobby to shield their eyes from the stage.

Another play, performed in the same month in Malay with subtitles at a tiny local theatre by a Penang-based company, was called 'Without the Utterance of Love' (Tanpa Lafaz Cinta). Written and directed by Yusof Bakar, the performance was part of a series, advertised in the programme flyer as 'Featuring stories about marriage, identity, love and inhabitants of the unseen world'. It concerned a couple who kept missing each other until they were eventually united after many years. It was unclear whether this drama was to be understood only in the domestic register in which it was played or whether the play and its title might be open to larger, more national interpretations.

Several months later, on a Sunday afternoon in April 2019, in a more prominent Penang auditorium, I attended 'Rebound', a show originally titled 'Sex in George Town' but which had been banned when it was first performed the previous February. The banning had subsequently been rescinded on condition the title of the show was changed. The performance featured quite explicit language and in parts seemed 'a bit raw' – as one of my local friends put it. Some of the several separate scenarios performed were witty and clever, and the main themes connecting them were the power play of sex (as well as the sexual connotations of power) viewed through an interethnic prism. These were different humorous takes on familiar ethnic stereotypes and the transgressions of inter-ethnic relations.

The first of the scenes featured an Indian boss (a businessman) and his Chinese assistant who had booked one room for them in a hotel

2 Marriage and Gender in the Political Moment

the night before a corporate meeting. Another was about two older Malay women, one of whom had a son married to a Chinese-Malaysian woman and broken relations with his parents. The other woman was a stereotypical village gossip with an iPhone and access to the other son's Facebook page. Another scene had a Chinese auntie – a masseuse – with a young Indian-Malaysian male client, who had a Chinese girlfriend who turned out to be the former's granddaughter. Because the young man was a lawyer with obvious prospects, he was able to win over the auntie's initial negative reaction to their relationship. Another scenario depicted Indian Muslim street cleaners in a well-known (and notorious) street in George Town chatting about their different marital problems: one whose wife could not get pregnant and one who had several daughters and didn't want sex. A different tone pervaded a more painful scene concerning sexual abuse. The central characters of a more humorous skit were a Malaysian-Indian and Malay couple who insulted each other with explicit imagery as a means to getting aroused. The penultimate scenario concerned a Scottish-French couple. The wife was shown lamenting, 'What is marriage? Why no sex? Once a month!' She finally ended up saying, 'Marriage is commitment and love – even without sex'. In the last view of this scene, the audience saw the husband lift his wife out of bed into a wheelchair. This was intended to be a surprise as she had up to that point been shown lying in bed and there had been no mention of disability. The final scenario concerned a Chinese-Malaysian escort girl and her client annoyed by the queue of other clients waiting to see her.

Evidently, 'Rebound' as a whole was partly concerned with familiar (and mainly humorously portrayed) ethnic and marital stereotypes seen through locally recognisable situations. But there was also clearly a more serious intent at work in terms of upsetting assumptions and the portrayal of gendered and conjugal power relations. I was struck too by the explicit sexual content and language, which were highly unusual in the Malaysian context. All three of the theatrical events I have described

Marriage and the Moral Imagination

were more outspoken in their overturning of stereotypes or their didactic intent than previous performances I had seen over many years in Penang. The audiences were relatively small and probably preponderantly from activist, creative and intellectual circles, but they seemed nonetheless positive and appreciative.

Marriage and Legal Practice

In the unusual political moment of the months following the elections of 2018, one could sense both a positive surge of excitement and possibility, and also some darker forces of resistance to change. During this period, in an attempt to gain a deeper sense of how matrimonial law figured in the public discourse to which I was attending, I interviewed two female lawyers in George Town about their work. Both had spent many decades working on marital and divorce cases and domestic violence and were concerned with women's rights. One of them has already been mentioned in the opening paragraph to this chapter. When I asked her about how she saw the current change of government, she expressed herself as full of hope for the future: 'I'm *very* optimistic – it's our best chance. I think they're willing to listen. Willing to put things into action. It's very exciting and very unexpected'. She acknowledged, however, that the government was 'a mixed bag'.

The important thing is they want to change. They have put a lot of people in the right places. People who have courage and were known before. That gives me hope. But they also have to overcome a lot of things they've put in place in the past. And funds – have all gone to waste. It makes you so angry. We want to build a new set-up for the country. But there's so much time to be spent fixing past things. But I'm also hopeful. That we can combat domestic violence is possible. I thought we couldn't defeat Barisan Nasional and we did. We are moving in the right direction.

When I asked about changes she had observed since first practising law in the 1980s, she told me,

2 Marriage and Gender in the Political Moment

Women are more independent; more willing to initiate actions. Sometimes they are the dominant characters; sometimes they are troublemakers – although legally they are the underdogs. When they're working and have salaries, they have more say – independent financially. I don't want it to tilt the other way. I see men being bullied, taken advantage of, threatened by wives.

The most significant legal changes this lawyer had observed, she told me, were the Marriage Reform Act of 1976, and in 1982 there had been further important legal change with the institution of monogamous marriage and better legal rights for women in terms of custody of children.[22] But in her view, things have not moved much since then. Women, she observed, were becoming more 'bullying'. But there was still a lot of work to do for women's rights – especially in terms of maintenance. It was difficult to enforce orders for maintenance. And this meant a situation where women were liable to be financially trapped and unable to leave an abusive marriage.

On the topic of same-sex marriage in Malaysia, she was very clear: there was 'no sign of gay marriage here!' There were couples who cohabited, however. And she knew of wives whose husbands refused to consummate their marriage. 'The wives feel tricked. Guys don't tell their parents and they agree to parents' pressure'. More broadly, she was struck by how, in spite of difficulties,

---

[22] The Law Reform (Marriage and Divorce) Act 1976 was passed in 1976, coming into force in 1982. It governed all non-Muslim marriage in Malaysia, replacing what had previously been separate marriage legislation for different religious and ethnic groups and placing them on the same legal footing. The Act provided for the solemnisation and registration of these marriages, instituted monogamous marriage and amended and consolidated divorce laws and arrangements over maintenance and custody. Amendments to this Act were passed in 2017 mainly to clarify legal jurisdictions, grounds and terms for the granting of divorce in cases where one partner to a non-Muslim marriage converts to Islam after marrying, but – as the preceding discussion in this chapter exemplifies – not completely resolving the legal complexities of such situations where unilateral conversion children has occurred (see Thambapillay 2020).

Marriage and the Moral Imagination

Everyone wants to get married. It's kind of amazing – considering there's a lot of oppression and imbalance. A lot is covered up; putting up appearances. Long marriages; you see happy couples at functions, and assume all is ok, then it's not. I don't believe in happy marriages – there's a lot of *compromise*. Nowadays, there's a lot of breaking up. I don't have faith in marriage. Not because I do divorce work. Because of my friends, the people I see. There's a lot of oppression. A need to concede. Often it's *one* person, not both. When you're married, it's *compulsory* to concede – not like individuals.

In this lawyer's opinion, part of the pressure was due to the presence of family in marriage, and this could lead to divorce. Imbalance was built into marriage and was the cause of oppression; families were implicated in this. These comments indicate an unsurprising awareness – given the wealth of experience which lay behind it – of the power dynamics of marriage and their negative implications. In the more intimate experiences of marriage depicted in accounts in Chapters 3–7. We will see many of these same themes emerge from the perspectives of the protagonists. Part of what is striking here was the juxtaposition of political optimism with pessimism about marriage. In view of how political events turned out, one might wonder about reversing these judgements.

The second lawyer, whom I interviewed some months later, in April 2019, had also been practising in Penang for many years. She had trained in both civil and syariah law, and the marital cases she worked on were predominantly Muslim marriages. I asked her about the changes she had observed over her career. Prior to her practice, she said, 'No women came who asked for divorce, or wanting to know their rights'. She spoke about an earlier era in the 1960s,

When my mum got married, no one, no one [i.e. no women] dared to go to the court or stand up for their rights. Later, when we had the Syariah Court (named the Mahkamah Kadi), we did have cases, but not many women came forward.

2 Marriage and Gender in the Political Moment

Later on, with more women going to universities, she said, more women were educated and came forward. But the judges (kadi) in the syariah court when she first practised, and prior to that, would not grant divorce to women. Instead, they would always ask the parties to settle out of court, and she indicated that this had to do with the chauvinistic attitudes of the judges in that era.

This lawyer described how the structures and enactment of syariah law had evolved over the previous decades:

With the proper structure of the 1993 enactment and the 2004 amendment and the Mahkamah Syariah [Syariah Court], women lawyers had begun to appear in court. Sometimes there were problems with a particular judge – he would ask: 'Why are you so aggressive?'. The other side would be represented by a male lawyer. He would brush me off as emotional – this was how he perceived it. Later on, with new introduction of enactments – earlier, there was only one law – the Islamic enactment. We didn't have family law. So, I tried to adapt civil enactments to syariah law. One or two judges appreciated that. I would say, 'This is what we do in the civil court, if you accept…'

Later, she told me, more judges were trained in both jurisdictions. There were younger judges and also more female lawyers. 'Now 60% of students in university in Malaysia are women. Nowadays, my clients are already well-prepared through the internet – more prepared. They more or less know what they're entitled to. Their expectations are very high'.

I asked about child marriage cases, but, as I had expected, this lawyer confirmed that there had not been child marriage cases in Penang. Most of her cases, she related, came from low-income, middle-income and professionals; some were cases involving children.

Sometimes professionals don't have *wisdom*. Women can come to the extent of saying, 'I don't want to look after the children' if the husband is having an affair. In those days [i.e. in earlier times] it wouldn't happen. I was shocked.

Now with the NGOs and activists – go out to the ground; they give talks about rights, actions for the Domestic Violence Act.

Marriage and the Moral Imagination

The lawyer talked about feminist activist groups that she supported, which ran sessions on women's rights: 'We educate the police about domestic violence cases. It's very helpful'. In the view of this lawyer, the civil court system and the syariah courts could play complementary roles. In domestic violence cases, an order from the civil court, presented to a judge in the syariah court, was helpful with a divorce being heard in the syariah court: 'The judge will see. So, it helps. Just a court order – the judge, sees, gives the divorce'. In such cases, the husband might not appear because of the court order. Husbands sometimes asked wives to withdraw the case from the civil court, she told me. But because an order from the civil court would be likely to have an influence on the syariah court in granting a woman's petition for divorce (on grounds of cruelty), she would advise a woman against withdrawing.

On child custody matters, the position of women had improved over the time this lawyer had been practising. Often women assumed that they could not get custody of children, she said, especially if they were housewives rather than professional women, but this was not the case. 'Many people think housewives are not entitled. In the syariah, the first custody right is with the mother, second, the mother's mother, *third* is the father'. And often, strategy came into play:

In one case, a woman married another man. We put the mother's mother as the applicant for custody. *Strategise* cases – it depends very much on how counsel handles cases. If they're a bit creative, for example, in applications for matrimonial property, can apply for half. Need to be a little creative.

This experienced legal practitioner in Muslim matrimonial cases voiced her opinion, which we will see echoed in Chapter 4 – that syariah law could be beneficial to women:

Under the syariah system women are *more* protected. It depends on the *implementation*. For example, the house, after divorce, three months [*iddah*] – finished. If the mother has custody of child and applies for matrimonial property after the three months, she can get the house because she

2 Marriage and Gender in the Political Moment

has the child. The husband has to provide shelter. But not in a civil court case. It depends on the judge *and counsel*. It's better if you know the judges and their pattern.

And interestingly in this context, she had a somewhat different take on the Indira case discussed earlier, which also reflected her perspective on the complementarity of the two legal systems and how this might be used to women's advantage. In her view,

Indira didn't need to go to the *civil* court. If a litigant is not a Muslim, can go to the syariah court and accept the syariah court decision. Counsel should have advised her to go to the *syariah* court, and they would decide in her *favour*. A test case… There was a risk for her – in her perceptions. If there's no court order, both should be allowed to submit to the order of the syariah court.

By the time of this interview, in April 2019, fractures in the new government were becoming more obvious and there was a sense of a growing backlash. When I asked this Muslim lawyer how she saw the future, she expressed a cautious optimism: 'I hope it will continue to improve for women. I'm not a political person; more NGO. The current situation is quite worrying – the PAS-UMNO coalition'.[23] Like others, she hoped the Deputy Prime Minister might introduce a child marriage amendment for all states as had been proposed by various NGOs and civil society groups.

What emerges clearly in the comments of these lawyers is not only the strong expectation that marriage will be a normal part of the life course but also an appreciation, derived from their practice, of the compromises and accommodations required to sustain a marriage. The nature of their legal experience gives these women lawyers a heightened consciousness

---

[23] A new alliance between the historically opposed parties of UMNO, United Malays National Organisation (the leading party of the long-term ruling coalition that the May 2018 elections had seen defeated) and PAS (Parti Islam Se-Malaysia) the conservative Malay Islamic party, was widely viewed by supporters of reform as a worrying political development at this juncture.

of the potential consequences of imbalanced power relations between spouses, and an awareness of the possibilities of different legal jurisdictions and ordinances that may be applied in Malaysia.

The Backlash: LGBT Rights

As has been clear throughout this chapter, while the elections of May 2018 had created a moment of unexpected optimism on the Malaysian political landscape, there were also strong signs of forces resistant to political reform. Strikingly, both tendencies could be expressed through the registers of marriage, women's rights and gender relations. The strength of resistance to reform became clear in the months following the elections. In March 2019, the annual march to mark International Women's Day was held in Kuala Lumpur. This was a small, peaceful affair involving a few hundred people – political demonstrations are strictly controlled in Malaysia. Nevertheless, it was immediately followed by a political storm.

The march, organised by a loose coalition of women's rights groups, took as its main theme '*Hentikan Keganasan, Hormati Perempuan*' (stop violence, respect women). It focused on five demands: ending all violence based on gender and sexual orientation; banning all child marriages; ensuring women's rights and freedoms to make choices over their own bodies and lives; ensuring a dignified minimum wage of RM 1,800; and destroying patriarchy and building genuine democracy at all levels of society. It was the visible presence of LGBT participants at the march that apparently provoked a backlash. Malaysiakini, the prominent English-language online news service, reported,

Among the 300 or so people present, some were seen holding rainbow flags, a popular symbol of solidarity for the LGBT community.

Some were also seen holding placards advocating just treatment of LGBT people, among them 'People of quality do not fear equality' and 'We exist'.[24]

---

[24] www.malaysiakini.com/news/467331, accessed 27 January 2021.

2 Marriage and Gender in the Political Moment

On the same day as the demonstration, it was reported that,

De facto Islamic affairs minister Mujahid Yusof Rawa says he is shocked that the Women's March in Kuala Lumpur today was used to defend LGBT rights, calling it an abuse of democracy.

'I was very shocked by the actions of some quarters today who abused democratic space to defend something that is wrong by Islam'.

'As I have said before, the government is firm that LGBT practices will never be accepted in this country. It is impossible for us to acknowledge something illegal', Mujahid said in a Facebook post today.[25]

Notably, other politicians who might possibly have been expected to be more sympathetic, piled in:

Bersatu supreme council member Wan Saiful Wan Jan, meanwhile, criticised the participants for 'polluting' the march and destabilising the country, while Wanita Umno [UMNO's women's branch] chief Noraini Ahmad claimed that advocating LGBT rights would lead to 'great destruction to social institutions'.[26]

The activist groups Sisters in Islam and the Women's Aid Organisation issued supportive statements but also noted that they had not been on the organising committee of the demonstration. The march organisers strongly condemned the singling out of LGBT participants in the march:

'This borders on incitement to hatred and violence towards a section of Malaysian society who are already at risk and facing multiple forms of discrimination'.

'We strongly reject such a move, and the continued escalation of this hostile and aggressive treatment'.

'A healthy democracy rests on the full and equal participation by all levels of society', read an excerpt.

For this, they attributed blame on the media as well as the 'political opportunism by individuals in positions of authority'.[27]

---

[25] www.malaysiakini.com/news/467258 accessed 27 January 2021.
[26] www.malaysiakini.com/news/467331, accessed 27 January 2021.
[27] www.malaysiakini.com/news/467331, accessed 27 January 2021.

Marriage and the Moral Imagination

No one I spoke to during my research was in any doubt that LGBT rights were an extremely sensitive issue in Malaysia, and even those broadly sympathetic did not expect legal reform in the near (or even distant) future. I was surprised therefore about ten days later, by a proverbial taxi driver in KL who was listening on his radio to a parliamentary debate in Malay about the Women's Day march. In response to my enquiry, he apologised for listening and simply said that it was good there was now more space for criticism.

What seemed striking in the furore was not just the visible emergence of LGBT issues in the public arena – where discussion of these is mainly foreclosed in advance. The virulence of statements from government politicians seemed to reflect the pressure which the new reforming government was under from conservative, Malay Muslim quarters. These tensions had already manifested themselves over LGBT issues some months earlier. In August 2018, during the same period as the liberal and open exchanges at George Town Festival events described earlier in this chapter, there were reports in the press of 'physical and verbal attacks against the transgender community' in Seremban, Negeri Sembilan and of an anti-LGBTQ campaign in the state of Pahang.[28] In support of this campaign, Pahang mufti, Dr Abdul Rahman, was reported to have said that 'LGBTQ activities had "caused family problems" and "destroyed the faith of Muslims"'.[29]

Meanwhile, an even more ominous scenario was playing out in the east coast state of Terengganu. On 12 August, the Kuala Terengannu Syariah High Court fined two women RM 3,300 and ordered them to be caned six times each 'after they had pleaded guilty to committing *musahaqah* (sexual relations between women)'. The sentence was postponed by the same court to 3 September.[30] This caning 'was witnessed

---

[28] 'Stop attacking transgenders', *Star* 20 August 2018.
[29] 'Mufti: LGBTQ activities have negative impact', *Star*, 20 August 2018.
[30] 'Caning of lesbians postponed to Sept 3', *Star*, 29 August 2018.

2 Marriage and Gender in the Political Moment

by more than 100 people in a courtroom at the Syariah High Court'.[31] It drew widespread condemnation from the Malaysian Bar Association, Amnesty International Malaysia, politicians, NGOs and women's groups, including Justice for Sisters, Sisters in Islam, the Joint Action Group for Gender Equality and the Women's Aid Organisation. The punishment, the first of its kind in Terengganu – and as far as I know in Malaysia – seemed to many 'a travesty and a grave miscarriage of justice', in the words of a joint statement by Justice for Sisters and Sisters in Islam.[32] The punishment and the public commentary generated by it starkly exemplify Michael Peletz's (2020a; 2020b, 234–39, Chapter 2) and Maznah Mohamad's (2020, Chapter 5) depictions of an increasing punitiveness to Islamic governmentality in Malaysia, especially around the policing of sexuality, marriage, women's dress and bodily comportment – and this in spite of a simultaneous discernible tendency for syariah court judgements in marital cases to be more favourable to women than in the past. Such cases vividly manifest the deep cleavages in Malaysia between the liberalising discourses of gender equality and LGBTQ rights, and conservative Islam.

Conclusion

This chapter has depicted some of the ongoing controversies and public discourse that figured prominently in the media and in cultural events in 2018–19. At this juncture of apparent political transformation in Malaysia, marriage and gender relations emerged as remarkably salient. In considering how marriage and political change might be connected, we should note the heightened rhetoric and imagery of the events and debates I have recorded here. The issues that emerged – whether child marriage, LGBTQ rights or religious conversion – were often depicted

---

[31] 'Caning was merely a lesson to others says exco', *Star*, 4 September 2018.
[32] 'MPs, women's groups cry foul over women's caning', *Star*, 4 September 2018.

in lurid terms. 'Child marriage' here blurred into something arguably somewhat different – paedophilia. Domestic violence and sexual abuse were dramatically presented through incestuous, homosexual child rape. LGBTQ rights, asserted in recognisably Western, 'modern' terms, were repudiated through an unprecedented resort to 'immodern' (Lambek 2013) syariah law and punishment regimes. Religious conversion and child custody became issues that referred to the Malaysian constitution. These matters were perceived to be at the very heart of the kind of nation Malaysia should be; they were unlikely to be smoothly resolved.

The discussions and shows I attended in Penang, and the media accounts I read, were unusually outspoken (and sometimes humorous). They instantiated long-standing religious, ethnic, rural-urban and class cleavages. Rhetoric about marriage and gender relations that coalesced around exemplary cases – for example, that of child marriage – had a powerful capacity to unite and also to divide the nation along these long-standing fault lines as well as vividly exemplifying Michael Peletz's (2023) depiction of a 'moral panic'. Debates and comments were relayed between different states of Malaysia, ricocheting between geographic and cultural sites with different histories and connotations. Events and performances could provoke unexpectedly virulent critiques and fiercely expressed opposition – as the examples of censored exhibition images, a banned play or a much-maligned Women's Day march show. And it seemed that any single issue had a propensity to evoke others – discussions about conversion could 'stand for' child custody or marital rights; child marriage could merge with polygamy; photographs of LGBT activists could become a matter of national honour. These were not easily contained stories, and all of them had complex legal ramifications.

Partly because of the strong linkages in Malaysia between ethnicity and religion and the political and legal status of both, these matters, as I suggested at the beginning of this chapter, defied the 'domaining effects' of 'modernity' – and of social science (McKinnon and Cannell

2 Marriage and Gender in the Political Moment

2013a; Yanagisako and Delaney 1995). In this respect, we can link them to contention over marriage in wider political colonial and post-colonial worlds – whether in the US, Botswana, Indonesia, India or elsewhere – and continued attempts of the state to regulate what kinds of relations are deemed legitimate. In Malaysia, as elsewhere, marriage and sexuality are a lightning rod for political tensions and controversy.

The porosity of events involving marriage or gender relations and of the controversies they aroused extended also to their temporal frames. It was difficult not to view the Women's Day March in Kuala Lumpur in March 2019 through the lens of the public caning of two women in a Terengganu courtroom the previous September. In this scenario, the echoes between one event and another seemed obvious. The Indira case, meanwhile, had taken ten years to proceed through the courts and harked back to divisions written into the constitution at Malaysia's formation as an independent nation. The historical resonances between two cases of child marriage many decades apart that I have placed side by side here were perhaps more submerged. I noticed no one directly referring to the earlier case when the 2018 one was discussed. But the echoes between them are nonetheless suggestive of the capacity of marriage to carry meanings across different historical moments. In Virginia, as noted earlier, Siobhan Magee (2025) has found a similar resonance between discussion of the recent legal institution of same-sex marriage and the lifting of the proscription against interracial marriage following the Supreme Court's *Loving v. Virginia* ruling. Such echoes reflect the centrality of marriage to political transformation – and its potential traction in efforts to impede change.

This chapter cannot be said to have nailed the question of how marriage and wider political transformation might be connected. In depicting some of the available repertoire, however, we can at least begin to perceive how certain issues emerged as salient and interconnected and why this might be the case. Observing how marriage or gender relations have the capacity to be explicitly politicised, and the pathways provided

Marriage and the Moral Imagination

by religion or ethnicity for this, may also shift our understandings of the 'political', encouraging a focus on more intimate and domestic experience. To grasp how change on a national scale is produced, lived and internalised, we thus need also to attend to marriage from the perspective of intimate, personal and familial experience. That is the subject of Chapters 3–7.

THREE

Marriage over the Generations

Amelia was a well-turned-out and articulate woman in her early sixties whom I met and interviewed in her workplace – a small family firm, founded in the late 1970s, situated in a middle-class neighbourhood of urban Penang. She described herself as 'born and bred in Penang', adding quickly, 'I suppose I will also die here!' Her parents had married in the 1950s; it was 'a mixture of a matchmaker and a romantic story':

Mother was watering plants in the garden. Father happened to ride a bicycle past and approached a matchmaker. I'm sceptical about that story – the housing estate was closed, so I'm not sure whether it's true. In those days it was important to have a matchmaker. I asked about love. More of a Chinaman concept – I don't know. I suppose my mother loves him. Marriage was a bit different [then].

Amelia described her mother as coming from a 'Nyonya' (mixed Chinese-Malay, or Peranakan) background; her father was Cantonese. 'In Nyonya culture', she told me, 'it was okay for a son-in-law to stay with the wife's side – *chin chai* [anything goes, whatever] – if there are special reasons'.[1] Amelia's mother came from a wealthier family than her father, but she had only received elementary school education while her father had gone to secondary school. They married in the

---

[1] Here the influence of Malay values favouring matrilocal residence (see Introduction) as well as the mother's family's greater wealth may have been relevant.

Marriage and the Moral Imagination

1950s, and it had not been a specially happy relationship. There were financial problems; her father had been 'quite an absentee father', she told me. Although the couple had lived mainly with her mother's parents, Amelia recalled two years spent living with her father's parents as having been particularly fraught because her mother, although she 'looked Chinese, was not Chinese'. She had not conformed to Cantonese cultural expectations – 'culture shock – they couldn't understand her'. But Amelia recalled a brief happy spell when the family had house-sat for neighbours: 'Their own home. I don't understand why he didn't get us a home of our own. My mother was not happy. Father, I don't know'.

In contrast, Amelia described her own marriage, dating from the 1980s and of more than thirty years' duration when we spoke, as happy and harmonious. She had met her husband-to-be in church through her sister who had converted to Christianity. Amelia had been a teacher at the time, and her husband's parents were wealthier than her own. Her marriage, she said, was very different from that of her parents:

The expectations are very different. My mother ... she was very powerless in marriage. Nowadays it's very different. My father's attitude was very different. In my marriage, we have a balance of power. My husband is very smart. He tells others, 'What is mine is yours; what is yours is yours'. Gives me independence. Probably because my mother didn't work. I always worked. First, needed the income. Now I'm in charge of the department...

***

This chapter is about the dynamics of marriage across generations. The central theme is change and continuity as they are threaded through marriage. It is conventional to think of marriage as a dyadic relation between spouses and, as such, one that occurs within, rather than between, generations. And yet, people I spoke to in Penang very readily made comparisons between their own marriages and those of their parents and grandparents or those of their children – sometimes in response to my

3 Marriage over the Generations

questions and sometimes spontaneously. In this chapter and the following one, I suggest that this intergenerational axis of comparison is a capacious and generative terrain of everyday, imaginative consideration and of ethical valuations and judgements.

The anthropology of marriage has for a long time taken it as read that marriage occurs between groups rather than individuals. Claude Lévi-Strauss's (1969) insights insisted not only on the centrality of marriage to relations between groups but also on the way such relations could be a source of structural continuity over time and generations (Lévi-Strauss 1969, 67–68). More recent studies, however, have tended to put an emphasis on individuals and on the affective dimensions of conjugal relations (see, for example, Cole and Thomas 2009; Hirsch and Wardlow 2006; Padilla et al. 2007). One prism through which these two ways of understanding marriage has been considered is that of 'arrangement' versus 'choice' or 'love'. The shift from arranged marriages to ones in which individuals are free to choose their own spouses, based on an ideal of egalitarian intimacy, has been taken as a fundamental attribute of modernity (see, for example, Giddens 1992). Jane Collier's (2020) study of changing families in an Andalusian village between the 1960s and the 1980s is one exemplary examination of the shift *From Duty to Desire* or 'the development of modern subjectivity' (Collier 2020, 24). The changes in marriage and conjugal relations that Collier documents occurred alongside fundamental economic and lifestyle changes associated with the abandonment of a rural agricultural base for urban employment. While in the accounts of some I interviewed there may be certain parallels with her depiction – especially if they were within just one generation of rural Malay life – the broader contours are also very different. Many of those I talked to came from families that had been resident in urban and highly cosmopolitan Penang for several generations. Their lives, arguably, had been 'modern' for some considerable time (see Lewis 2016). Nevertheless, the way people spoke to me about marriage articulated important changes.

Marriage and the Moral Imagination

Increasingly, studies of marriage, particularly in South Asia, have problematised the dichotomy of 'arrangement' versus 'choice' (Donner 2002; 2016; Fuller and Narasimhan 2008; Osella 2012; Parry 2020, Chapter 11). In Sri Lanka, for example, Asha Abeyasekera (2021) describes how middle-class people may use a language of choice or arrangement to characterise their marriages and to emphasise change from a parental generation whose marriages were arranged by their seniors to a younger generation free to choose their own spouses. But the reality is more complex. In practice, members of an older generation often had more autonomy in spouse selection than seemed obvious, while those of a younger generation may take more account of their seniors' preferences than their initial descriptions seem to imply. As Abeyasekera argues, what has changed here is more the mode of representation than actual practice. A marriage that was in fact 'chosen' can be made to look 'arranged' – and thus conform with 'tradition' and with conventional morality. The differences between these sharply delineated types are thus more fuzzy than they appear. And, importantly, as Clark-Decès (2014) shows in her beautifully rendered study of preferential kin marriages in Tamil Nadu, 'love marriage', in spite of its 'modern' attractions, is not necessarily seen as a preferable option to kin marriage – partly because of the latter's assumed foundation in equivalence and shared love.

In Penang, quite a lot of people spoke spontaneously of their parents or grandparents having 'arranged' marriages or some hybrid version of these, and most middle-aged and younger people described themselves as having followed their own wishes. While this is a pervasive way of understanding marital change, taking account of the insights of scholars of South Asia, I seek to explore this topic in a more modulated and less essentialised way than afforded by the binary of 'choice' versus 'arrangement'. Conversations in Penang brought home to me the ways that parental marriages are good to think with – or to evaluate ethically. This recalls the argument of Cheryl Mattingly (2014, 17–25), drawing on

3 Marriage over the Generations

the work of Alasdair Macintyre and Charles Taylor, that I took up in the Introduction – that narratives are a means to reflect on what constitutes a good life. Formulating and articulating such narratives requires imaginative work.

In this chapter, I ask, quite broadly, what gets transmitted between the generations through marriage? What changes? What is replicated? As well as abrupt deviations, could we think in terms of parallels, diversions, detours or echoes? And is it possible to discern all of these patterns – sometimes in the very same marital stories? As in Amelia's telling, one very prominent theme in accounts of marriage within families was the hierarchical content of relations between spouses. Women especially, but not only women, tended to bring this up in the context of speaking about their parents' or grandparents' marriages. The arc of history here was generally understood to be moving towards marital relations that are more egalitarian than in the past. Husbands were seen as having less control over wives than in previous generations. This was readily associated, as in Amelia's case, with increasing levels of education for middle-class women and greater participation in the labour force. However, for reasons explored in the Introduction, I do not take this progressive account of marriage unproblematically at face value – although I do take the understandings on which it is based seriously. Notably, in Amelia's rendering of her own marriage, it was her husband who 'gave her independence'. Partly because of the scope for variations in individual marriages depending on families, personalities and circumstances, and partly because of the strength and resilience of patriarchal values – most unambiguously expressed in patrilineal Chinese and Indian kinship norms – a progressive direction of travel towards an egalitarian ideal is hardly assured. A further complication for Malay marriages is that, as outlined in Chapter 1, while earlier descriptions emphasise gender complementarity in Austronesian bilateral kinship and a tendency for hierarchy to be based on principles of age and generation rather than gender differentiation (Carsten 1997; Karim 1992; 1995; Karim 2021; Ong and Peletz 1995; Peletz 1996; 2009), the institutionalisation of a more conservative interpretation of Islam in Malaysia over recent decades has arguably eroded these values and amplified more patriarchal interpretations of religious and family life (Maznah 2010a; 2013; 2020; Norani 2005; Norani, Puthucheary and Kessler 2008; Peletz 2020b).[2]

If the conversations and interviews recorded here are varied enough to make generalisation difficult, from another point of view, the range of ethnicities, religions and backgrounds they encompass is an inducement to consider tensions between divergent trends. Rather than providing a seemingly linear narrative of 'marital change amongst such-and-such a group', it becomes difficult to ignore deviations from obvious patterns. The examples and exceptions that emerge are perhaps more akin to how marriage and family are experienced by most people in their everyday lives than a more essentialised or pared-down sociological depiction. It is this everyday quality of how marital change across generations is generated, encountered, reflected upon and absorbed that I highlight here in order to explore its implications for familial and ethical lives lived in historical context.

In the following sections of this chapter, I draw on the accounts of those I interviewed to explore how patterns of marriage revealed replications, changes, diversions, loops, echoes and tensions across the generations of families. In the concluding section, I take up again the theme of autonomy and choice versus arrangement, but in the context of a more modulated understanding of time, generation and kinship as they are calibrated through marriage and through ethical evaluations.

---

[2] In spite of these shifts, Karim (2021) notes the persistent value placed on gender complementarity in marriage, inheritance and residence practices among Malays, and the longstanding importance of economic productivity and autonomy for Malay women.

3 Marriage over the Generations

Replicating Marriage

Many of the accounts of marriage that I was given were folded into life stories and family sagas. Their generational aspects seemed to arise organically in conversations and interviews. One young man spoke vividly of how his attitudes had been shaped by being the youngest child, which meant that he had spent a lot of time in the kitchen where 'there was always something going on', and of his mother's influence in transmitting an interest in cooking and in new ingredients that had been brought back from his parents' travels. This was the background in which his understandings of marriage and gendered relations were forged. In numerous accounts, I heard about personality traits or features of family life that struck their narrators as having recurred in successive generations and shaped their marriages.

One woman in her late fifties, Mei Ling, told me of three generations of 'strong women' who had shown grit and determination as the main income-earners ensuring their family's livelihood. Her grandmother had come to Malaya from China on a 'social visit' with her father as a ten-year-old child, and decided to stay behind with her father's sister when he returned. The grandmother's arranged marriage ended in widowhood when she was still in her thirties, but she managed to support eleven children through small-scale rural rice farming. Her daughter, Mei Ling's mother, struck out at aged fifteen to 'make a better life' in Penang and established 'her own business', a hairdressing salon in her marital home where she was the main income-earner, and the father was a house-husband looking after their seven children. Mei Ling attributed her own dispositions to her mother and grandmother – she had 'slept next to her grandmother' as a child, she told me, and would ask her about her childhood in China. Mei Ling had not gone to university, but she had carved out her own successful business in the educational sector and she too was her family's main earner, supporting her husband and numerous nephews and nieces. The couple had no children – by choice:

Marriage and the Moral Imagination

'Because of my expectations. I put energy into my business. It was hard. I grew up with very independent [ideas]. It's difficult to have children and business'. She spoke too about her belief that 'men and women should be equal – and in marriage'. This she attributed to her upbringing: 'Difficult to think the husband is superior because I saw the roles at home – my father at home, my mother at work'. Mei Ling's husband made interjections here and there through this account, commenting on the 'gender reversal' of his wife's grandmother and the transmissions in his own family – of 'bad temper – a family trait'. He attributed his own attitudes to being the 'peace child' in his parents' difficult marriage: 'I was always the baby of the family and [had my] own share of the drama between them'.

Li-Mei, a woman in her forties who worked as a nurse, told me how she had met her husband at a dinner – a 'match dinner'. She had gone to accompany a friend who planned to meet someone there. She and her husband were from somewhat different backgrounds, she said; his parents were hawkers while hers were more educated. Li-Mei hadn't planned to marry as soon as she did, but she had got pregnant and the wedding had been rushed. Her rather schematic account of the wedding was similar to those of many others: a 'Western' white wedding, a tea ceremony and a dinner of 30 tables for 300 guests. The expenses were shared between her and her husband. When I asked Li-Mei about her relationship with her husband, she said, 'It's a bit similar to my parents in terms of the relationship. I do the cooking. The cleaning – I do it'. What began as a seemingly conventional story, however, soon took on a different quality in which replication was a central theme. Her husband had communication difficulties, she told me, 'perhaps because of his educational background and family background'. Maybe he had 'learning problems'. 'I feel like I take charge a lot. But if not, I feel like we collapse'.

Marriage had turned out very different from how Li-Mei had expected it to be. She and her husband had become distant from each

3 Marriage over the Generations

other. Her brother too, she mentioned, had marital problems, which she perceived as a result of his wife's neglect of their children and a divergence of interests between the couple. And then the tone shifted again. Reporting that, after her marriage, she had become more involved in Buddhism, she told me,

We believe in Karma, next life.
I wish they [her children] will not have marriage when they grow up. I hope they can end [the cycle]. I'm not saying that married life is not good. But the circle is continuing, and [there's] a lot of suffering like that.

It gradually became clear that Li-Mei's parents had had an unhappy marriage and quarrelled a lot in her childhood – which initially she had described as 'happy'. 'They didn't talk to each other', she said.

Sometimes I regret getting married. I'm trying to adjust to suit him.... I don't want to ask more from him. That's why I go into Buddhism – Buddha will know. Maybe in a previous life, I owed him. That's how I tell myself. That's why I hope my children won't have marriage – so that in the next life they won't have to stay like that.

I was initially puzzled at the direction this conversation had taken and its tone. As the interview neared its close, however, what appeared to be a formative experience around which other events had been arranged and understood emerged. A family tragedy had resulted in Li-Mei's sister's sudden death in her presence and that of her brother when both parents had been away from home. 'I was ten years old. I didn't feel really sad. Maybe I was too young to understand about death. But I was very close to my sister'.

There was no doubt that this (probably unpreventable) death had shaped Li-Mei's understandings of how her own life and the marriages in her family had subsequently unfolded. The narrative was unusual in conveying such a sombre family history – although others too told of unhappy marriages, their own or those of their parents or other close

Marriage and the Moral Imagination

relatives. Her guilt and sorrow, and that of her parents, formed part of this story and, by her own account, had directed Li-Mei's choice of career as well as her turn towards Buddhism. What seemed to stand out in this narrative was the way that the experience of unhappy marriages across the generations of one family could be connected to this traumatic event and absorbed through perceptions of karma. Marriage, generations and the idea of replication were apparently linked through an inevitable cycle of repetition. Breaking this cycle of suffering, in Li-Mei's view, could only be achieved through drastic intervention: her children might have to avoid marriage entirely and separate themselves from their parents. While such an explicit articulation of the inevitability of generational replications of marriage and the obstructions to happiness that ensued was outside the norms, many other accounts featured more submerged recurrent elements of personality traits and relationships running through their family histories.

Changing Marriage

Although the lens of replication undoubtedly provides a powerful way for people to make sense of marriage across the generations of their families, it was certainly not the only optic available. In a more upbeat vein, many people, like Amelia in the opening account of this chapter, spoke in terms of contrasts and change when comparing their own marriage to that of their parents. More equal marital relations between husband and wife were generally perceived, as was the case with Amelia, to be the concomitant of rising levels of women's education and engagement in paid employment outside the home.

One woman in her forties, whom I got to know through a close friend from her schooldays, told me about the three generations of her family. All of Saw Peng's four grandparents had been immigrants from China who had come to Penang in the 1920s and 1930s. Her parents had married in the 1970s:

3 Marriage over the Generations

They went out as a gang, as a group. It was not an arranged marriage. My mother was 21; my father was 22. They met one or two years before they married. My mother was sewing in a shop. Father was working at Weld Quay. They were from similar backgrounds – quite poor. They spoke different dialects – Hakka. They speak Hokkien to each other.

After the marriage they lived with my mother's parents. My grandmother was quite friendly so my father didn't mind. My uncles were also there, married. It was a big house.

My childhood was very happy because we were a big family. One uncle had seven children, the other had two children. My parents had four children. My uncles' wives worked – cleaning. We saw my paternal grandparents twice a month. It was quite happy.

While her mother had been 'a housewife – she had no chance to get an education', Saw Peng herself had initially started working while studying for secretarial qualifications after leaving school at sixteen. But then, after getting together with her husband-to-be through neighbourhood ties, she had married in her early twenties. Her husband had been to university, and they decided,

Teaching college would be good, my husband thought, because you only work half a day. So I went to teacher's college here in Penang because I wanted to take care of the family. I only did it on condition that I got a place in Penang – I got!

She had duly qualified as a primary school teacher – work that clearly gave her satisfaction. Both she and her husband had grown up in the same neighbourhood of urban Penang. Reflecting on her own and her parents' marriage, she said,

My marriage is different from my parents' because I'm working; because I've got an income. Very independent. My mum had to ask my father for money. I can take care of my parents. My mother is very conservative. She thinks boys are better than girls – and my grandmother. I don't and my husband also. Children are all the same. So, they gave education to boys not girls.

Marriage and the Moral Imagination

In contrast, she said, 'I hope my daughter will work. I make decisions; my husband just follows. My husband is quite a nice man! Big decisions we discuss – we respect each other'.

This was an intergenerational story of marriages and family lives that was deeply embedded in one of Penang's larger, urban, working-class Chinese neighbourhoods. Both of Saw Peng's parents came from poor backgrounds. One of her grandfathers had worked as a stevedore; her father worked in cargo shipping. Over the generations, a trajectory of upward mobility accompanied the account of more equal gender and marital relations. This was taken to be a matter of hard work and responsibility:

Responsibility is very important. Trust is very important. Without trust, can't continue. My husband is very hard-working – makes a happy family. Can influence children if serious.

But equally important was the value of independence that she was trying to inculcate in her children and which she said had propelled her to decide to move away from the house of a mother-in-law 'who would have done everything' for her grandchildren. 'This way they learn to launder clothes, they can cook – the boys too'. Here we see how a story of marriage is inseparable from the values that are understood to underlie it and make familial relations, as well as individual persons, strong and resilient.

While many middle-aged and younger women spoke of the differences between their own marriages and those of parents or grandparents in positive terms, changes could also be seen, perhaps especially by men, in terms of a loss of tradition or customs. One Chettiar businessman whom I got to know, who was a strong proponent of the importance of upholding his community's distinctive heritage in Penang, enthusiastically told me about his family history. One of seven siblings, Mr Muthiah had been born in the 1950s on the east coast of Malaysia and had come to Penang for his schooling as his father had done before him. His father had had an arranged marriage in the 1940s for which he had returned to India:

3 Marriage over the Generations

They came from the same village, neighbouring houses. They were not related. In that period there were *no* love marriages. It was an arranged marriage; they were neighbours. It was a community wedding – over one week, because of transport'.

His parents 'had a good relation', he told me, 'It was a happy, harmonious marriage'. Speaking of his own generation of siblings, he said with some pride:

All of us had arranged marriages, except the youngest. Normally, if we have daughters, they (the father) will come and propose marriage. Wedding is of *families*, not individuals. Divorce was unheard of in my father's time, and in my time, even if they don't like each other. The ones who arrange – everyone's involved. Not easy to separate, so complicated. All the families are interrelated. Too many intertwines – cannot pull up!

Like his father, Mr Muthiah had gone to India to find a wife and he had married in the late 1970s:

We met. We couldn't go out. Her brothers and my mother – we went out, ten of us! We were allowed one hour to ourselves at a different table. It seemed OK – to both of us.

Reflecting on changes in current marriage practices, he commented on the tendency to marry later:

When my father was alive ... my father, his policy was: *before* you're independent, must marry. Afterwards, won't listen – which I think is true. If you don't have independence, no financial strength, not independent. Afterwards, won't listen.

What was of particular concern here in terms of parental control was out-marriage from the community:

My community is changing a lot. A lot of families no longer in control. They [young people] get educated abroad and meet people. Marry outside – in my time, it was unheard of. A lot are in the US in IT, doctors. When they get educated, they lose track. Good or not – we don't know.

Marriage and the Moral Imagination

Before, you were outcast from the community. Now parents accept, but [still] outcast from the community. [Parents have] fewer children – they can't disown them... [i.e. in the event of marriages of which they disapprove] But before, people had six or seven children. If one got lost, didn't bother.

Although the register in which this was described was distinctly less positive, here again change was perceived as being linked to women's education and employment:

The last twenty years have been amazing changes. The next ten – don't know what will happen. So many marry outside. They are happy marriages overall – both educated; both earning. Ninety per cent of women are highly educated – to degree level – and work. Then they are independent, and decide what they want to do. They agree sometimes to arranged marriages...

His own marriage had been more like that of his parents. His wife had been educated but not independent – and this was crucial: 'If she was independent, [it would be] a different scenario'.

For the future, things seemed uncertain – both in terms of marriage and community:

In ten years' time, my perception, the community thing, I don't know how we will sustain it. One of my nephews – we're trying to get him married. It was very different when I was twenty-two, twenty-three. I would have married a Malay girl. Now I think, I would have been very stupid. At different stage of life, think differently. I would have lost my family. Now I think, I was *lucky* – my father sent me off. My brother – his children married, got divorced. All the children are very independent. Parents have no say. In my community, all the aunties and uncles have some say. Young people don't want it... I don't know if it's for good or bad. We'll have to wait and see.

In this narration, marital change over several generations was articulated partly in the idiom of 'arrangement' versus 'love', and also in terms

3 Marriage over the Generations

of a perceived greater independence of young people from their parents, and of wives from their husbands. These shifts are bound up with anxiety and loss – conceived in terms of the risk of divorce, the dissolution of wider family ties and, most serious of all, the threat of disintegration of community.

Echoes and Divergences

So far, we have looked at marriage across the generations in terms of a simplified dichotomy of replication or change. Some stories seemed to fit easily into one or other of these framings. But of course, things are not always so straightforward. Many, if not most, of the family histories I was told about encompassed elements of both continuity and divergence from how things had been done in the past.

I interviewed Dr Hasnah in her university office in 2018. She struck me as bright, cheerful and articulate. Born in the early 1970s, she had been brought up on the east coast of Malaysia. She and her four siblings all went to boarding school (one route of social mobility for Malay children of academic aptitude), which, she said, meant that they hadn't grown up close to each other. Her father had been a teacher who had gone to university late as a mature student. Her mother had been a nurse. They had married when both were in their mid-twenties. The story of her parents' marriage came from her father; she said:

He was quite good-looking when young. I don't know how they met. She was a nurse and he a teacher in the same town. My [paternal] grandmother was in Pulau Penang on the haj. She saw my mother. They came from similar backgrounds – about the same. People then [the late 1960s] left school at about 13. They both did that. And went for training. Both were working.

Dr Hasnah described her parents as having a 'pretty much equal' relationship, 'not one person dominating the other – they both had a say'.

Marriage and the Moral Imagination

They were always close, they're even closer now than before. They spend a lot of time together. My father used to spend a lot of time with friends, away. Brought satay and came home at 11, 12 o'clock. Most of the time they had a good relationship...

But there had been a more difficult period while her father had a more prestigious post:

People said he should take another wife as well because he had a bigger job and more power. A Kelantan thing – men friends encourage it .... A 1980s Kelantan thing. He was tempted. There was a bit of conflict in the marriage, then it was resolved. He didn't ever marry.

Apart from the possibility of a polygynous marriage, there was another unexpected late twist to this seemingly conventional Malay marriage story that had endured for fifty years. It emerged in the relations between generations. Dr Hasnah's mother had retired early, in her forties, and her father in his fifties in the 1990s. After this,

They sold their properties and bought a house in KL. All my siblings are in KL – all in one house. They live with three sibs – three sisters who all married and are all divorced. They are all working. There are five children in two houses turned into one. It's nice for my sisters and nice for my parents. They help with the children, and the children help with them...

My second sister's children are 20 and 23, so not small. They still live together. The youngest is nine. Five children and only one is a boy. My father is very supportive of his daughters. And they are also supportive. Usually older people go to the village...

This form of parental mobility whereby elderly parents give support to divorced daughters is one we will meet again in Chapter 4. We could see it as a contemporary manifestation of older trends of Malay matrifocal residence (see, for example, Carsten 1997) adapted in the context of urban living and employment. The theme of gender equality came up too in Dr Hasnah's narration of her own marriage. She had married in her late twenties; her husband had been thirty. They had met while she was studying through mutual friends in KL and had married after she completed her PhD and began working. The wedding had been held together with her sister's – a way to save on expenses; it was 'a regular Malay wedding', she said. Theirs was a happy marriage, but there had been problems with the childcare for their three young children – a live-in Indonesian maid turned out to have been 'seeing a guy'. 'We were concerned for safety of the children'. Eventually, her husband resigned from his job – 'He became a house-husband', she said, 'he looks after the children'.

In the beginning we told them it's a temporary thing. Though we knew it might be permanent. I was not happy with childcare. I was very concerned about the children. I planned that one of these days he would resign. Worried we could not afford it. Then when the situation came up with the maid, we did the calculations, whether we could afford it. Then he gave one week's notice. His boss was very concerned but decided it was ok. Ten years [we've been] like that. For me, it's a much better quality of life. Everyone is much happier, healthier. Don't have to worry.

Dr Hasnah later mentioned that she had attained a higher level of education and achievement than her husband, and this apparently connected to the decisions about their household division of labour. This could be seen as a result of women's improved educational and employment opportunities – which, for Malay women, represents an extension of older patterns of female economic productivity and autonomy (Carsten 1997; Karim 2021). But she focused more on what she and her husband had in common: both were originally from the east coast, and both had been to boarding school and then studied abroad. Both valued marital equality and independent decision-making. Reflecting on the intergenerational aspects of this, she noted that both had fathers who had been teachers, and both she and her husband put an emphasis on education for their children.

Both my father and husband are quite liberal men, respectful. My parents get on with my husband. We don't ask for financial help. They leave us

Marriage and the Moral Imagination

alone. Psychologically, because I'm in the university also – they don't tell me what to do. My parents have some traditional values. They expect me to make the coffee for my husband...

Considering the future and that of her children, the theme of gender equality became even more pronounced:

We think about future generations. I would like to raise children who are different – especially in terms of gender equality. In the house we try to teach them this. In the family, whether male or female, everyone should have equal say. Not just the oldest brother making decisions for others. We talk about it only as it comes along – it's not planned. My husband doesn't look like a liberal man.[3] But he's ok with it. I think it's harder for men to break with gender expectations. We have three sons. They all aspire to be academically successful.

In this family story, traced over fifty or more years, we can see how explicit values of gender equality have emerged from rather 'traditional' Malay norms. Although Hasnah sees her parents as expecting her to 'make the coffee' for her husband, the parental marriage was one forged from similar backgrounds, in which, notably, both spouses worked outside the home, and they had what she described as 'a pretty much equal relationship'. An apparent crisis, when her father's status had taken a sharp upturn and he was pressured to take a second wife – in line with what many in Malaysia would see as conservative Muslim east coast values (see Chapter 1) – had been averted. We can see echoes of the parental marriage in the values that have shaped Hasnah's. The divergence was in Hasnah's explicit espousal of ideals of gender equality in the running of her own household and the upbringing of her children. This seemed congruent too with the co-residence of her divorced sisters and their parents in KL. The set-up she described in

---

[3] I did not enquire what she meant by this, but it is possible that Dr Hasnah was alluding to conspicuously conservative Islamic religious attire.

3 Marriage over the Generations

her own and her sisters' houses suggested strong elements of continuity but also the mark of more recent and explicitly feminist-inspired ideals of gender relations.[4]

Looping Effects

While theories of modernity might lead one to expect a linear and progressive intergenerational movement towards more egalitarian relations of conjugal intimacy, this was not necessarily what was articulated in the marriage stories I was told. Amelia, whose account begins this chapter, seemed certain that her own long-lived marriage was an improvement on that of her parents in terms of the gendered balance of power, female independence and values of mutual respect it embodied. She attributed the harmoniousness of her marriage, which she viewed as 'extraordinary', partly to the fact that she had always worked, and to her own nature as someone 'quite stubborn and assertive'. She spoke too about how her mother-in-law had been the dominant partner in her husband's parents' marriage – so perhaps this had provided a good model for him.

Amelia's views on marriage, however, were hardly radical:

The key to any good marriage lies with the man. Because women always respond to love. So, if a man knows how to love, the woman responds to make him happy.

She talked about the informal pre-marital counselling that she had for many years given at her church. 'Looking around, it breaks my heart. So many marriages are difficult', she told me, and here she became visibly upset. Going on directly to speak of her daughter, who was married with children, she lamented that,

---

[4] It is thus in line with the conclusions Karim (2021, 110) draws about the persistence of *adat* Malay values of gender complementarity in the face of a more conservative Islam.

Marriage and the Moral Imagination

My daughter, she has gone backwards. Not wrong to stop working. [But] She has become totally dependent on her husband. Now he's the lord, master and boss. I don't think it's healthy.

Amelia attributed these attitudes partly to the possessiveness of her daughter's mother-in-law, who resented the time that her daughter spent with her own parents:

She [her daughter's mother-in-law] sees herself as a mother-in-law not a daughter. To have a good relationship, you need to understand. Probably she's jealous. She knows my relation with my daughter is very tight. My daughter has to lie to see me. Going backward. My daughter is caught in a fight. His mother should try not to jeopardize my daughter's relation with her husband.

Beyond assessing the importance of women's paid work and independence, these reflections illuminate how modes of conjugality are perceived as situated within a nexus of intergenerational relations that may support or undermine a marriage. The models that parental marriages provide are important, as are the attitudes and interventions of a woman's mother-in-law. Rather than the steady march of progress, marital relations here are understood to have 'gone backwards'. Notably, Amelia deployed imaginative effort to comprehend how a marriage might succeed or get into difficulties. She also considered the standpoint and understanding of others – as well as their imaginative limitations. Her daughter's mother-in-law was thus to blame for a failure in empathy in not putting herself in the position of a daughter.

Amelia's poignant narration of these intergenerational stories of marriage was unusually clear in tracing what she saw as the progressive and retrogressive movement of marital relations over many decades in her family. Others spoke in more muted terms, but their accounts were nevertheless laden with valuations, ethical assessments and judgements that made sense of their own marriage and those of others through the imaginative work of comparison. These comparative assessments were often made in a temporal or generational register.

3 Marriage over the Generations

I got to know Harindra, a middle-aged man born in Penang, through his work in the artistic sector, which connected him to mutual friends. On the face of it, he seemed an unlikely exponent of 'conservative' values. Despite paternal pressure, he had avoided the family business, instead taking up tertiary education abroad, and had lived in Singapore, Canada and elsewhere for many years.

My father was very upset. He wanted me to go into business. I'm the only one in the family who's pursued arts.

Harindra's paternal grandfather, he told me, had migrated to Penang from a Gujarati village in India around 1920 and had set up a trading business for spices and textiles, later turning to other goods. He spoke of the particular values associated with his grandfather's place of origin:

The people there have a very different sensibility from the rest of India – gentleness and austere. It's where Gandhi came from – Jainism, Hinduism – very austere values. *Everyone* in the fourth generation – my grandfather had seven sons and one daughter – all the children are vegetarians.

The grandfather, who had returned to Gujarat to take a wife in an arranged marriage, had been a profound influence on Harindra. Through his grandfather, he told me, he had become interested in Indian philosophy and Hindu scriptures. In his father's generation, all the siblings had had arranged marriages – all of them had been happy, he said.

My generation is different. The marriages are in India, generally in urban areas, and rural to an extent. The orthodoxy is not there. My father's generation – [they had] arranged marriages. My generation was not forced. You are introduced. I rejected so many because I never wanted to get married. My father took my biodata and introduced me. But I never wanted.

I was very young, full of ideals. I wanted to devote myself to humanist issues. In my generation it's become a routine for parents to introduce someone compatible to the families. But to a large extent, the young generation

Marriage and the Moral Imagination

have family and community in mind. There's a kind of consensus. Take me, for example, I would not choose anyone who was not compatible with my family.

After working as an artist abroad for some years, he had been pressured by his father to return to Malaysia and had then found a job in Penang. But through all this, he said,

I maintained the values my grandfather had taught me. Even [abroad] – loose morals. My grandfather taught me. I took [my training] in a very disciplined way. I was very moved by the discipline. But all the time I was true to my grandfather's values.

After his return to Malaysia, his relatives had diligently sought out a bride for him.

When it was time to choose a bride, I had many options whom my father found. I said no to all of them. My mother's sister's daughter knew my wife's family – informed my family… It was difficult because my father and grandfather *expected* me to accept.

Harindra had not made things easy, but eventually something struck a chord:

Exchanged biodata, astrology. Went to the family with my brother and a friend/cousin. We went into a big room, and met as a group – all the youngsters.
    I was smitten not so much by her as her family. Her father reminded me of my grandfather. He was very educated, soft-spoken. My father-in-law and brother-in-law were top lawyers. Another brother was a financial consultant. But what mattered most were the *values*. My father asked, 'let's have a second meeting'. I was 28, she was 24.

There was a subsequent visit a few months after this initial one:

I met her once, it went ok. We took an autorickshaw. She was very careful. We went to a grove by the lake. I told her I didn't want to marry. We had light talk.

3 Marriage over the Generations

Perhaps not surprisingly after this somewhat hesitant beginning, a crisis ensued:

We went to a hill at the centre with a view. A friend and his wife took us there. It was evening; there were prayers at the temple. We started talking about philosophy. She said. 'You have to decide. We can't keep meeting like this'. I said I'd get back within 24 hours. Then next day I went to my mother's brother's house. My father got on with my future father-in-law. My wife found me interesting – quite principled, sincere.

I disappeared. My father was looking for me. My father's friend was looking for me. He came to my mother's brother's house – he knew I would be there. My uncle didn't know the situation. The friend gave me a lecture: 'Do this to someone else! Don't keep people waiting – someone's daughter. It's a good match. Make sure you don't lose it'. I didn't want to commit. I had my own ideas – travel. My friend pressured me; he scolded me – it was a good thing! Everything was right with the family, and with her too. I called my uncle; I said, 'I just lost my freedom'.

Despite these initial hesitations and hiccoughs, Harindra and his wife had married in the late 1990s. The wedding had been a 'very traditional one', he said. After being a housewife for many years, his wife had eventually taken up work in Harindra's father's family business. It was clear that this much-travelled, spiritual and highly educated man had found satisfaction and solace in what one might see as a turn towards the past and tradition:

[There is] So much similarity between my parents' marriage and mine. Even today young people prefer a full-scale traditional wedding – Bollywood films encourage it. I wanted the rites and rituals, and the post-rituals.

...

Whenever we go to India, we go back to Gujarat to relatives. When my father-in-law was alive, we went on a trip with him. I'm very thankful my parents taught me Gujarati – when I go back, I can speak, people invite you in.

I've been to Indonesia, Kedah, Kelantan – villages. I speak Malay. Elderly Gujaratis in the village, or the elderly in the US – it's the same kind of sensitivity – native US, the same kind of sensibility. If I had not gone into [the arts], I would have gone into anthropology. I go to places and meet people…

Marriage and the Moral Imagination

Nevertheless, even in what we might see as a 'conservative' turn, Harindra acknowledged that there had been shifts between the generations of his family in terms of conjugal relations:

In my grandfather's generation the husband was lord. My father's generation, less so. My generation, the wife dictates! Though my ego does come in, my wife can smash it down.

And towards the end of our conversation, he amplified:

The role of females has changed. My wife is working. My mother and aunties were all housewives. [The family] business is doing very well, so there's no pressure to work. My auntie from Singapore – there's always only one in that generation who worked…

Given Harindra's personal trajectory, his extensive travels and his artistic and intellectual preoccupations, one might perhaps have predicted that he would marry abroad and possibly make a life outside Malaysia. Here a respect for 'tradition' encapsulated in vegetarianism, spiritual values and arranged marriage has been subtly incorporated into an unconventional life in which he successfully resisted pressure to join the family business. Significantly, marriage here too, in spite of its apparent 'traditional' basis, expresses change. The importance of women working outside the home, and the autonomy and independence this gives rise to, is given weight in this narrative as in others. Perhaps most striking in Harindra's marriage story is his avowal that he was first 'smitten' by his prospective father-in-law, who reminded him of his grandfather, and by the family rather than the proposed bride herself. What mattered to him most were the values of the family. More broadly, the idea that a prospective spouse should be 'compatible with family' emerged clearly in this and many other marriage stories I was told.

I have alluded to 'looping effects' to capture the way that Amelia's and Harindra's depictions of marital change across the generations in their families did not necessarily take a straight course but could loop back to echo or recapitulate aspects of marriage in previous generations. Harindra's assertion of the similarity of his own marriage to that of his parents, or Amelia's depiction of her daughter's marriage as a throwback to earlier generations, are examples of this. But in new or different social contexts, these aspects acquired different meanings and significance. An adherence to patriarchal values or aspects of an arranged marriage might thus appear in some respects anachronistic. But the processes of history and the life course encapsulated in these stories indicate that the melding of new and old elements of marriage was a subtle, shifting and complex process. How exactly such stories might play out in forthcoming generations was difficult to predict.

Conclusion

What can we learn from the half dozen or so intergenerational stories of marriage presented here? I have intentionally presented protagonists of different ethnic, religious, educational and class backgrounds. And one obvious theme is the variability of trajectories in terms of individual life courses and family histories. Structural constraints help to shape marriage, but marriages also shape the contexts in which they are lived – partly through the incorporation of new elements into a family. The marriage stories I have presented were ones that seemed in some respects striking; they stood out as trajectories that both fitted within and diverged from pre-scripted scenarios. As we will see in Chapter 4, there is much to learn about marriage from what takes place at the margins of the conventional.

In selecting particular protagonists, I have also had in mind others who might have made an extended appearance: an old lady in her eighties who, considering three generations of marriages in her now far-flung family, including the marriages of two daughters outside their ethnic community, wondered at the extent of change: 'Each generation is quite different – because of the times – times change', she said. Another, in her

Marriage and the Moral Imagination

seventies, and able to trace eight generations of her family in Penang, told me of the three marriages of her father, a man from a Teochew-speaking dialect group who had been born in the late 1890s. From his perspective, she told me, 'Teochew girls don't exist. When my father was asked how many children he had, he only named the boys'. Another person I interviewed, an artist in his forties, related how he had come to marry only recently, after an online search in China. His wife had come to Penang from China as a marriage migrant, and relations with his own mother were sometimes difficult.

There are a lot of differences – the social structure; politically, nationally, structure and education. She is ten years younger [than me]. She was happy to leave. That's why we make it. That's the crucial point.

In a quite different vein, a Malay university lecturer preparing for her retirement spoke about the marriages in her family in terms of the core Muslim values they embodied and the 'waste of money' of lavish wedding ceremonies. Contrary to her own earlier expectations, she had found herself pursuing a career, and she saw the marriages of her children as expressing similar Muslim values to her own:

To me, you have to work hard at marriage. It's not romantic. You have to know skills to handle a marriage. Have to know love language – the *many* languages of love.

It is impossible to convey all the possibilities of these marriages and of the ways they were talked about or the lives they reflect. And this is partly because each marriage story opens out to take its place in a life story, a family history, as well as wider events. Like a palimpsest, marriages are revealed through stories of successive marriages. Parents' marriages were understood through, and weighed against, the experiences of childhood and of one's own marriage and, vice versa: people made sense of their own marriage through considering those of others, especially their parents. In this way, as Pierre Bourdieu notes, rather than being

3 Marriage over the Generations

'an autonomous unit', each marriage is part of a series, taking its place in a 'matrimonial history of the family' (2008, 153). Perhaps the most explicit example of this process was Li-Mei's reflection on her own and her parents' marriages as both the cause and result of suffering reproduced over generations. Here, marriage is not only key to reproduction but also to the reproduction of suffering from generation to generation. The only way to break this non-virtuous cycle, as she saw things, was to avoid marrying.

I began this chapter by drawing on anthropological discussions of marriage under modernity in terms of the binary of 'arrangement' versus 'love' or 'choice'. We have seen that, for many of those I interviewed, this is a powerful lens through which to articulate marital change over the last fifty years or so. What has been illuminated here, however, are the more subtle processes through which change is generated, experienced and absorbed by individuals and families. This is inherently an intergenerational process of accommodation and friction. Families, especially parents, are important when individuals 'choose' their partners; the highly valued aspiration that a spouse should be compatible with one's family is not easily or lightly ignored. And this has implications in terms of the progressive accumulation of change.

The modulated shifts, echoes, diversions and looping effects that are documented here show how marriage – even under conditions of 'modernity' – is an intergenerational process that is deeply embedded in family ties. The resilience of what we might see as 'conservative' values, however, should not necessarily be understood as an obstacle to change. This resilience is only part of the story. Partly because of the way that adherence to family, communal or religious values can occur alongside other shifts – especially women working outside the home – ideals and practices of marriage are widely perceived to be different today from how they were in previous decades. The increasing independence and autonomy associated with women's employment in the labour force have brought fundamental transformations in gender and marital relations.

Marriage and the Moral Imagination

In this sense, the effects of education and employment opportunities for women seem more significant than ethnic or religious differences and are spoken of, at least by women, in positive terms. At the same time, 'traditional' ways of doing things may mask or divert attention from changing forms – and norms – of conjugality. And here it is telling that men seem more prone to speak in terms of cultural loss than women.

Inevitably, marriage introduces new elements into familial and individual lives. The stories of successive marriages over several generations of families recounted here illuminate the ways that marriages are experienced, comprehended and evaluated through intergenerational relations. Such stories, which enfold judgements and comparisons, are a potent medium for ethical engagement (as discussed in the Introduction) and for narrating change. How people situate themselves in such narrations is prone to reconfiguration through a life course and from generation to generation. In this way, marriages mark time and kinship; they can be a way to reveal life stories and family histories as well as express changing expectations through time. Ethical and imaginative engagement with marriages in the past, alongside new expectations and circumstances, precipitates change even as these changes may be absorbed within older forms. This process is one that Siobhan Magee (2021), in the context of marriage in the southern US, has called 'creative conservatism', but it may also allow more radical departures from earlier norms. In either case, the presumed normativity of marriage provides a capacious cloak to cover ongoing transformation. Narrating histories of marriage, and the qualities of ethical imagination that this draws upon, is thus part of the process of creating history – as we will see in the rest of this book.

FOUR

Marriage in the Flux of Self-Fashioning

Two women, one in her sixties, the other in her thirties; both have married foreigners. One is a scientist, the other a businesswoman. One is a Malay Muslim, the other is from a Sri Lankan and Keralan Catholic background. One reflects back on a long and successful marriage; the other is in the immediate emotional aftermath of a marriage that has broken down. What could these women have in common? What can we discover about marriage as part of the life course from their stories?

The lives of Anna and Rashidah, the protagonists of this chapter, apparently have little obvious that connects them. They were two women of different generations, backgrounds, ethnicities and religions, working in quite different sectors, with whom I connected in Penang through different pathways, interviewed more than once in 2018–19 and met up with again in 2022. Both women struck me in initial interviews as exceptionally articulate and energetic; they seemed to have carved out unexpected lives largely through their own talents and efforts. Although the interviews concerned marriage, paradoxically, the role of marriage in these biographies was unclear. It was not obvious in either case that it had been as central as one might expect to the achievement of highly successful careers or life stories. What then was the significance of marriage in these trajectories? It is this puzzle that I address here to consider whether these two scenarios can illuminate how marriage may be a site not only of intimate transformation

Marriage and the Moral Imagination

but also of more overt political change, a matter considered further in Chapter 7 – and how this can be masked under a cloak of apparent conformity.

Marriage, as discussed in the Introduction, links personal and intimate lives with the political, partly through its embeddedness in religious and state institutions and its reliance on these for legitimation. Underlining how personal, intimate lives are framed by wider politics, the state has an all too clear interest in asserting its legitimising powers to secure and reproduce normative family forms. Yet the obviousness of the connections between the state and personal trajectories that coalesce around marriage may obscure the minutiae of how these connections actually operate. In this chapter, I draw on the life stories of two apparently exceptional women – both of whom had apparently 'made themselves' in sharp distinction to any expectations that could be associated with the circumstances of their upbringing. What can these two marriage-and-life stories tell us about what marriage is and does, or the possibilities it offers for transformation of the self, of intimate worlds and of the wider public sphere – in Malaysia and elsewhere in the contemporary world?

These two protagonists, Anna and Rashidah, who both lived in urban Penang, were born in different eras – one in the early 1950s, the other in the mid-1980s. Anna was from a Keralan and Sri Lankan (Ceylonese) Catholic background; Rashidah was a Malay Muslim. Anna grew up on rural rubber plantations; Rashidah was born in Kuala Lumpur. By birth, ethnic affiliation and religion, they could hardly have been more different. And yet something impelled me to place these two life stories side by side to see whether some wider understandings about the place of marriage in the life trajectories of upwardly mobile women might be gleaned from them. As adolescent girls, they were, in different ways, somewhat marginally situated, and both were from relatively poor and uneducated families. And both of course were women, which might, from some points of view, constitute a unifying feature of their marginality.

4 Marriage in the Flux of Self-Fashioning

Gender is a crucial feature of what makes these stories exceptional, and gender relations mark changes that have taken place in Malaysia over the last forty to fifty years. Far from being straightforwardly unidirectional, I outlined in Chapter 1 two separate and apparently contradictory trends in gender relations over this period. On the one hand, there has been a very marked rise in women's education and participation in the workforce (Jamilah 1994; Lee 2014; tan beng hui and Ng 2014). This has been accompanied by a gradual co-option of a rhetoric of gender equality in public policy and governmental discourse. Connected to these shifts, there has been a growth and expansion of middle-class feminist and civil society activist groups (Ng, Maznah and tan 2006). In contradistinction to the implications of gender equality discourse, however, a more conservative and patriarchal Islam has simultaneously made strong inroads in Malaysia and has gained a wider institutional footing in formal bureaucratic, legal and governmental procedures and policies (Maznah 2010b; 2013; 2020; Norani 2008; Norani, Zainah and Zaitun 2005; Peletz 2020b).

The interviews about marriage that I conducted among middle-class people of different ages and ethnicities in Penang reflect some of these wider trends and patterns emerging over the last fifty years. Some of these social changes are evident in Anna and Rashidah's stories recounted later. Narrating a marriage – one's own or those of close family members – inevitably occurs in past, present and future tense (Carsten et al. 2021). Such narratives involve reflecting on how things have changed, and they have an explicit or implicit temporality. They also imply and reveal ethical judgements – choices or stances taken in the past about an imagined future as well as retrospective assessments of actions taken long ago. These might be about small, seemingly 'everyday' matters or about larger issues, and they may be implicit in the way stories are arranged and told rather than made obvious in declamatory statements. Values and judgements, memories and sentimental attachment may be silently embodied, as I show towards the end of this chapter, in the material objects accrued in the course of a marriage. Objects may encapsulate in a quite implicit manner the emotional registers of childhood or marriage; or they may enable a recuperation or readjustment of difficult relations in the past without this being explicitly articulated. As discussed in the Introduction, I want to convey here, following Veena Das (2020), how the 'everyday' or 'ordinary' is elusive rather than obvious, that it does not reveal itself directly, and cannot be taken for granted. For most people, kinship as it is lived and imagined is a realm of the everyday that is suffused with ethics. In this way, as Das emphasises, the ethical is not a separable realm but instead thoroughly permeates everyday life (2020, 145).

Marriage seems particularly rich in opportunities for ethical assessment and reassessment because it involves navigating and sometimes diverging from the past as well as imagining and planning a future. It can appear as a caesura in the life course, when actions with particular consequences are taken or not taken. Retrospectively too, it provides a point of entry for retelling a life and for reflecting on the repercussions of earlier decisions and actions or their possible alternatives. Inevitably, the ethical judgements that pivot around marriage are also relational ones.

I have suggested that the stories that I focus on in this chapter trace exceptional trajectories rather than more common ones, and this prompts questions about the location of the exceptional. Marriage may encapsulate conformity or innovation – or aspects of both of these. But as we see in this chapter, it is not necessarily clear that exceptional lives, however they may reveal themselves, will be expressed in obviously exceptional or innovative marriages. On the contrary, marriage might provide a conformist 'mask', or cover, for an unusual life. I take inspiration here from another essay by Das (2018b), in which she critiques understandings of new forms of social engagement that privilege separation from earlier attachments as the condition for achieving new

4 Marriage in the Flux of Self-Fashioning

autonomous agency.[1] Das explores ethnographically the possibilities within the everyday for generating new kinds of attachments and outcomes – in other words, 'the potential of the everyday itself to produce a different everyday' (Das 2018b, 58). In this chapter we see how exceptional trajectories can be embarked upon while still maintaining older familial ties, and indeed these may provide a recourse when new relations founder. Planning for, and reflecting on, marriage, I suggest, might be occasions when this potential of the everyday to generate opportunities for innovation emerges especially clearly.

Operating as a 'hinge' between conformity and transgression, we will see how marriage across ethnic boundaries may be absorbed into more conventional webs of connection or, alternatively, eventually trigger the reassertion of pre-existing familial ties to smooth over the disruptive effects of a marital breakdown. Marriage here has curiously elastic properties; it may amplify a transformative movement in terms of social mobility, but it may also disguise the transgressive effects of the disruption of conventional familial bonds. Judgements, reflections and comparisons are part of the ongoing process through which marriages that are on the limits of what is conventionally acceptable are absorbed and enfolded into families and communities. Gradually over time and generations, this precipitates an expansion of possibilities within families and across communities.

The idea that the emergence of new forms of agency takes place in the flux of everyday life, and without necessarily rupturing previous ties, is highly pertinent to the two stories that I trace in this chapter. The narratives related here show how marriage can be simultaneously radical and conservative and how 'the everyday' permits a folding of new relations

---

[1] The essay, 'On Singularity and the Event: Further Reflections on the Ordinary', is an extended engagement with Caroline Humphrey's discussion in 'Reasssembling Individual Subjects' (Humphrey 2018). I thank Resto Cruz for drawing this work to my attention and for the generativity of his reflections on social mobility and kinship over time and across generations.

into pre-existing ones. Elsewhere in the Southeast Asian region, Resto Cruz (2020) has recently discussed the longer-term implications of social mobility for kinship over generations through the lens of cousinship (for urban Malays in an earlier era, see also Nagata (1976)). This brings us back to the question of how to place marriage in the projects of self-fashioning that I describe here – a question I return to at the end of this chapter together with a further consideration of the exceptionality of these biographies. Constrained by the past, but also offering openings to innovation, marriage here is not simply – as we might expect – a means to social or economic mobility. Rather than seeing marriage as the route to the successful attainment of unusual life projects, we see how it may instead be enfolded *within* a larger ethical project of self-transformation.

A further question arises about the wider implications of these personal or familial life trajectories. I suggest here that what we deem to be matters of personal choice or familial matters do not simply *reflect* or echo wider social changes – such as those in gender relations discussed earlier. Partly through the way that they encompass ethical judgements and practices that are relational in nature, they impinge particularly on families. Actions and precepts that coalesce around marriages, apparently pertaining mainly to intimate personal lives, have a tendency to accumulate and amplify in a range of attitudes and stances taken by members of different generations of a family, and also to travel between families – partly through subsequent marriages. The ethics of gendered lives and relationships are also, simultaneously, contested – as we saw in Chapter 2 – in the contradictory public discourses and social trajectories mentioned earlier. Thus we might view the ethics of marriage as a particularly fraught zone of political, familial and personal concern, debate and transformation. Marriage, in life trajectories such as those described in this chapter, is both subject to wider transformative processes and, itself engenders ethical judgements that are at once intimate and political, and which have the capacity to effect both personal and political transformation.

4 Marriage in the Flux of Self-Fashioning

In the sections that follow, I trace Anna and Rashidah's lives through their accounts of their parents' marriages and their own childhoods to adolescence and leaving their families, to making their careers and marrying, and finally to reflecting back on the marriages they have both made. Their own ethical assessments, as well as those of their relatives, are revealed through their narrations, and also in their accounts of the material stuff, the objects, accrued through the course of their marriages.

Parental Marriages; Childhood Backgrounds; Moving Away

Anna described a difficult childhood. 'It was a typical Kerala wedding – Catholic but it also had Indian traditions', she said. Her father had come to Malaya as a child in the 1920s from Kerala; her mother was Sinhalese – her family had come to Malaya from Ceylon. Her mother was sixteen at the time of their marriage; her father was twenty-eight. Anna's mother died when she was a small child, and her father then lived together with her mother's older sister in an informal marriage. Her stepmother eventually came to favour her own two children over her sister's. Anna vividly described growing up on several British-owned rubber plantations in the 1950s and 1960s where her father was in charge of the plantation workers and was also an assistant at the plantation clinics. The family moved frequently, depending on where he was working. She described her father as 'very strict' and, as the oldest daughter, she had many domestic duties to perform, including making breakfast for the family at 5.30 before going to school and cleaning. 'The boys didn't do anything. I used to get angry with them', she said. She also had a sometimes irascible father to placate who tried to keep her away from boys as she was growing up: 'My father said, "don't stand at the windows". If you did, you were slapped. You were not supposed to look at boys'.

Anna recounted her vivid memory of humiliation as a young child at a Christmas party held in the estate manager's bungalow.

Marriage and the Moral Imagination

The boss of the plantations was British. Christians were invited at Christmas. We got presents; there was a Christmas tree.... We got invited. Dad said, especially, 'be polite'. I called the lady 'aunty'. She got angry, shouted, 'I'm not your aunty'. After that, I kept quiet.

New pink dresses every year were another kind of ordeal. And in Anna's account of her childhood, I sensed the constraints of domestic labour and a harshness to the tenor of familial relations. But it was also clear from these depictions that Anna was, from early on, something of a rebel at heart. She described listening to the Beatles and putting up her hair to make it look short – 'my father gave me a tight slap'.

Rashidah was brought up in a different era – the 1980s and 1990s. The traces of the colonial past that are viscerally present in Anna's recollections of childhood are more attenuated in Rashidah's. Both her Malay parents came from large rural families with twelve or thirteen siblings in each case. 'Their backgrounds were pretty much the same', she said. 'They came from the same village'. Neither was educated beyond primary school. They had an arranged marriage in the mid-1960s that was celebrated in their villages in a way that sounded familiar to me from my research in Langkawi in the early 1980s (Carsten 1997). 'They met for the first time one week before the marriage', she told me. Her mother was fifteen and her father twenty-five when they married. The families were poor and there were no photographs from the wedding, and this too seemed familiar as I was generally the photographer for the weddings I attended in Langkawi. After their marriage, Rashidah's parents went to Singapore, and her father was in the British army for ten years. Subsequently, they moved to Kuala Lumpur, and he worked as a lorry driver for a large state company while her mother made cakes for sale to supplement the low family income. This kind of mixed earning was also familiar to me from earlier rural research. Rashidah didn't describe her early childhood in great detail, but she conveyed that, although poor, it was an affectionate one: 'Theirs is a very harmonious marriage. I've never seen them in an argument'. Her mother was easy-going, she said,

4 Marriage in the Flux of Self-Fashioning

and her father had a kind of questioning attitude to life and a curiosity about the world that she thought might have influenced her. 'He was always reading newspapers, listening to news. Maybe I am more curious from him. My mother is more happy-go-lucky, I get that from her'. Rashidah did well at school, and at thirteen was selected to be sent to a state boarding school until she was fifteen – one typical way in which Malay children of perceived aptitude may find themselves on a path that diverges from that of their families.

Of an earlier generation, and non-Malay, Anna's career path was not forged through education – although one aspect of her paternal inheritance was to prove crucial: fluency in English. Her adolescent years were increasingly tied to servicing her father's domestic needs as he moved from job to job on the rubber estates while the rest of the family became less mobile. Irked by the sense of confinement and increasing drudgery, as well as an obvious need to supplement a meagre family income, at the age of sixteen, when she finished secondary school, she struck out. Seeing an advertisement in the newspaper for trainee blackjack croupiers in the newly establishing gambling industry, unbeknownst to her father, she applied for a job. Once again, her description of how she made the move away from her father's control, beginning with a clandestine visit to Kuala Lumpur for a job interview, telling her stepmother it was for a position as a cashier and under cover of visiting relatives, was dramatic and memorable. The relatives proved unwelcoming; severe floods considerably exacerbated the difficulties, but Anna was successful. The would-be employers were initially sceptical about her background: 'You're Indian. Are you sure your parents will allow it?' they asked. Somehow she convinced them. A combination of lively intelligence, talent, quickness and good looks might have played their part. After a period of initial hardship and very tough living conditions, gradually her earnings increased from a meagre RM 150 per month, while training, until after more than ten years, she was earning the sizable sum of RM 5,000. During this time, although her relations with her father were rather distant, she regularly

Marriage and the Moral Imagination

sent money home and became the mainstay of the family income, renting and furnishing a house for them in Kuala Lumpur.

Rashidah spent less time than Anna in describing her childhood and adolescent years. For reasons that will become clear, she had other aspects of her story that she wanted to convey. By her own account, her parents, although religious, were not extremely strict, and her mother did not adopt a Muslim head covering, *tudung*, until the 1980s, when many Malay women who had not previously done so began to veil as a sign of more observant Islamic practice. In line with this movement, Rashidah described how, during her stay at religious school, she herself had conformed to a strict form of female Muslim attire with her wrists covered but, as an undergraduate in Australia, she had unveiled. At a certain point at boarding school, she became interested in science and had gone on to a science college for a year from the ages of sixteen to seventeen, followed by a preparatory college. Achieving excellent results in science in her exams, she gained a scholarship to study for a first degree in Australia, and subsequently a PhD in the US.

These accounts enable us to get an initial sense of the geographic and social distance our protagonists began to travel from their families of origin. Neither of them followed pre-scripted paths. A combination of talents, aptitudes, determination and hard work, as well as increased access to higher education for women in one case, enabled them to take their initial steps away from scenarios that might have been more predicted by their family backgrounds. Notably, they both initiated their careers without marrying. In this respect, marriage seems to have been tangential to their self-fashioning.

Marriage and Its Sequels

After some years, the limitations of Anna's career as a successful croupier became constraining. Although she earned a good income, there was no sense of progression. Her father began insisting that, at the age

4 Marriage in the Flux of Self-Fashioning

of twenty-eight, it was time for her to marry. Her two younger sisters wanted to marry, and he told her that, as the eldest, she should marry first. In the late 1970s, she left the casino to work in a hotel in Kuala Lumpur and from there was once again selected to help run a travel agency based in a hotel in Kuala Lumpur, and subsequently transferred to a hotel at Penang's popular beach resort. Spending time for her work in the lobby of the hotel, she noticed Michel, a Frenchman who had come to work for a large electrical company in Penang, who also frequented the hotel lobby and bars: 'I thought he looks quite cute'. Eventually, the two were introduced by the hotel chef. 'I thought it would be a casual thing', she said. Anna was at the time renting a suburban house, and her housemates included an Australian working at the nearby Royal Australian Airforce base in Butterworth. When the room was vacated, Michel moved in as housemate. In time, the two became partners. Michel, when I spoke to him, reflecting on this period, spoke of the attractions of Anna's great cooking.

The story of how their marriage came about had elements of romantic comedy. A visit from Anna's father to her Penang rented home, accompanied by her brother as moral support for his sister, was recounted as farce – with Michel initially keeping to his bedroom. They lived together for a few years. In time, Anna decided to move out 'because they were going nowhere'. Michel, before rushing into anything, announced that he needed to go to France to talk to his parents. On his return, he asked her to marry him, and they registered their marriage officially. There was a reception at a hotel in Kuala Lumpur and the matter of Michel's somewhat lapsed Catholicism to attend to. The local Catholic priest said that 'even though we were married, we were living in sin'. After receiving instruction, the couple were married in church, Anna by then in an advanced state of pregnancy. Eventually, the couple had two daughters, and, for a time, Anna gave up work to attend to the children and homemaking. After some years, she established her own successful business, which combined her expertise in tourism, Penang heritage, cooking and an interest in antiques. One of the many notable features in Anna's story was the successful and affectionate relationship she had forged with her father-in-law, partly through her aptitude for language learning and her interest in things European.

Rashidah's story also involved marriage to a foreigner, but the mood of this narrative was more sombre. The couple met and lived together while Rashidah was studying for her PhD in the US. Stephen accompanied her back to Malaysia, where she took up an academic post in Penang while he worked as a freelance media consultant. Her family meanwhile remained in Kuala Lumpur. Cohabiting in Malaysia was a different matter from doing so in the US, and illegal for Muslims. In order to continue the relationship, the couple were obliged to marry. Rashidah's mother counselled her to marry swiftly, and the couple duly did so after two weeks back in the country. At the time, she was twenty-eight and Stephen was thirty. Under Malaysian law, marriage to a Muslim required Stephen to convert to Islam – although, as she recounted, this did not extend to him changing his name or to following the precepts or observation of Islamic practice in daily life. Rashidah told me that she made all the arrangements for the wedding celebrations herself, quite quickly and online: 'It took me two weeks to organise a wedding.... There was the solemnization and the meal straight after'. There was some discussion as to what to do about the customary marriage payments from the groom to the bride's parents (*belanja kahwin*). Stephen had been reluctant about this, she reported, 'because it sounds like the family is selling their daughter'. Eventually, as if to underline their ideological distance from the practice, a nominal sum was fixed on: 1234.56RM, which she said she had given to her mother 'out of my pocket money, not his'. This was much lower than the norm for a woman with her qualifications and with a number pattern that made it seem somehow less serious. Meanwhile, her husband-to-be transferred a more substantial sum to her account.

Unfortunately, as Rashidah told me quite early on in a first interview, the marriage did not prosper. Already, when they were still in the

4 Marriage in the Flux of Self-Fashioning

US, she had discovered through emails on his computer that Stephen had been having an affair. 'There were arguments for and against staying. I gave him a chance. He promised he wouldn't do it any more. I was devastated. I gave him a chance', she said. Back in Malaysia, she had been offered the opportunity of a one-year post-doc abroad after their marriage. She suggested that he accompany her, but he resisted, citing the cold climate in Europe, and what would he do about their dog? Rashidah spent the year abroad on her own while Stephen stayed on in the house that she had bought in Penang. On her return, it became clear that he had engaged in a long-running affair using the house as a base while she was away. Rashidah's account of her discovery and the ensuing events was dramatic. She decided at once to turn him out of the house and put her scientific training to the service of her anger by gathering forensic evidence of Stephen's adultery for laboratory analysis, and strategising on the best way to obtain a divorce through the Syariah Court in Penang, which has jurisdiction over Muslim marriages. As she put it succinctly, 'Don't mess with a smart woman!' The application for a divorce had been speedily granted not long before I met her, and, at the time, she was engaged in filing for compensation for the financial support she had given Stephen over the years of their marriage as well as the return of property through the same courts. Meanwhile, she pursued her career with seriousness, went regularly to the gym and engaged in a social life that sometimes involved going out with groups of friends.

Although Anna's and Rashidah's marriages have turned out entirely differently, one could discern in both women's trajectories their purposeful and energetic attitudes and a proactive approach to marriage, careers and the life course. The impetus to marry in both cases seemed to have come at least partly from the immediate circumstances – pregnancy for one, the impossibility of cohabiting for the other. But one could sense too the unspoken assumption of expectations to marry as part of the normative life course and its successful achievement.

Marriage and the Moral Imagination

The 'Stuff of Marriage': Registers of Retrospection

Many people are unused to speaking to others openly about their marriage or other close family relationships – although I suggest that there is a sense in which internal dialogue or silent reflection on these relations is nevertheless an often unnoticed part of everyday life. Apart from spoken and unspoken narratives, however, there are other registers in which we might trace ethical reflection on marriage. Here I argue that certain kinds of objects – the 'stuff of marriage' – may silently condense attitudes, dreams, memories and judgements about relationships. Objects may endure through time, encapsulating positive or negative emotions; they may be treasured and kept, but they may also be disposed of or replaced. New kinds of objects, embodying middle-class and modern lifestyles, may reflect a shift from families of origin. Older ones may take on a patina of nostalgia. The kinds of marital objects I have in mind are houses, furnishings, jewellery, clothing, cooking implements, photographs and other kinds of material that pervade everyday lives and are often brought into a marriage (for example, as a trousseau or dowry) or acquired during its course as inheritance, gifts or joint purchases. Such objects may sometimes be directly spoken about, but, importantly here, the ethical values and sentiments they embody or evoke may remain oblique or hidden, surfacing only at moments of marital rupture or bereavement. Notably, the evocative capacities of this kind of object are a rich terrain for novelists and memoirists – Edmund de Waal's *The Hare with Amber Eyes* (2011), Elif Shafak's *The Island of Missing Trees* (2021) and Geetanjali Shree's *Tomb of Sand* (2021) are just three obvious examples.[2] They show how everyday objects constitute another register of the elusive or taken for granted everyday that is suffused with ethics in the manner that Das has suggested. And they also speak to the way the everyday may generate new kinds of relations.

---

[2] It is not coincidental that all three of these are stories of both familial and national rupture.

4 Marriage in the Flux of Self-Fashioning

I was intrigued by the way that homes, furnishings and objects figured in both Anna's and Rashidah's accounts of their marriages and could do so in either positive or negative registers. Anna spoke warmly and in some detail about the different houses she had made since she married. It seemed clear that homemaking had been a source of pride and pleasure and had been bound up with her marital status. She described the kitchens and gardens of different houses and the household furniture acquired. A much-loved house in one neighbourhood eventually had to be left because of the persistent intrusion of snakes from the garden, which might have endangered the children. I interviewed her in the premises of her own small business in the tourist trade in Penang that she had established some twenty years after her marriage. There she had recuperated countless antique objects and old photographs about which she spoke movingly as somehow reconnecting her to her childhood homes on the plantations (see also Day 2018; 2023). This work of recuperation, I sensed, was also part of a process of patching over and reconciliation with the difficult relations of her childhood. Looking around her, towards the end of our interview, she said, 'On the estates, I had to clean. We had water filters, grinders for rice flour, pounders for coconut chutney. We used to use old gadgets'. Indicating the old railway lights hanging as ornamentation in her premises, she said, 'The lights at railway stations, I saw them and bought them'.

At first, it seemed that household objects had not really emerged as a theme in Rashidah's account of her marriage. But on reflection, my initial impression had ignored how the marital home and its property figured as the subject of harsh dispute rather than nostalgia. Although she did not speak of her house as entwined with her marital status in a positive register, it was her money that had paid for the house and furnishings, as Rashidah told me, and she was determined to keep them and to receive compensation for anything removed. Her account of the initial fight in Penang, on the occasion when she had discovered her husband's affair and had thrown him out of the house, featured furnishings, clothing and other household objects. There were the minutiae of domestic items taken to the forensic labs for analysis in her pursuit of evidence to use in her divorce case. And then there was the Harley-Davidson motorbike for which Rashidah had paid the instalments through the marriage. She had demanded the key for this when she 'kicked him out of the house', she said. 'I told him to give me the bike keys and get out. He said "no". I took his clothes and threw them out. He pushed me against the sofa. I called the police and filed a report'. With its resonances of status, value, masculine mobility and freedom, the bike seemed a peculiarly 'sticky' object whose attachment was difficult to sever. The focus of lengthy and complex paperwork in order to establish the case for its return, it cropped up in several of our conversations and updates on the divorce case and considerably preoccupied her.

It is not accidental that in both Rashidah's and Anna's accounts of their marriage, houses, furnishings and marital property should figure largely. For both women, homeownership had been directly linked to marriage and to the fulfilment of successful life trajectories in normative terms. The status afforded to women through the constellation of home, family and marriage was expressed even in the face of marital breakdown.[3] But the way that houses and household objects incrementally absorb and accrue positive and negative emotional value here is suggestive. Like other kinds of 'marital objects', such as wedding albums, trousseau items, wedding dresses or jewellery, houses and their furnishings encapsulate the emotional tenor and historicity of the marital relation itself. They have the capacity to embody and convey qualities of these relations over time (Carsten 2019b; Trautmann, Mitani and Feeley-Harnik 2011). Such objects may overtly express the success of a marriage and the status of a husband and wife; they may be imbued with memories and become part of an inheritance down the generations. Here Anna's retrospective collection, and her recuperation and ordering of

---

[3] I am grateful for the suggestions of an anonymous reviewer on this point.

4 Marriage in the Flux of Self-Fashioning

a difficult past suggest a complex temporal disposition that can travel both forwards and backwards in time. But we might take the location of these items – away from Anna's marital home – as equally suggestive. It recalls Rebecca Empson's (2007) discussion of contrastive modes of display and concealment in Mongolian homes of photographic montages of agnatic kin, women's embroideries and the hair cuttings and umbilical cords of children secreted in household chests. These different kinds of objects signify different kinds of relations and the separations they entail: 'Things kept inside the house become the site or body through which relations are maintained' (Empson 2007, 68).[4] Such objects, which convey attachment, are suffused with the loss of particular relationships.

What is highlighted by the juxtaposition of these two marital scenarios is that, although we may be disposed to emphasise sentimental attachments and the positive valency of objects as they accrue relational value, their negative capacities are equally potent. As in Mary Bouquet's discussion of family photographs, objects can have an 'associative' power that may be constitutive of kinship (Bouquet 2001, 86–87). A marriage undone necessitates fragmentation and dispersal of its property, and marital objects may absorb and convey the negative qualities of the dissolving relationship, but this does not diminish their emotional power. Here Lauren Berlant's rendering of 'the cluster of promises … embedded in a person, a thing, an institution …' is pertinent (Berlant 2011, 23). The 'condition of maintaining an attachment to a significantly problematic object' is the essence of what Berlant calls 'cruel optimism' (2011, 24). Marital objects instantiate how emotional and ethical qualities may be silently incorporated and accrued in the intimate material world, bridging different temporalities and transmissible over time and space. Such objects express and contain memories, which are readily absorbed in their physical properties without the requirement of explicit

---

[4] My thanks to Charles Stewart for making this connection and for emphasising the link to different kinds of relationships.

articulation. Their everydayness, like the everyday of a marital life, is elusive in Das's sense, unarticulated, suffused with ethics and also often fragile and transitory.

Not surprisingly, given the divergences between these two life courses and marriages, as well as the disparate ages and life stages of the protagonists, different aspects and elements emerged in their telling. Anna dwelt on the circumstances of her childhood; Rashidah was quite brief on this theme. Anna took pleasure in recounting the unusual path her career had taken as a young woman and the early events of her relationship with Michel. Rashidah's account omitted to say much about any early romantic engagement and concentrated heavily on her anger and sense of betrayal at the discovery of Stephen's infidelity and her ensuing actions. One interesting theme that emerged here was the ease and speed with which the syariah court had granted Rashidah's application for divorce. This might not have been the case, she thought – and her lawyer had advised – if she had applied only on grounds of adultery, which she said 'is not a strong case in the syariah court. But lack of support is'. The case was strengthened both by her former husband's lack of observance of Islam and because, far from financially supporting her, as required of husbands under Islamic marriage law, she had supported him. The judgement of the syariah court here, and Rashidah's own assessment, are in line with Michael Peletz's conclusion (2020b, Chapter 5) in his study of marital cases in these courts, that there is a tendency to view women's requests for divorce favourably, in contrast to procedures in the 1970s and 1980s (see also Jones 2023, 206 for a comparable case in Indonesia, and Chapter 6 this volume).[5]

---

[5] See Peletz (2020b, 198–204) on the expansion and liberalisation of grounds for women to gain unilateral access to *fasakh* divorce (by annulment) in syariah courts in Malaysia enacted between 1983 and 1991, and historical changes over several decades congruent with the emergence of a new Malay middle class, a rise in women's education and independent earning capacities and ideals of companionate marriage – all of which are relevant to Rashidah's case.

4 Marriage in the Flux of Self-Fashioning

Anna's two daughters are now in their thirties; both are living and working outside Malaysia. Neither have (yet) married, and it is unclear whether they will do so. 'They gave me an ultimatum', Anna related, 'don't talk about marriage'. Anna and Michel's marriage seems a harmonious one. Both continue to work hard in their late sixties, but, she told me, they always take one day off a week and in the evening make sure to go to a favourite bar at one of Penang's beach hotels (perhaps reprising the early days of their romance), so that they have regular opportunities to talk with each other. On several occasions, Rashidah mused aloud about her parents' marriage and the mystery of how they had managed to achieve more than fifty years of harmonious cohabitation while, for herself and her siblings (one of whom was twice divorced and one still unmarried), this seemed so unattainable. Unsurprisingly, given her mother's early death, Anna's account of her parents' marriage was quite brief and schematic. She had more to say about how her stepmother (aunt) was treated by her father: They 'were very loving together in the beginning. Later he got irritated. I still remember when my [step]mother cooked curry, he would take it and throw it on her – hot. We would cry'. Reflecting on our interview in a subsequent conversation, Anna told me, 'I did tell him he shouldn't do that, and he shouted at me'.

Comparative assessments about the different marriages in different generations of their families were woven through Rashidah's and Anna's retrospections almost imperceptibly and in the natural flow of their conversations. Inevitably, these carried ethical claims. One could sense that Anna felt her own marriage was a significant improvement on those of her father, while Rashidah strongly conveyed that she viewed her parents' marriage as a notable achievement – in marked contrast to her own. In this sense, although Rashidah may have viewed her own educational and career trajectory as a success story, her marriage had a more ambivalent import. At the time that it was contracted, one could assume it would have participated in, and at least partially expressed, her successful trajectory in normative terms – although this might have been tempered by the fact that she was marrying a foreigner and a non-Muslim. In asserting the positive values embodied in her parents' marriage in the aftermath of her own divorce, one could see a different kind of personal and familial ethical claim being made – against the devalued morals of her husband. But of course this is to take a snapshot at a particular moment. At the point of her wedding, Rashidah would presumably have articulated a different and more rosy view, and what would transpire in the future was unknowable.

Conclusion

What can we learn about contemporary marriage in Malaysia or elsewhere from the two stories recounted here? In some respects, they seem to make an unlikely, or non-obvious, pairing. I suggested at the start of this chapter that this was partly due to the differences between the two main protagonists: their ages, the era in which they had grown up and their ethnic and religious backgrounds. We might add to these divergences the relative success or failures of their marriages. What draws the two stories together is that they both feature women who have somehow 'made themselves' in ways that have involved forging careers and marriages that are in sharp contrast to what might have been expected from their familial backgrounds. As career women, they could serve as 'figures of Southeast Asian modernity' in the sense described by Barker, Harms and Lindquist (2014; see also Jones 2009; 2021; Jones, Hull and Maznah 2015), and this might be the most obvious aspect of their exceptionality.

What of the place of marriage itself in these accounts of self-making? In both scenarios, marriage appeared as the sequel rather than the precursor to career-making – the latter already being well under way before either Anna or Rashidah married. In this sense, marriage does not seem to have been the engine for self-transformation in either case but, instead, was encompassed *within*, and affirmed a story of moving beyond, social

4 Marriage in the Flux of Self-Fashioning

and familial backgrounds. Here the wider changing opportunities for women and movement into the labour force in Malaysia over the last fifty years, outlined in Chapter 1, are significant. We could view these stories simply as accounts of their protagonists' lives, reflecting a particular era and place rather than being 'about' marriage as such. But beyond the fact that both Anna and Rashidah initially responded to requests to be interviewed about marriage, I think this would also miss some of the more subtle intimations of what marriage is doing in these two scenarios.

Both women's marriages were part of already-ongoing trajectories that were apparently removing them from the sphere of their natal families socially and geographically. In both cases, we might see marriage here as a kind of linchpin of conformity and transformation. In both accounts, marriage was required by conventions governing the immediate circumstances – in one case, 'living in sin' and pregnancy, and in the other, the illegality for Muslims of cohabitation outside marriage. The marriages were thus conformist in the obvious sense that they fulfilled and affirmed normative expectations of the life course in Malaysia – as is often the case elsewhere too. But they also substantiated and amplified the transformative trajectories that were already under way. Anna and Rashidah both married foreigners of different ethnicities from themselves. Notably, Anna's choice of partner did not cross any religious boundary, while Rashidah's required her husband's conversion – though by her own account it was not any difference in religious inclination or observance that undermined the marriage, and she described herself, rather frankly, as without religious leanings.

As we will see in Chapter 5, marriage to foreigners and across ethnic or religious boundaries can be construed as 'transgressive' to varying degrees in the Malaysian landscape, and certainly it can have the capacity to challenge existing familial or communal relations. But significantly, both Anna and Rashidah maintained ties with their families. Anna mentioned at various points her brother's crucial supportive role in her tense relation with her father and spoke of her own continued remittances to her family. Rashidah was living on her own when I first interviewed her, but, to my surprise, when I returned to Penang in 2019 after an absence of a few months, she related how her elderly parents and unmarried sister had moved to Penang from Kuala Lumpur to live with her on a long-term basis. This move did not seem to be predicated on any lifestyle changes on her own part, and it was clearly much welcomed as a gesture of support. Thus, Rashidah's independent marital homemaking, after the failure of her marriage, eventually and counterintuitively, became a means to reattach herself to her natal family. Substantiating Das's (2018b) argument, the achievement of new forms of social engagement for Anna and Rashidah, in terms of marriage, work and lifestyle, was not premised on the rupture of previous ties – although these may have undergone some temporary disruption.

We could see marriage here as having the capacity both to amplify transformative movement and simultaneously to restrict it. Non-conformist or 'transgressive' marriage may create or instantiate disturbances in lives and relationships – as, for example, described by Perveez Mody (2008) for love marriages in Delhi (see also Jones 2009; Jones et al. 2015), but it may also mask these disruptions or allow them, like ripples on the social surface, to become gradually absorbed into familial relations and wider expectations, which, as Mody also intimates, may then adjust incrementally. These different destinations are arrived at through the deployment of serial ethical judgements, and in light of the memory of the past, and the imagination of possible alternatives. These processes may be explicitly articulated or implicitly incorporated into whether and how, for example, decisions to marry outside normative bounds are accepted, or not, by parents or other relatives. Marriage may accentuate and enlarge or, alternatively, reduce social differences. We might say marriage allows departures from social norms precisely because of, and through, its normativity. Of course, what determines which, if any, relations may break in this process, or how disruptive marriages are likely

4 Marriage in the Flux of Self-Fashioning

to be, may partly depend on the direction of travel they allow in terms of social status as well as other factors – as will become clearer in Chapter 5. Both Anna's and Rashidah's life courses have, thus far, been tales of upward social and economic mobility. Their lives have instantiated the expansion of the middle class that has been such a notable feature of recent decades in Malaysia, as it has elsewhere (see, for example, Collier 2020). The selves being fashioned are socially successful ones. And this might have increased the likelihood of their families maintaining ties with them.

Comparison is one means through which we can observe the minutiae of how marriages are imagined, planned and accepted or rejected by spouses and their relatives. Both the stories that have been recounted here have incorporated comparisons, evaluative judgements, memories and imagination exercised within and between generations. Apart from those that I have relayed from the accounts of Rashidah and Anna, there will have been others too, of their relatives and friends. Such comparative labour, involving the critical assessment of intimate relations and their viability, is both implicitly and explicitly also ethical and imaginative labour. It exemplifies Das's (2020, 145) discussion of the way that ethical judgements are diffused through everyday life rather than necessarily being constituted in exceptional acts.

Through the accumulation of such judgements, we can see marriage as encapsulating and enabling elements of both conformity and transformation. It is important to recognise that while some evaluations may be explicit, others may be unarticulated – resonant, for example, in the accumulation and safeguarding of objects that are suffused with the emotional qualities and memories of marital or other relations in the past. Over time, the gradual acceptance of new forms of marriage may adjust or expand the realms of what can be accepted into the everyday. We might thus expect a wider expansion of horizons in Anna's and Rashidah's families, particularly in the following generation, to ensue from their marriages. The non-marriage of Anna's daughters into their thirties and their

Marriage and the Moral Imagination

residence outside Malaysia suggests just such an enlargement of possibilities. The steps taken by Rashidah's parents and sister to show their support for her by relocating to Penang (which could be seen as reciprocated in housing and other material contributions they received) are indicative too of the elastic accommodations that can be a quality of kinship relations under difficult circumstances. This might prompt us to consider how more radical social transformations – for example, the gradual and ongoing acceptance of same-sex relations and marriage within kinship and legal regimes in Europe and North America – have been made possible. A striking feature of the struggle for same-sex marriage, as Judith Butler (2002) and Tom Boellstorff (2007) have commented, is the manner in which it appears at once radical and conservative. Marriage is from some points of view inherently a conservative and conformist institution. And yet, examined more closely, it also holds within it the promise and possibility of change for individuals, families and wider societies. Rather than assuming that new family forms are necessarily brought about in direct response to wider politico-economic change or state policy initiatives, the trajectories of Anna and Rashidah, together with the accounts of 'mixed marriages' in the chapter that follows this one, suggest that new forms of marriage and conjugality may gradually become acceptable through an accumulation of the smaller ethical and imaginative evaluations and adjustments that are part and parcel of everyday life.

The two stories presented in this chapter illuminate how marriage provides a lens through which protagonists themselves assess and make sense of their lives both prospectively and retrospectively. It can be a way to tell a life, encompassing childhood, work and economic circumstances. And it can illuminate the turning points of a life – not having an illegitimate child or the discovery of a spouse's infidelity. Ethical judgements are implicitly and explicitly incorporated into how these accounts are rendered. Such judgements are conveyed too by the material objects that embody the marital relation, which provide an everyday register for their unarticulated expression. The way these stories

4 Marriage in the Flux of Self-Fashioning

are recounted here has been shaped too by particular anthropological conventions and concerns, adding further layers of interpretive complexity (Reece 2023). As an aspect of intimate familial lives and, simultaneously, a state institution, marriage affords a privileged lens into how this connectivity operates and its implications. The self-fashioning depicted here is personal and familial, but the possibilities and expectations it expresses at 'the boundaries of what is normative' have the capacity over time to travel outwards, as we will see further in Chapter 7, and gradually to become part of an expansion and transformation of wider political possibilities.

FIVE

Negotiating Difference in Marriage

Conjugality and 'Mixing'

Husin, a well-educated man in his thirties, talked enthusiastically about traditional Malay marriage rituals – those at his own and at his parents' wedding – when I interviewed him early in 2018. With considerably less approval, he compared these to the enthusiasm of younger relatives for lavish weddings with a 'Bollywood theme', using 'Chinese wedding planners'. I was puzzled when he mentioned his uneasy relationship with his in-laws. From a Penang-based family of several generations' depth, Husin seemed quintessentially Malay. But he spoke animatedly about how irritated he became when his wife's family referred to his 'Indian' appearance and ways and how, in their manner, they revealed that they felt themselves to be superior to his own family: 'I'm a Penangite – mixed blood with Indian. They kind of looked down on us ... consider us "not pure Malay". I got over it after nine or ten years of marriage. They kind of like to remind me'.

Marriage, to varying degrees, is always about bringing together spouses of different backgrounds. This is another way of phrasing the insights of Lévi-Strauss's opening chapters to *The Elementary Structures of Kinship* (1969) in which he sets out his argument that the principle of exogamy is the precondition for all marriage, and for social life in general. In fact, however, things are more complicated than Lévi-Strauss maintained – partly because marriage may actually be represented in terms of endogamy rather than exogamy (Bourdieu 1977; Carsten 1997). But beyond

5 Negotiating Difference in Marriage

this, in many parts of the world, exogamy – or marriage across religious, ethnic, racial or caste lines – may be experienced as fraught, and be a matter for policing whether by the state, local communities or families – or all of these. In Chapter 2, I noted how such policing of marriage and of non-marital sexual intimacy was particularly evident in colonial contexts. Anti-miscegenation laws and surveillance of such relations were a notorious and seemingly obsessive feature of the South African apartheid regime. Ann Laura Stoler's (2010) work on colonial Indonesia shows how the progressive hardening of barriers to marriage and intimacy across racial lines through the nineteenth and early twentieth centuries regulated and defined relations between colonisers and their subjects. And in the United States, we saw how legal barriers to 'interracial' marriage were not formally lifted across all states until the US Supreme Court ruling of *Loving versus Virginia* in 1967 (Cashin 2017; Magee 2025).

Legislation governing who may marry whom may thus be critical to maintaining certain kinds of political order and subjugation – the ban on marriage for enslaved people in the US or the apartheid regime's control of marriage and sexual relations across racial categories in South Africa are obvious cases. The role of marriage at the intersection of intimate lives with wider political structures is thus particularly telling. In India (another post-colonial context), a particularly toxic discourse has emerged around inter-religious intimacy between Hindus and Muslims. Allegations about a so-called 'love Jihad' propound a conspiracy theory in which Muslim men are waging a religious war against Hindus by illegitimately seeking Hindu women as marital partners. This discourse has been propagated by Hindutva religious zealots for political purposes to gain support for anti-Muslim legislation that targets 'forced' religious conversions, including intermarriage. Perveez Mody (2022, 278–82) draws together how such rhetoric builds on older tropes and anxieties surrounding blood, mixing and inter-caste marriage, as well as communal tensions, and mobilises colonial laws regulating 'unlawful conversion' in which prior public notification of both marriage and conversion were made legal requirements (see Anderson 2015; Gupta 2016; Hansen 1999; Nielsen and Nilsen 2021).

Legislating over who may marry whom necessarily also has the effect of legitimating the offspring of marital unions – or declaring some illegitimate. In the case of Israel, Susan Martha Kahn's (2000) study of state-subsidised assisted conception shows how this interest in legitimacy requires strict control over the sources of fertility. Here, citizenship is dependent on Jewish identity and the latter runs in the maternal line by Jewish religious law. For migrants applying to take up citizenship, or those wishing to marry, Jewish identity must be proven. The rabbinical courts not only control access to marriage (as civil unions are not recognised) but also have jurisdiction over determining what kinds of gametes are legitimate for use in assisted conception in order to produce babies that will be recognised as Jewish under Jewish law, and thus eligible citizens. This convergence of contemporary practice with religious law in fact entails a surprising degree of flexibility, which Kahn carefully teases apart – particularly over the sources of male sperm since Jewish paternity is not a necessary requirement to produce Jewish babies. Nevertheless, as she shows,

> Clearly, non-Jewish sperm is not considered to be neutral to these rabbis. Its inability to confer paternity and to create paternal relatedness does not cancel out its ability to 'pollute' the Jewish kinship that already exists. In other words, the fact that non-Jewish sperm has no positive value does not mean that it has no negative value. (Kahn 2000, 107)

These examples, in which marriage, maternity and paternity, as well as the control over reproduction, are all critical, make clear that one reason for the state's seemingly excessive interest in policing marriage is that barriers to intermarriage serve not only to maintain or harden boundaries between different categories of people. They are instrumental in actually constituting and reproducing the categories by which individuals and groups are defined.

5 Negotiating Difference in Marriage

In this chapter, I pursue the issue of 'mixing' in marriage, as locals in Penang phrase it (using the English term), to consider how differences of various kinds are negotiated, accommodated or managed. As the cases cited earlier suggest, we have rather more information about the political importance and control of marriage in colonial or post-colonial contexts than we have studies of actual experiences of marriage across ethnic, religious or racial lines, such as those that are the subject of this chapter. Penang, as we saw in Chapter 1, through its colonial and trading history, has been the site of an extraordinary confluence of people of different origins, cultures and religions for more than 200 years. In a world thoroughly permeated by distinctions of ethnicity, religion, cultures, class and language, marriage has a uniquely far-reaching (and often fraught) role in producing and reproducing distinctions or managing the connections between individuals, their families and communities. The mixing and separation that marriage enacts may easily be perceived as transgressive from the point of view of maintaining the boundaries of social distinctions. In looking at marriages across religious, ethnic, cultural and class boundaries, what emerges is the way that marriage expresses and encompasses different degrees of distinction. One could discern familial dispositions to marry within a relatively small and tight community or sub-community – whether Malay, Chinese or Indian – and, in contrast, those where over several generations there had been more 'open' marriages across sub-communities or even across ethnic or religious lines. Strikingly, and as I noted in Chapter 1, the familiar categories of Malaysian ethnic identity (Malay, Chinese, Indian, etc.) with their roots in colonial history tend to fracture into smaller sub-categories under the scrutiny of marriage. Some of those I interviewed were actively concerned with conserving the material and cultural heritage of their own particular group (although their own marriages might have been outside these boundaries), Peranakan, Chettiar, Mandailing, Jawi Peranakan, Hakka or Teochew – or any of the many others that are woven into Penang's history.

Marriage and the Moral Imagination

Many marriages crossed over the lines of sub-community, and some over religious or ethnic lines. Some said that such marriages were on the increase because of contemporary urban educational and employment patterns, which meant that people were 'mixing more'. These were impressionistic accounts whose reliability was difficult to ascertain but are confirmed by demographic work on marriage in Malaysia. This suggests that, despite a long history of intermarriage in the pre-colonial and colonial eras, only about 1 per cent of marriages in the 1980s crossed interethnic lines (Pue and Nidzam 2013; Jones and Tan 1990). Such marriages have, however, since increased to around 4.5 per cent in the 1990s and to 11 per cent in 2019 with urbanisation and consequent greater interethnic contact posited as the most important underlying factors (Nagaraj 2009; Tey 2021).[1] In a scenario of unequal prerogatives and rights, the questions that animate this chapter are, which boundaries emerge as particularly salient for marriage? How is this salience expressed and negotiated? And what larger lessons about marriage can we draw from the accommodations or difficulties over mixing that are discussed here?

In Chapter 2, I discussed the long-running and high-profile case (over ten years at the time of my research in 2018) of Indira Gandhi, a Hindu, Tamil woman whose husband had secretly converted to Islam and, without telling his wife, had also converted the couple's children in her absence before absconding with their youngest child and successfully filing for divorce in the syariah courts. The possible repercussions of conversion to Islam are amplified in such notorious cases, which are prominent in media accounts (see Maznah et al. 2009). In January 2018, the Supreme Court had finally ruled that the conversion of the children was not valid as the children had not been present and the mother had not been heard. Thus, after ten years, the case had finally been won by

---

[1] See also Tan (2024). Figures cited in this paragraph are from demographic work that draws on and analyses information from the Malaysian census and relies on official ethnic categories. This tends to give a broad rather than a nuanced picture.

5 Negotiating Difference in Marriage

Indira, and the conversion was nullified. The children were ruled to be still Hindu. As lawyers and commentators pointed out (see Chapter 2), the disputed powers of the two sets of legal authorities to rule on this case turned on matters at the heart of the Malaysian constitution. These have their roots in a colonial system that separated Islamic authorities and jurisdictions from civil matters, and which was supposed to safeguard the position of Malays in an ethically plural context, but were here turned to new purposes – at the level of the personal and familial, and of the nation state.

There is little question that marriage between non-Muslims and (Muslim) Malays is likely to produce tensions and familial friction. Beyond religious and cultural differences between the families, the privileged legal status of Islam in Malaysia, the facts that marriage to a Muslim legally requires conversion of the non-Muslim partner and that Muslim status (unlike that of other religions) is not reversible mean that the religious/ethnic status of the two spouses is on a different and legally prescribed footing. Increasing emphasis on what Maznah Mohamad describes as the 'ring-fencing the Muslim subject' (2020, 159) by the Islamic bureaucracy in order to delineate who is or is not a proper Muslim impacts all citizens whether Muslim or not. In what follows, these tensions are most clearly articulated by non-Muslims. Michael Peletz notes wider trends in Malaysia, including

…stepped-up efforts to stigmatize and criminalize not only inter-faith marriage, apostasy, and Shia teachings, but also the use by non-Muslims of terms, such as 'Allah' that are seen as 'belonging to' Muslims, as well as varieties of non-heteronormative practices and identities. (Peletz 2020b, 221)

As discussed in Chapter 1, Peletz sees this as part of a more general (and sometimes contradictory) polarisation of interethnic and interfaith relations in Malaysia. There are thus strong barriers (in spite of apparent permeability) to such interethnic/interfaith marriages (see Leow 2016, 180), which may be viewed with anxiety by parents of intending spouses.

Nevertheless, beyond the high-profile cases depicted in the media and in public discourse, it is worth considering what may occur in less dramatic circumstances – in long-running marriages between (Malay) Muslims and non-Muslims that do not end in divorce, and which seem to be happy and successful.[2] If all marriages, to different extents, require the negotiation and accommodation of difference, is it possible to consider 'difference' in terms of a continuum of lesser and greater salience? The stark terms of publicly enacted legal contestations (the outcome of conversion carried out in secret by one spouse) might be at one extreme of such a continuum; more modulated, small adjustments and their everyday frictions – which may play out in gendered ways – might be a more common form of consensual scenarios.

Over time, marriages between those of different ethnicities, religions or classes may be incorporated into familial worlds, their contours being subsequently reassessed and recalibrated at the time of a marriage in a later generation. Evaluations and distinctions, as ways of judging and managing connections, are inevitably part of the process of marrying. But the strains and difficulties of managing difference, and equally, the importance of continually producing distinctions, take their toll. Some connections prove impossible to manage; some marriages, across wide gulfs of national, class and/or religious background, floundered and in the end broke down. 'Too much mixing' – as one friend rather ruefully expressed it in relation to her own marriage across ethnic and national boundaries, which had ended in divorce. Others were more successful, depending partly perhaps on the degree of autonomy and separation of the main actors from their families, on particular strategies through

---

[2] There is little published work on actual experiences of inter-ethnic marriages in Malaysia, but see Lindenberg (2009) for an account of Chinese-Malay marriages in Kelantan; Tey (2021) and Pue and Nidzam (2013). See also Foong and Teoh (2022) for analysis of attitudes to inter-ethnic marriage in Malaysia based on a wider qualitative survey. This work suggests that these attitudes are broadly becoming more positive (Tan 2024).

5 Negotiating Difference in Marriage

which differences were accommodated and managed and on the circumstances, temperaments and personalities of those involved.

The intention of focusing on 'mixing' here is not to impute the existence of any essentialised essences or 'pure forms' – whether ethnic, cultural, 'racial' or religious – even though the idea of 'mixing' could be taken as inevitably relying on such essences. Despite the implications of Husin's evocation of the 'pure Malay' using idioms of blood – with concomitant intimations of snobbery – the category of Malay has been shown to have historically encompassed considerable regional geographic mobility, demographic diversity and intermarriage (see Carsten 1995; 1997; Kahn 2006; Laffan 2022; Milner 2008; Thompson 2003; 2007). In this sense, 'mixing' has been central to Malay kinship and marriage. But significantly, Malay marriage is premised on ideas of endogamy and similarity, so that this 'inter-Malay' mixing is submerged, diffuse and unarticulated. In Langkawi in the 1980s, marriage occurred in idioms of siblingship. Many marriages were between second or third cousins; they in turn produced new sibling sets when couples had children, so that one had the sense of a circular process of transforming marriage into siblingship. Although it was possible to show that many residents in the village where I did fieldwork had parents or grandparents who had come to the island as migrants from elsewhere in the Malay world, marriage had an incorporative and flexible logic, which assumed similarity rather than difference. It was a process of incorporating outsiders, and of dissolving distinctions rather than creating them (see Carsten 1997, Chapter 7). In contemporary urban, multi-ethnic contexts, however, distinctions between Malays and non-Malays are more prevalent and potentially salient. Because they are reinforced by Islam's privileged legal status, marriage – rather than dissolving distinctions – can in fact sustain them (see Leow 2016, 180).[3]

---

[3] See also Leow's (2016, 206–2012) illuminating discussion of Malaysia's post-colonial language policy, establishing Bahasa Malaysia as the national language, with its aversion to multilingualism and linguistic hybridity. She draws a suggestive parallel between the 'obsession with monolingual purity' and the 'accounts of colonial and the

Marriage and the Moral Imagination

Weddings, as Husin's comments reflected, brought up contested ritual forms, evoking origins and essences, as well as generational differences. As noted in the Introduction, at these 'vital conjunctures' (Johnson-Hanks 2002), the ethical and comparative work around marriage often becomes explicit and performative rather than being embedded in everyday conjugal relationality. My aim in this chapter is to consider in local terms how marriage is built on the management and negotiation of perceived differences, and the ethical and comparative judgements on which these are premised. An exploration of the axes of difference that matter most, or are most inimical to marital and familial harmony, as well as those that are more easily accommodated, provides insights into the larger and longer-term significance of marriage in contemporary Malaysia – and more widely, in contexts of cultural diversity. The contexts in which marriages are historically set are constantly shifting. Against a backdrop of transforming patterns of employment and urbanisation and also of shifting gender ideologies, the negotiation of perceived divergences between individuals, generations, families and communities, I suggest, reflects and informs wider transformations over several decades in Malaysia that we met in Chapter 1. In this way marriage is constitutive of the nation-state (see Chapter 2). Experiences of 'mixed marriage' and ideas about conjugality provide a way to understand how intimate worlds may envision and enable social transformation and contribute to new versions of social futures.[4]

Negotiating Permeable Boundaries

We have already come across cases of marriages across ethnic or religious lines. In Chapter 4, we encountered Anna from a Sri Lankan and

> race dangers that hybridity and métissage – interracial unions – posed to the "colonial order of things"' (2016, 211; Stoler 1995).
>
> [4] By way of comparison, see Cashin's (2017) discussion of the relation between 'interracial intimacy' and harmony across 'races' and ethnicities in the US.

5 Negotiating Difference in Marriage

Keralan family who had been married to a French engineer for over thirty years, and Rashidah, a Malay who had recently divorced her American husband after a much briefer marriage. Both Anna and her husband were Catholic, whilst Rashidah's marriage had necessitated her husband's conversion to Islam. We will keep these two cases in view through the discussion that follows. But rather than exploring marriages through the theme of self-fashioning over the life course as in Chapter 4, here I consider them through the lens of divergence and 'mixing' within and between generations. How do such marriages play out? What are their likely difficulties, or the possible conditions for their stability or breakdown? Exactly because 'mixed marriages' are by their nature less conventional, on the boundaries of the normative, they tend to encapsulate singular histories. So, there is no obviously typical scenario to pick out, and patterns may be difficult to discern and articulate. I begin with cases where it seemed possible to accommodate an obvious divergence of backgrounds between spouses.

I had known Pee Wah and Daniel for some years when we sat down together after they had finished work one Friday afternoon for an interview about their marriage. I had been intrigued by what seemed to be the unusual circumstances of their marital arrangements, and had persuaded them, perhaps somewhat reluctantly but with their customary good humour, to answer my questions. The interview was a slightly hurried affair as they were anxious to get home and begin their weekend. Pee Wah was in her forties and had been born in the mid-1970s; Daniel was around ten years older. For both partners, it could be considered a late marriage. She had been brought up in Penang in a Mandarin-speaking family; he was from Perak, in the third generation of a family originally from Kerala. Daniel had been educated in English-medium schools in Perak and Pee Wah in Chinese-medium schools in Penang. Neither of them came from wealthy families. They had originally met at their workplace and had been married for about fifteen years at the time of the interview. Pee Wah and Daniel spoke English to each other, bearing out the importance of English in expressing 'a transethnic Malaysian identity' (Mandal 2001, 160) we have already encountered. They had one child, a school-aged daughter.

When I asked about their wedding ceremony and those of their parents, Pee Wah told me that her parents had had a Chinese ceremony in a Catholic church – her parents had met in church. Daniel said his parents had also had a Catholic wedding in a church in Kerala; this was an arranged marriage, but he didn't know too much about their wedding. Daniel and Pee Wah's own wedding had been in a Catholic church in Penang, and they had also had the customary Chinese tea ceremony. They told me that no one from Daniel's side had attended the wedding, just Pee Wah's relatives and friends of her parents. One reason for my interest in finding out more about this marriage was that I already knew something of the couple's living arrangements. They maintained two separate homes with Daniel living in a high-rise flat on his own while Pee Wah and their daughter stayed in the house of her parents. At the weekends, Pee Wah and their daughter would come to stay in Daniel's apartment. When I probed a little as to why they maintained this dual-living arrangement, they told me it was because her parents helped take care of their daughter, whose school was near their home, while Pee Wah and Daniel were at work all day. Asking why Daniel didn't also live at his in-law's house elicited a detailed description with some humour of the disposition of space in the house. All the rooms were occupied or taken so that only the kitchen or hall remained – an uncomfortable proposition, I was told. Also, he needed to take care of the cat and the fish at his own house, he said. The cat (a long-term feature of Daniel's life) was elderly, somewhat aggressive and didn't get along with their daughter.

Much of this I had already known. But I was somewhat surprised when Pee Wah mentioned that her parents had never actually met Daniel's mother (his father had died some years earlier). She explained that there would be difficulties in communicating as her parents didn't speak

5 Negotiating Difference in Marriage

English. From domestic space and their daughter's care, the couple went on to mention other factors that made their arrangements convenient. Their daughter liked being outside in the garden at her grandparents' rather than being cooped up in her father's apartment; her grandparents could easily collect her from her Chinese school, which was near their home. Each spouse preferred to eat different kinds of food. Daniel explained how his wife 'still sticks to Chinese food; very seldom takes nasi kandar [popular Penang-style steamed rice accompanied by curries and vegetables]. She doesn't take curries. Our daughter is following her. Chinese food is okay; I prefer vegetarian'. To affirm these differences, Pee Wah added, 'I can't take spicy food'.

These were familiar themes from life in Penang. Culinary styles and preferences in food are a frequent focus of conversations about ethnic difference (Carsten 2019a, 169–76, 195), and I pursue this theme later in this chapter. I knew other working couples where the wife lived with her parents and the husband lived separately, and some women who resided with the children and whose husbands lived elsewhere – though none of these spouses also worked together as did Pee Wah and Daniel. Pee Wah said, 'It's okay – we work together; we see each other at work'; though, in fact, their working environment was busy with numerous other people present, and behaviour would have been quite constrained by the norms of workplace etiquette. Pee Wah also drew attention to the fact that Daniel's father had lived separately from his family until his retirement, as he had run a clinic on a rubber plantation. As she indicated, in this way their own residence pattern recapitulated that of a previous generation.

We could view this couple as performing a particularly delicate choreography in their living arrangements. A marriage across somewhat fluid ethnic boundaries is here maintained by keeping an amicable distance between spouses – and between son-in-law and parents-in-law – with their mainly separate residence permitting different culinary preferences and house-holding styles. Their chosen pattern of life also apparently prioritised relations between the wife and her parents, and between their daughter and her maternal grandparents, over the conjugal bond. This was a version of what occurred in other marriages where spouses lived separately (see Chapter 6), but here ethnic distinctions (enacted in houses, schooling and food), rather than mixing, were enfolded into patterns of co-living and separation. While I have teased out the divergences captured by this story, we should also note the convergences of work and religion that were foundational features of this marriage.

In the case of Anna's marriage, which I recalled earlier, we saw in Chapter 4 that, here too, ethnic difference was bridged by the shared Catholic background of husband and wife. For Anna, however, the establishment of an aesthetically pleasing marital home in a series of houses was central to her assessment of a successful marriage. And her husband Michel mentioned how Anna's culinary skills were part of what had originally attracted him to her. It might be significant to their story of joint conjugal homemaking that this couple were geographically and in other ways somewhat distanced from both sets of parents – Anna having partially removed herself from her family who lived elsewhere in Malaysia and Michel's on a different continent. Anna and Michel's marriage and that of Pee Wah and Daniel show different modes of accommodating differences in familial and ethnic backgrounds of spouses, and the delicate choreography and balance this entailed. Both marriages were apparently harmonious, but the ways in which the two couples had 'solved' the dilemmas posed by marriage across ethnic lines held different implications in terms of the past, present and future of familial relations.

Salient Distinctions

The marriages considered so far involved a careful staking-out of modes of life, which was not necessarily overtly articulated but might be implicit in the manner in which divergent backgrounds of husband and wife

5 Negotiating Difference in Marriage

were recognised, reconciled (or not) and incorporated into conjugal life. In the case of marriage between Muslims and non-Muslims in Malaysia, however, religious difference must explicitly be dealt with in legally prescribed ways. Distinctions between Muslims and non-Muslims, which largely overlap with those between Malays and non-Malays, are strongly marked politically, religiously, spatially, legally and socially. As already noted, marriage between Muslims and non-Muslims in Malaysia legally requires the religious conversion of the non-Muslim spouse to Islam. Unlike other religions, it is not possible in Malaysia for Muslims to renounce their religious ascription. Further, all matters of family life for Muslims, including marriage, divorce, inheritance and child custody arrangements, are dealt with in the state-level syariah courts, whereas for non-Muslims these fall under the civil code. All of this entails different kinds of implications for 'mixed marriage' between Muslims and non-Muslims than for marriages that encompass other ethnic, religious, social or cultural differences (Lindenberg 2009; Maznah, Zarizana and Chin 2009).

For the parents and wider family of spouses, marriages between Muslims – who are predominantly Malay – and non-Muslims of different ethnicities are likely to initiate more obvious tensions than marriages between people whose backgrounds diverge in other ways. This is not infrequently a topic of everyday conversation. One friend of mine to whom I was talking about my research recalled the difficulties that her sister's marriage, thirty years earlier, to a Chinese man whom she had met at work, and who converted to Islam, had caused in their family. Recalling her father's reluctance to accept her sister's husband, she told me how her father had put pressure on his son-in-law to appear Malay, for example, by wearing Malay-style clothes and not eating with chopsticks. My friend had objected at the time on the grounds that these were 'cultural matters'; she had told their father he should 'distinguish religion from culture', rather than impose his views. Such stories are unsurprising in a Malaysian context – though most of the Malay people

Marriage and the Moral Imagination

I interviewed maintained that they wouldn't mind if their child married a non-Malay – on the grounds that such a marriage would necessarily entail religious conversion, and so would not present difficulties. Whether such theoretical acceptance reflects reality or not, it indicates the categorical nature of the boundary between Muslims and non-Muslims in Malaysia. From the Malay point of view, marriage to a non-Muslim is not necessarily problematic – precisely because, in such cases, this boundary's permeability is prescriptive on religious grounds and occurs in only one direction. This can also be considered as one aspect of a more general expansive and incorporative logic in Malay kinship.

For non-Malays (who are primarily non-Muslims), however, marriage to a Muslim, premised on conversion to Islam, is likely to be experienced differently. This is often clearly articulated by parents when considering the possible marriages of their children. At various points, I was told by non-Muslims about parents who had warned them explicitly that they would be happy with any marriage as long as their prospective daughter-in-law or son-in-law was not Muslim. One elderly Chinese woman, a widow, told me of her disappointment when her son had married a Muslim. She expressed this partly as a matter of no longer being able to carry on the rites of ancestor worship, a visceral and affective break in the connections between generations. Because the children of a marriage between a Malay and a non-Malay (or between a Muslim and a non-Muslim) are automatically categorised as Malay (or Muslim), this is keenly felt by non-Muslim grandparents.[5] But there was also a more general sense of loss – of participation in family rituals, of talents and of future possibilities for her grandchildren (see also Lindenberg 2009; Peletz 2020b, 184).[6]

---

[5] See also Tey (2021, 143); Nagaraj (2009).

[6] For further discussions of the sense of encroachment and unease experienced by non-Muslim Malaysians at the expansion of Islamic spaces, prohibitions and legal jurisdictions, see Baxstrom (2008); Nonini (2015); Peletz (2020b, 24–26, 183–86, 188–91; 2023); Willford (2006; 2014).

5 Negotiating Difference in Marriage

From another point of view, however, I was struck by the unconventional career paths, sometimes involving the creative arts or academia, that were taken up in Malaysia or abroad by the adult children I knew of from several 'mixed marriages'. Their backgrounds had not necessarily been infused with intense religiosity as their grandparents had feared, but had been rather liberal and open to new ideas. This echoes Sumit Mandal's (2001) research among members of Malaysia's creative arts communities and the connections he draws between their activities and political transformation. His interviews suggest not just the importance of the arts as a crucible of changing attitudes but also indicate the importance of family background and the prevalence of hybrid ethnicities among his participants.[7]

Wahidah, a Penangite in her forties who was brought up in a Hokkien-speaking family and educated in an English-medium school, recalled when I interviewed her how she had met her Malay husband soon after leaving school. 'It was difficult', she said:

He was a different race and religion. So, I didn't introduce him to my parents yet. Till it got serious, and we decided to marry. We dated for seven years. He proposed many times. I had to decline. I was not ready – I was too young. I was concerned that my parents would object. In the end, I proposed to him instead!

Wahidah's maternal grandmother had been from a Thai Buddhist family, but both Wahidah's parents were born in Penang. Her family had followed Thai Buddhist customs in her childhood. She had had several marriage proposals from Malays, Indians and others, she told me: 'They were all non-Chinese. Not all were Muslim'. She related this to her appearance, which, Wahidah said, did not appear as characteristically

---

[7] The 'mixed' or hybrid ethnicities of Mandal's participants and their families across the three generations of families he considers suggest a theme worthy of further exploration.

Marriage and the Moral Imagination

Chinese (and, she thought, perhaps made her more attractive to those her beyond her own ethnic background).

I weighed the pros and cons. I was looking for a long-term relationship. Which was with a person who loves me more than I love him. It's a good criteria for long-term relations!

The idea that a woman is best off with a man who loves her more than she loves him, articulated to me on a number of occasions, points to women's perceptions of their own potential vulnerability in marriage and is discussed further in Chapter 6.

Conversion to Islam was one factor that weighed strongly in Wahidah's decision-making, she told me:

Conversion was another reason I took so long. I had to understand, and make sure I was ready to embrace religion.... It felt very different. Certain things I had difficulty in accepting. The pre-marriage course – whatever they were teaching, we were not actually practising. So, I didn't feel so bad.

Wahidah spoke of how the reactions of the couple's two sets of parents differed:

Religion was not an issue for his family. They know I have to convert. My mother-in-law was concerned I wouldn't be able to adapt to their family. But they never interfered. My parents were definitely upset. They tried to persuade me. They reminded me of what would follow if I became a Muslim – a change of name, not being allowed to eat non-halal food, dress. But they were not so severe as to break the relation.

Looking back over her marriage of more than twenty-five years, Wahidah expressed her satisfaction at how things had turned out. Her four children were now all grown-up or nearly so. It was clear that she attributed the success of her marriage, resonant in the production of children and the promising educational and career paths on which they had embarked, at least in part, to the accommodations that she and her husband and their respective families had been able to make:

5 Negotiating Difference in Marriage

There've been no problems with [maintaining] contact with my family. For big celebrations, they invite and we come together. For Chinese reunion dinner, we come. Roughly to expectations. Otherwise, we wouldn't have been together so long!

These accommodations had been arrived at over time; the first part of the marriage had been more difficult for her:

We share decisions. When we were younger, he was more controlling. We've reached an age where we trust each other more. The early part was a bit different. I couldn't go out without his permission.

Wahidah spoke too about the areas of life that had been important in these accommodations of her marriage – work, maintaining her independence, cooking and the sharing of household tasks. She had had her children early, and that had given her more freedom later – although she mentioned that she would happily have stopped at two, but her husband, who came from a large family, had wanted more.

Also, advice from my mother: 'Don't give up your career'. She went through that herself because she was a housewife. I had a lot of good advice – from my mother and my best friend's mother: 'Invite your husband into the kitchen to cook there'. My husband – *he* does the cooking. My husband is a *great* cook. Not just Malay food – different types of dishes. My eldest son cooks, my second son likes to bake. Shared responsibility – everybody in the household has chores to do. We bake together sometimes – a family thing.

Here, apart from the importance to her own autonomy of maintaining her career, a united project of cooking and feeding involving the whole family was singled out as instantiating a warm and harmonious domestic life – in contrast to Daniel and Pee Wah's difficulties in accommodating each other's culinary preferences described earlier. It is worth noting that while the latter couple did not have to bridge religiously enforced dietary differences (thus perhaps giving them a certain latitude), Wahidah's marriage required the adoption of halal precepts for cooking and eating, and this lends added weight to her depiction of how this had been achieved.

Summing up what had made her marriage a success and a source of satisfaction, Wahidah told me,

> My in-laws are okay – they practise, follow their culture and religion but don't interfere with us. So, my husband supports me. I chose one who loves me more. I would give that advice to any woman choosing a life partner.

Here the principle of 'non-interference' by parents, whose categorical difference is clearly marked, emerges as crucial to marital success. Instead of being based on measured conjugal distance as in the case of Pee Wah and Daniel, the harmony of Wahidah's marriage seems to rest on a certain degree of flexible detachment from both sets of parents. 'Detachment' might be a misleading term here as in fact Wahidah described to me the close involvement of the two sets of parents, both living in close proximity to the couple, in the care of their grandchildren. Crucially, perhaps, the couple had not co-resided with either set of parents. And, as we saw, she also spoke warmly of how she had not been forced to distance herself from her own parents. So, in this case a strong affective bond between husband and wife and active ties with both sets of parents are supported through flexibility and 'non-interference' in certain matters.

That a certain degree of pragmatism (including, for a woman, marrying someone who was strongly emotionally attached to her) might help to assure the success of a marriage that bridges salient and categorical religious boundaries is hardly surprising. Here gendered ideals may also be pertinent. We might expect to find that, in accordance with the patriarchal premises of marriage, women are more likely to do the accommodating than men. But the bilateral principles of Malay kinship referred to in Chapter 1 may also encourage a somewhat more balanced and complementary disposition on the part of men to accommodate to their wives (see Karim 2021). Wahidah had not spontaneously mentioned

5 Negotiating Difference in Marriage

dress to me as a contentious issue, but I had noticed when she arrived for our meeting at a local Starbucks, that she was not wearing the head covering that is conventional for Malay women. At one point in the interview she had said, 'My in-laws and parents don't meddle in our lives. They don't tell me how to dress'. When I asked her about head-covering towards the end of our interview, Wahidah's answer seemed to encapsulate the pragmatic spirit of her marriage: 'Sometimes I cover, sometimes not. My husband's fine with it'.

Managing Difference

What enables a marriage across wide social differences to endure? What factors are liable to produce conjugal tensions and difficulties? The answers to these questions preoccupy all kinds of people and are a matter of everyday speculation as well as the subject of novels, magazine articles, films and popular discourse – in Malaysia as elsewhere. One reason that many of the interviews and informal conversations I had about marriage in Penang were fruitful and illuminating was that, for those I spoke with, this seemed a self-evidently interesting topic, often one of direct concern (see Introduction). In Chapter 4 we saw how Rashidah, whom I mentioned at the beginning of this chapter, speculated as to why her parents' marriage had endured harmoniously for fifty years, whereas her own marriage and those of her siblings had all broken down. In some respects, those I spoke to might in general terms have attributed such different outcomes to fate, chance or luck. But we also saw in Chapter 4 that, for those closely involved, marital breakdown tended to be ascribed to particular causes. Rashidah, a Malay married to an Australian, attributed the breakdown of her own marriage to her husband's serial and long-term infidelity rather than to any religious or cultural differences. It was only when it reached the divorce courts that the matter of her husband's non-adherence to Islam emerged more prominently.

Marriage and the Moral Imagination

The nature of the historically and legally evolved distinction between Islam and other religions in Malaysia means that this is a difference that matters differently, and more categorically, than those between other religions, ethnicities, cultures or classes in Malaysia. This is not simply a matter of the degree of permeability of boundaries since conversion is an accessible and meritorious process from an Islamic perspective. But partly because of the syariah legal system that has jurisdiction over Muslim marriage and family life, and partly because – unlike with other religions – there is no possibility of renouncing Islam, the qualities of permeability are not the same: It occurs in only one direction and has irreversible repercussions into succeeding generations. The anxiety clearly expressed by some non-Muslim parents about the marriage of their children to Muslims reflects their awareness of the possible long-term individual and familial implications of this difference.

As already noted, the apparently widening powers and jurisdiction of Islamic legal and religious courts over recent decades and the increasing occurrence of disputed cases following conversion are matters of considerable unease for non-Muslims in Malaysia. As we saw in Chapter 2, it receives attention from lawyers, activists and other commentators in the media, and it forms part of the background to anxieties voiced by non-Muslims about possible future marriages of their adult children to Muslims. Parents seemed more obviously concerned with the potential risks of such marriages than their children. We have also seen in the accounts recorded earlier that these differences could be accommodated in everyday terms. What was highlighted in interviewees' assessments of the successful bridging of categorical distinctions was not religious faith or observance *per se*, which is apparently negotiable between spouses who begin their marriage with some basis for a common outlook, but matters of housing, relationships with wider family, the authority of a husband over his wife, tastes and preferences in food and dress. These connected issues can be understood as pertaining to embodied ways of living, which are perceived to have ethical dimensions. This bears out

5 Negotiating Difference in Marriage

Clive Kessler's (1992, 139) assertion about the nature of Islam's effectiveness in maintaining boundaries being linked to the bodily restrictions imposed by rules governing food consumption and gender relations (see also King 2021, 39; Lindenberg 2009). Because of the importance and range of Muslim food restrictions and the categorisation of food as halal and non-halal, or haram, this is a particularly salient distinction across Muslim/non-Muslim boundaries. The corporeal transformations required by conversion to Islam, reinforced in ethical precepts and law, are thus linked to changes in relationality and personhood.

But we saw earlier that food is also a prominent theme in accounts of marriages that bridge other ethnic distinctions without a religious dimension. Indeed, culinary differences between spouses figured as a point of tension in several of the marriages I investigated. When I asked one couple who had experienced marital difficulties over many years how they divided domestic tasks, they told me that neither of them cooked. Roger, the husband, explained that, because his wife was Cantonese, she liked boiled, bland food. Hokkien himself, he found her food tasteless. Their solution was to go out.

Culinary distinctions can emerge as different styles and ways of cooking but can also indicate different modes of parenting. One Malay woman, a full-time working mother married to a fellow Malay, described to me how her husband's sister was living together with them to help look after the children. The arrangement was not altogether comfortable. This interviewee spoke about how her husband and sister-in-law had had a different kind of upbringing, and therefore had a different attitude to meals from her own. In her husband's family, she said, the children would buy food for themselves rather than having it cooked for them at home. In her own family, her father spent a lot of time with his family. The distinction, one could sense, held moral implications.

In some respects, the divergences I have highlighted here are distinctions of degree – with some being more salient or difficult to bridge than others. While different culinary preferences between spouses might be thought of as a trivial matter, the propensity of food to carry bodily, moral, ethical and religious connotations, and for commensality to be an index of social proximity or distance, means that differences of 'taste' have the potential to reverberate across spheres of social life.[8] For some people, such differences might entail a relatively easy adjustment, but non-Muslim parents whose son or daughter married a Muslim would be concerned about the implications for continuing to eat with their own child, his or her spouse and any eventual grandchildren. Commensality is both fundamental to everyday sociality and an important part of larger family and communal celebrations, such as weddings or Chinese family reunions. When a Muslim couple was co-resident with a non-Muslim parent, substantial changes – at least in the home – would need to be made by the parent. We could see food, then, not just as a barometer of sociality across boundaries but also as one expression of potential fracture between spouses, with their respective families and between communities. At the extremes, matters of degree held the potential for more categorical divergence. The emphasis on religious conversion for non-Muslims who marry Muslim spouses and the non-negotiability of Islam, as well as its privileged position in Malaysian law, mean that marriage across this boundary is likely to be of special concern.

Fractures and Continuities between Generations

A theme that emerges prominently from the earlier discussion is the importance of intergenerational ties alongside conjugal ones. Where marriages obviously bridged wide differences in terms of class, religion or ethnicity, one could discern an effort to negotiate some kind of balance between conjugal ties and those with a couple's respective

---

[8] By way of example, see Chaudry's (2021) account of the moral connotations of food transfers across perceived caste differences in 'mixed' cross-regional marriages in rural north India.

5 Negotiating Difference in Marriage

parents. At one extreme, a couple might live far from one or both sets of parents – and employment might be part of the pragmatic story behind this. At the other, co-residence with one set of parents, or their residence in houses that were in close proximity, suggested the importance of intergenerational ties and often implied that one set of parents played a greater role in the life of a young family than the other. Generally, grandparents are expected to be highly involved in the lives of children and grandchildren. In cases of 'mixed' marriage across obvious cultural or religious boundaries, which set of grandparents played a more crucial role might indicate the relative weight of the background and culture of each spouse in the upbringing of their children. This might be a potential source of friction in a marriage or its inter-generational relations, particularly in the case of the conversion of one spouse to Islam where children are apparently less the embodiment of 'mixing' than of the unilateral conversion of one parent. In some circumstances, it seemed that maintaining a degree of geographic distance from parents and parents-in-law could be conducive to marital harmony. But the case of Wahidah who converted to Islam upon her marriage also suggests the opposite – that her successful marriage was constructed on the involvement of *both* her own (Chinese) and her husband's (Malay) parents. In contrast, Rashidah's marriage, as we saw in Chapter 3, which was childless, was lived at a considerable distance from her own Malay parents, and even further from her partner's Australian ones. Significantly, after her divorce, Rashidah's elderly parents and her divorced sister had moved from Kuala Lumpur to live with her in Penang.

We might then see conjugal relations as evolving through the course of a marriage in tandem with those between spouses and their parents, but not necessarily along highly predictable lines. Marriage 'by choice' and across permeable ethnic, religious or class boundaries does not here mean that couples are necessarily dislocated from their families of origin. And even when geographic or social distancing has apparently occurred, this may turn out to be only a temporary phase, which can be

Marriage and the Moral Imagination

mitigated or resolved differently later on. In the case of Anna's marriage to Michel, we saw in Chapter 4 how, although she had not completely severed relations with her family of origin, she had already put herself at a distance from them before she met Michel. When Anna talked about her marriage, she mentioned with particular pride the fond relation she had been able to forge with her father-in-law who lived in Europe and whom she met only at well-defined intervals. Meanwhile, for Pee Wah and Daniel, it seemed that conjugal harmony had been constructed out of the co-residence of Pee Wah, her parents and the couple's daughter, with regular but circumscribed visits to her husband, Daniel, who lived separately.

These different scenarios in marriages across divergent backgrounds illustrate the variety of arrangements couples arrived at. They are suggestive of the continued expectations of involvement of parents and grandparents in the lives of their married children even when the latter's marriages bridge wide social differences. The careful choreography that maintaining relations with parents might require was often expressed at the start of a marriage by the manner in which a wedding was celebrated. Spouses marrying across different communities or sub-communities had to make choices about what elements of marriage rites from their respective backgrounds to include or to drop. This might matter more to each spouse's parents and grandparents than it did to themselves, and there were obvious risks of causing offence as well as wider communal sensitivities to consider.

Usually, couples would pick out some core elements from a repertoire of rites and symbols to include in their celebrations. We saw how Pee Wah and Daniel had married in a Catholic church, and had a Chinese dinner for her relatives and her parents' friends. In a manner that was not unusual, they thus combined Catholic and Chinese customs. Such creative ritual adjustments and recombinations were likely to be more difficult across Muslim–non-Muslim boundaries. I was therefore surprised when Wahidah told me,

5 Negotiating Difference in Marriage

We had both a Chinese and a Malay wedding. The *akad nikah* [Muslim marriage ceremony] was first – registered in the state mosque. Then a Malay ceremony – one *kenduri* [marriage feast] in his house.⁹ It was a big thing because it was a mixed marriage. The whole community came. We underestimated the numbers. It was really huge – around 1000 or more? Maybe 3000? They sent out 1000 invitations. The turnout was more than expected. We ran out of food! It was in a community hall. My family came. On my parents' side, they were very excited to come and attend because it was a different culture. After that, we had a Chinese wedding in a hotel – a tea ceremony first. Then a formal dinner – just close family. Around 130 people – only his immediate family because it was for my Chinese relatives. The planning was stressful. There were various outfits. A traditional Malay outfit for the Malay ceremony; a cream-coloured one for the Chinese.

Although this was unusual for a Malay wedding in that it retained Chinese elements, it does replicate numerous other cases that I was told about in which the core, iconic elements of ceremonies were picked out – for example, the *akad nikah* and *kenduri* in the Malay case, the tea ceremony and a dinner in the Chinese – and planned in a sequence that also indicates the relative priority they had been given. While Wahidah's account strongly emphasised the positive connotations of rites celebrated across ethnic, cultural and religious boundaries, her assessment that 'the planning was stressful' was indicative of the difficulties and potential risks of causing offence.

This kind of selection of particular highlights, and accommodation of divergence by picking out different cultural elements, was not just a feature of the weddings of spouses from different ethnic backgrounds. It might occur in other contexts too, for example, when the respective families of a Malay couple came from different states on the peninsula with slightly different betrothal and wedding customs, or when Penang-based family members had adopted different religions. One

---

⁹ A Malay marriage would conventionally be celebrated with two *kenduri* – one at the bride's parental house and one at the groom's.

Marriage and the Moral Imagination

man in his thirties went into considerable detail about the considerations and planning of rituals adapted for his own wedding about ten years earlier. In this case, they had to accommodate Taoist elements that were important for some older family members and Christian elements that were paramount for himself, his mother and his wife. He began by giving a brief depiction of his parents' wedding before proceeding to his own:

My parents had a Taoist wedding, with a tea ceremony. The groom goes to the bride's house and asks her parents for her hand. They have the tea ceremony, then go back to the groom's house. My paternal grandparents had passed away, so it was just his grandmother. There was a wedding dinner in a restaurant. They were aged twenty-three and twenty-four. Both were working. Both finished secondary school. They had no further education. They lived with dad's grandmother – she was born in 1900 in George Town – and his younger brother.

We married in …. a church wedding, at [names church]. The dinner was sixty-eight tables – at a restaurant along the coast. It was all in one. I paid ten tables extra; my side twenty-one tables plus ten. My in-laws paid the rest. There was no dowry. Either you give dowry – in China that's the traditional way – or gifts, or it's more common nowadays to pay for extra tables.

Both of us are Christian. My wife's side is still Taoist – it includes both cultural and religious elements. No one could advise us. A lot of the so-called 'traditions' are recent – from films and TV. For example, preventing the groom from entering [the bride's house]. I find it offensive. It contradicts [my] idea of marriage. We sat down with a cultural expert. For example, the umbrella for a wife leaving her house. We tried to get to the bottom of everything. Her grandmother is still around. She was a bit worried. We sat down with her and auntie and discussed what was most important – we said we would do it if it didn't contradict our beliefs.

The groom going into the [bride's] house – we didn't do that because the bride's father gives her away in church. I collected her, and her father, and my best man in a VW mini. Her father walked her down the aisle. We had a tea ceremony only in *her* place after the church ceremony. Actually, for

5 Negotiating Difference in Marriage

a Chinese wedding, it's supposed to be at the groom's house. The bride's house should be the night before, and just the bride serves – to thank her parents. And the dinner just on the groom's side. Her family *lose* their daughter to the husband's family. So, her grandmother said just the tea ceremony [was important].

Between the two of us, we adopted the thinking that she wasn't marrying out. [We were] joining two families. So, we made it a point that the tea ceremony had to be done. We still joke that she hasn't served tea in our house.

My mum insisted that the wedding had to be in church. White dress.... On the surface, it's similar to my parents – except for church. But it's a more subtle process – very different. We didn't hire an old lady to do things, or wedding planners.

In this account of a wedding, we see how elements of Taoist ritual were incorporated, but what was important to the main participants was that this should be a Christian rite. Some underlying implications about the relation between husband and wife or the wife's severing connections to her natal family and joining her husband's that were not consonant with the couple's ideas were therefore avoided. The narrative also shows how wedding rituals require explicit discussion and decision-making about which elements to include and which to change or omit. Here recombinations of older elements and innovations to wedding rituals assert the couple's new (corporate) identity and are also part of a process of change and distinction from earlier generations. Assertions of difference from past generations can thus enable a process of mixing in successive ones. In contrast, where a couple choose to live apart (as in the earlier case of Pee Wah and Daniel), we could see this mixing process as to some degree stalled or more partial. And we might suppose that their daughter is more likely to be drawn to the largely Chinese influence of her upbringing than the Indian elements.

In many respects, the kinds of adjustments described here are more obvious versions of the way that all middle-class urban couples, even

Marriage and the Moral Imagination

those marrying from apparently similar backgrounds, devise wedding ceremonies that are partly based on their own preferences and wishes and partly accommodate religious ascriptions, obligations to parents and different familial customs. Marriage across wide class or wealth differences also required negotiations around weddings, but in those cases the wealthier family would have the greater influence in how the rites and celebrations were conducted. Here once again, there was an obvious contrast to the Malay marriages that I saw celebrated in Langkawi in the 1980s where partners were broadly of similar wealth and standing, and there was an explicit emphasis on marrying 'close' (*dekat*), connoting background, geographical proximity, degree of religiosity and consanguineal connection. The format for weddings was to a large degree prescribed. Although negotiations could become tense over the exchange of gifts involved, and care needed to be taken to avoid causing offence to the other side – demonstrating that equal standing might be fragile or unstable – one reason why I did not always enjoy participating at weddings was the sense that I already knew what was going to happen.

In contrast to the lack of surprise that pervaded weddings in my earlier fieldwork, in Penang when a marriage was expected to encounter the strong disapproval of parents and wider relatives, there was another, often shocking, possibility open to some couples. This was to go abroad to marry – or to marry while abroad. I knew some couples that had done this or who had contemplated doing so. Rather than being a way to bridge differences of religion, ethnicity or class (or a combination of these), because of the strong expectations around familial involvement in marriage, this kind of elopement was a drastic step and a sensitive topic even many years later. It expressed the insurmountable nature of the breach between the families of spouses, and was unlikely in the short-term to lead to reconciliation in the face of strong parental opposition to a marriage. Rather, it seemed an index of difficulties and strained relations that were often spoken about in a register of pain and loss.

5 Negotiating Difference in Marriage

Conclusion

This chapter began with a discussion of the surveillance and control of 'mixed marriages' in colonial and post-colonial contexts. Such control is crucial to the constitution and reproduction of political power, especially in regimes of ethnic or racial separation. But I have argued that we know more about the politics of marriage than its lived experience, and this means that we are liable to miss its everyday, creative significance. We know more about colonial categorisations and the control of boundaries between different racial, ethnic or religious groups than we know about intimate processes of accommodation and living together or the longer-term significance of such accommodations. In a more modulated register, I have explored the relative permeability and salience of boundaries in Penang between those of different ethnicities, religions, languages and cultural background. We saw in the opening vignette how 'mixing' may be more or less imperceptible to an outsider but is nevertheless woven into the fabric of life in Penang and its history – as is the case in many parts of the world. Sometimes the forms that 'mixing' takes, and the ways in which it is spoken of, evoke essentialised essences of 'race', 'blood' or other categories that were sedimented into colonial governance but have evolved to take new connotations in contemporary Malaysia (Carsten 2019b; Leow 2016, 111–12). Sometimes, we catch glimpses of a more positive embrace of difference that might offer unexpected possibilities for the future.

Marriage proves a productive lens through which to understand processes of negotiating and accommodating differences in Penang and more widely in Malaysia – as it does elsewhere. We have seen how some boundaries are more salient than others, and more prone to categorical distinctions. Those between Malays and non-Muslim others are particularly freighted. These boundaries are distinguished legally, religiously and in other ways. Their permeability is governed partly by the historically produced regulation of ethnic categories in Malaysia, which means

Marriage and the Moral Imagination

that 'Malayness' and Islam have a privileged significance distinct from other categories. This distinction is thus the reverse of the Indian case that I referred to at the beginning of this chapter in that Malay Muslims are in the politically dominant position. Nevertheless, this is a difference that makes a difference, resulting in transformations to bodies and persons as well as to familial relations. We have also seen how apparently 'domestic' and mundane processes of making a home, cooking and eating together are fundamental to producing new familial arrangements and accommodations that can nourish (or restrict) changing social imaginaries.

I have drawn a contrast in this chapter between the Malay marriages that took place in the 1980s in Langkawi, based on a logic of siblingship, similarity and the incorporation and suppression of difference, with the contemporary context of urban Penang. In the former case, differences of status or geographic origins were to a considerable extent submerged or erased through a process of incorporation, which could at times seem coercive. This was not straightforwardly the case in urban Penang where differences were often acknowledged as more obvious. I argued in Chapter 1 that experiences of doing anthropology have something in common with marriage. In both marriage and undertaking anthropological research, Langkawi seemed to provide a strongly incorporative model. This was sometimes an uncomfortable experience for a novice fieldworker, and the same could be said for new marital partners. The marked preference for the first period of marital residence to be in the bride's parents' house rather than that of the groom's parents meant that household labour was usually undertaken together by closely related women rather than by a young woman under the supervision of her mother-in-law. The women that I became close to in Langkawi understood all too well that, separated by a long distance, one would miss one's parental home.

In a context where, according to local perceptions, people are 'mixing more' due to conditions of urban life and work, marriage can be expected to occur more frequently between those of divergent backgrounds. The small and large adjustments that enable such marriages to endure take place alongside more intransigent separations and fractures – the results of accommodations not made. A truism of anthropology has been that marriage occurs between groups rather than individuals. This is sometimes difficult to discern in the apparently highly individualised contexts of North America or Europe. In this chapter and in earlier ones, we have observed the continued involvement of the parents of spouses and their wider families in conjugal life in Penang. Where differences between families cannot be bridged, couples are more isolated, and marriages are often more fragile.

Alongside its importance for individuals and families, marriage has a longer-term historical significance. The changes that it encompasses and makes possible, including new social imaginaries which conjugality enables, emerge with particular force under conditions of rapid social change. Increased urbanisation, women's education and participation in the labour force are part of this story in many places in the world. In Penang, an unusually diverse population of historically formed communities with boundaries that are both distinct and also permeable is another part of this story. Attributing causality to micro- or macro-processes of social change in this complex setting seems difficult. Marriage can be viewed as both an event and a process. Depictions of past weddings and marital relations illuminate a temporality which is inherently relative. Present marriages are compared to past ones in different generations of a family in terms of the tenor of conjugality and how nuptial rites are celebrated. The process of getting married presupposes imagining a future together – one in which participants may hope to replicate the marriages of their parents or to distinguish themselves by enacting alternative scenarios – or sometimes both of these at once.

The concurrent present, past and future tenses in which marriages are lived and imagined by spouses and by their families (Carsten et al. 2021)

Marriage and the Moral Imagination

emerge both in the way that weddings are planned and enacted and in longer-term domestic processes of homemaking, cooking and eating. But weddings and domestic processes also come up against communal expectations and state policies, which set limits on what is acceptable and legal. We saw in Chapter 2 how the high-profile case of Indira Gandhi's divorce and custody proceedings threw into question different interpretations of the Malaysian constitution, a document that was itself devised and written at a particular moment in historical time and is subject to later reinterpretations. In this way, apparently personal or familial matters have the potential to erupt into the very definition of the nation-state.

This chapter has focused less on the high-profile and bitterly contested cases that feature in Malaysian media accounts (see Peletz 2023) than on marriages that could be viewed as occurring 'at the boundaries of the normative' – between spouses whose differences of background were negotiated and accommodated – as is the case perhaps for many or most marriages. The perception that 'mixing' is on the increase suggests that this is part of a wider social process of creative accommodation. Placing different kinds, degrees and qualities of conjugal adjustment side by side brings into focus their continuities and contrasts. In this respect, one might view elopement as a vivid expression of the transgressive force that is part of the potential of marriage. But families that were shocked by elopement in the past are likely with the extended passage of time and the birth of children to reconcile with those who married in secret and without their relatives as Perveez Mody (2008) also describes for elopements in Delhi. What was transgressive in the past can, in the merging of familial and historical time, eventually become enfolded into the normative. Perhaps it is indicative of this historical trajectory that elopement was brought up most by some of the older people I talked to. Younger activists, on the edge of what was allowable, speculated instead about the possibility of more open non-normative sexual relations (see Chapter 7). More commonly, the changes and

5 Negotiating Difference in Marriage

accommodations that marital 'mixing' requires are delicately balanced, modulated and often non-obvious. 'On the surface', as I was told in relation to inter-generational shifts, things might seem similar to how they were in the past, but underneath, 'it's a more subtle process – very different'. While we might view such ongoing processes of change as integral to marriage, the tensions they give rise to also result in instabilities and uncertainties – as we will see in Chapter 6.

SIX

Those Who Leave and Those Who Stay

Marital Uncertainties Narrated through Time

The historian's temptation is to capture the uncertain past, to contain and divide it into chapters, ages and epochs, to organize and tell the story coherently, to locate and make an inventory of its motives and outcomes. And we are, of course, each of us, the historian of our own lives. The future, on the other hand, provides excellent opportunities for our predications and fantasies. With it we can indulge our optimism by planning the years ahead, as though time were a carpet one could roll out into the unknown. The past and future stimulate our imagination; the present overwhelms it. What is there to do with this ongoingness that neither pauses nor tires, this ceaselessness that is like a blinding light flickering so rapidly that the naked eye cannot perceive its reverberations? (Matar 2019, 35–36)

***

One of the paradoxes of marriage that was illuminated in numerous conversations and interviews I had with people in Penang is that, although imagined and hoped for as a means of achieving security, it could often turn out to be the source of unexpected uncertainty and instability. Older married women, as we saw in Chapter 5, sometimes told me that their mothers had counselled them to marry a man more in love with *them*

'Those Who Leave and Those Who Stay' is taken from the title of Book Three of Elena Ferrante's Neapolitan novels, translated by Ann Goldstein (2014), originally, *Storia di chi fugge e di chi resta* (2013).

6 Those Who Leave and Those Who Stay

than they were with him. This was the best way for a woman to ensure the long-term stability of her marriage. Although some acknowledged this was an old-fashioned way of looking at things, the attitude encapsulated the gendered nature of the uncertainties surrounding marriage. It also captured the underlying tensions between security and uncertainty that are inherent in conjugal relations.

The quote from Hisham Matar that forms the epigraph for this chapter eloquently suggests how, as 'the historians of our own lives', we endeavour retrospectively to order events that may have overwhelmed us in the present, and to imagine new futures in their aftermath. Shocks and uncertainties experienced in the present tense stimulate such reformulations in ways that are often unwelcome at the time. Marriage can be a particular locus of such retrospective and future reimagining partly because of the way that it encompasses hopes and expectations by introducing new and inherently risky elements into the heart of intimate lives. For individual actors, it has the capacity to enfold disappointment and regret as much as positive anticipation. In this way, marriage is a stimulus to creative ethical reflection. Beyond this, intimate relations have the cumulative potential to reformulate wider ethical and normative understandings of what is appropriate or acceptable behaviour.

If the expectations and hopes in marrying include achieving security, what happens when things unravel? Uncertainty in marriage can take many forms, and is often produced by external circumstances, such as warfare or migration or both (see Maunaguru 2019). In this chapter, I focus on the unexpected as it is generated not so much by profound political or economic upheaval, but within more everyday marital circumstances. The chapter title is taken from Elena Ferrante's novel (the third in her *Neapolitan Quartet*), set in Naples in the 1970s, in which the marriages of the two female protagonists founder under the strain of violence, emotional suffocation, divergent worldviews and expanding horizons for women. Unpredicted turns in the lives of Lenu and Lila are not ones that favour marriage. Instead, as perhaps was true for

Marriage and the Moral Imagination

many Western women in that era, they highlight the importance of female friendship.

Here I use the term 'uncertainty' to convey a broader, more modulated and nuanced sense than 'instability' (or other terms) to highlight how unpredictable events may impact a marriage, as in a life course more generally, as well as to emphasise their unknown or unexpected outcomes from the point of view of protagonists. Such upsets do not always or necessarily make a marriage unstable – some marriages have the capacity to absorb or withstand unexpected occurrences to a greater degree than others, and this resilience may in part relate to the stage at which they occur. We will look at uncertainty as it unfolds at different points in a marital life: during betrothal and early married life, in the middle years and in older age, and at how it is processed and absorbed through time. Uncertainty, I suggest, also carries generative possibilities; it can connect to wider transformations of the kind described in Chapter 2. We will see how such political transformation may be tied to narratives of marriage in the chapter that follows this one.

Although, as explained in Chapters 1 and 5, I seek to avoid essentialised renditions of ethnicity, there are some divergent cultural features of marriage and conjugality to note here. Unmarried Malay and other Muslim couples are under strict public and legal surveillance in Malaysia and are highly circumscribed in their behaviour and interactions. These follow Islamic proscriptions and enactments that do not apply to non-Muslims – although the latter may also experience considerable familial and communal scrutiny. Malays and other Muslims are likely to become formally engaged at an earlier stage in their relations than many non-Muslims, partly to allow some interaction and to signify the propriety and seriousness of their intentions (see also Nurul Huda 2020; 2022; Smith-Hefner 2019). However, these engagements are often unstable – an instability that in an earlier era also extended to early married life, and which I recognised from my research in Langkawi in the 1980s. Ethnographic accounts show that divorce at the time research was carried out was common and relatively unstigmatised (see Carsten 1997; Djamour 1965; Firth 1966; Peletz 2020b, 248 n.5; Nurul Huda 2022). Notably, the frequency of divorce among Malays declined sharply in the latter part of the twentieth century, which demographer Gavin Jones (2021) suggests was probably correlated with rising age at marriage, increased rates of 'self-choice' of spouses, less poverty and increasing external efforts to combat the notoriously high rates of Malay divorce, including the introduction of compulsory pre-marital Islamic courses for Muslims. Maznah Mohamad has conducted research on these courses as part of her work on the proliferation of a 'divine bureaucracy' in Malaysia over recent decades. Her feminist critique centres on the ideology of a patriarchal Islamic 'masculine protectionism' these courses inculcate as well as their lack of effectiveness in preventing marital instability (Maznah 2020, 202–18). Comments from research participants I spoke to suggested rather wry attitudes to the obligatory nature and the content of these courses on the part of at least some participants.

Divorce rates among all groups in Malaysia rose sharply in the first decade of the twenty-first century, levelling off for Malays after that. Jones suggests that this rise of what he calls 'modern divorce' – where incompatibility of spouses is the most frequently cited cause – can be attributed to a number of factors, including the strains of urban living, increased women's education and participation in the labour force, a rise in dual-income households and less stigmatisation of divorce among Chinese and Indian Malaysians. While divorce rates for Muslims were still more than double those of non-Muslims in Malaysia in 2017, the overall trends in divorce rates in the first decades of the twenty-first century show considerable convergence (Jones 2021).[1]

---

[1] For more detailed discussion of the demographic trends of divorce in Malaysia, including its 'spectacularly high levels' among Malays (Jones 2021, 53) in the mid-twentieth century (and probably earlier) and trends among different ethnicities, see (1981; 1994; 2021); Jones, Hull and Maznah (2015); Tey (2015).

Marriage and the Moral Imagination

These patterns are broadly reflected in the narratives of those I interviewed. In what follows, there are more Malay stories of broken marriages or engagements than Chinese or Indian Malaysian ones, and I return to this point in the conclusion. But the purpose of this chapter is not to describe or account for ethnically and/or religiously divergent patterns. Instead, I take uncertainty as my central and more general theme. Beyond the experience of its destabilising effects for the main protagonists, I ask what does uncertainty do in a marriage? How is it processed? Rather than seeing it in inherently negative terms, I explore the ways uncertainty and instability may provide openings for judgements and visions that cast relations in new lights. Here the force of the unknown in the form of unexpected, untoward events precipitates transformative understandings (see also Pandian 2019, 66–67). These may take years to gradually assimilate, crystallise or articulate, and they should be perceived as having a long-term temporality in which the delineation of new configurations of relations emerges partly in retrospect, sometimes between generations. At the time that events occur, outcomes are unknown, and temporality here manifests itself in multiple registers: as expectations, hopes or prayers. Later, it may appear as relief or regret – sometimes invested in the marital relation itself or transposed to children, grandchildren or others. In contexts of South Asian marriage with strongly patriarchal values, and where women often migrate to marry, anthropologists and sociologists have shown how the ethics of endurance, forbearance, suffering and patience (*sabar*) frame women's experiences (Chaudhry 2021; Qureshi 2016; 2019). Here, as Chaudhry shows in the rural context of Uttar Pradesh in India, conjugal love, intimacy and support may grow within and despite the inequalities of marriage. Such ethical stances have an inherent temporal quality; time here has an agentive and transformative force and takes relational forms – as in Ammara Maqsood's (2024) depiction of 'the work of time' in urban middle-class marriage in Lahore. Temporality, then, emerges as a central thread of the stories

6 Those Who Leave and Those Who Stay

told in this chapter and has a wide applicability to marriage beyond the specific context of Malaysia.

Starting Out: Unstable Betrothals

I first met Nadia in her office in April 2018. I immediately warmed to her outgoing and friendly demeanour and her articulate intelligence. Like many of those I interviewed, she seemed to have something on her mind that she wanted to talk about, and there was a discernible tension in her manner. Nadia was in her early thirties and had been born outside Malaysia but brought up mainly in Kuala Lumpur. Her parents came from very different backgrounds, she said; on her mother's side there were 'good family values', while her father's parents had divorced. Her father had spent time outside Malaysia studying for his university degrees when she was a young child and had been accompanied by his family. Over some years, she had got interested in religion, and had also been 'practicing meditation, mindfulness and positive thinking'. This had made her feel 'more stable, more rational'. Quite rapidly, she turned from talking about her parents and her background to explain that she had got engaged six months earlier, and the marriage was to take place in a few weeks' time.

The wedding that was being planned was to be a double occasion with her brother.

I'm doing all the planning [for the wedding]. Me and my brother. The venue has been hired by my brother. The rest of details – flowers, gifts, decorations – me. My brother is having photos done. Catering is done by the venue.

'There are financial constraints because of house renovation – my parents' house', Nadia explained. There were to be two wedding feasts (*kenduri*), one at her own parents' house and, subsequently, one at her fiancé's parents' home. A double wedding with her brother was a

Marriage and the Moral Imagination

recognised way of saving on expenses. Aspects of Nadia's story fitted very well with the understandings of Malay weddings that I had gained from rural fieldwork in the 1980s when wedding feasts were also the occasions for house renovation and improvement (Carsten 1997, 36–39). But Nadia said, 'Engagement hasn't been a smooth process. The emotional issues have been stressful'. The previous September they had decided on an April wedding. But in December, her fiancé 'said he wasn't ready for marriage'. He had wanted to postpone by two weeks.

I told him the venue was booked for 15th April. He said he wanted the 28th April. We didn't quarrel. I told him to talk to my mum. She said he was spiritually sick – he should see the Ustaz. A bit depressed. He says he loves me 100 per cent but not ready for marriage. January and February for him to recover. I was being supportive. In March, he texted my mum that he wasn't ready. Panic attack. Because of the uncertainty we couldn't send out invitation cards. We had one lot with my name, one lot just with my brother's. One month before [the wedding], we said the cards were ready. He said he was ready. One week later he had a panic attack.

This was a story of repeated and seemingly unprovoked panic attacks, which had obvious destabilising effects:

His father and sister came to KL to apologise to my family. Then he said he was sure, and there would be no more changes.
    Door gifts are usually customised with the bride's name. I had to pick some without names. It made me uncertain as well. I tried to strengthen myself spiritually; prayed for guidance. It's still 50-50. I will see him tomorrow. There's a chance it might be cancelled. Not sure.

In this interview, the intensity of uncertainty over whether the wedding would proceed and the acute anxiety to which this gave rise were palpable. The ways in which this was expressed were at once thoroughly contemporary – in the sending of texts, the allusion to 'panic attacks' and the problems of door gifts – while the account of how both sets of parents behaved was recognisable from an earlier era:

6 Those Who Leave and Those Who Stay

My mum never criticized him. She just said we shouldn't upset the family. I said, 'We'll call it off'. He said he wanted to go ahead. I don't understand why he's not happy. He's not dating anyone else. He wants to postpone more. He wanted to postpone to December – to full recovery. Mum said [there were] 'two decisions: yes or no'. Making him feel forced is not fair for me. I have always to think of plan B – what happens if it's cancelled. I'm not afraid if we need to cancel. I want someone like a best friend; I want to be emotionally stable. I said, 'I have to find a mechanism for me'. Meditation helps. I really like his family; he really likes mine – especially my mum. It felt like my mum was his mum. Didn't want to lose that.

The ideal role of Malay parents in cases of dispute or disagreements of a young couple is well recognised by those involved – they should try to patch things up, if necessary taking the side of a son- or daughter-in-law rather than their own child. Of course, this is not necessarily what transpires (see Carsten 1997, Chapter 8). In any case, it was clear that Nadia's mother as well as her fiancé's parents had tried hard to shore up relations. In spite of their efforts, and although the planned wedding was only a couple of weeks away, as the interview closed, it was hard to predict whether it would in fact go ahead. That much was at stake was clear in Nadia's remarks: 'It really stresses me – what people will say'.

Keen to discover how things had turned out, I interviewed Nadia again on my next visit to Penang some three months later. 'The drama continued until the day before the wedding', she told me. 'We drove to KL. I was busy getting the dress. On the night before we had the same tension. I thought my life was over'. And still on the following day,

I wasn't sure. I saw him come to the hall – things changed. My mum came with me. For the *nikah* [the Muslim marriage ceremony] I was on the *pelamin* [wedding dais]. He smiled.

The first session [recitation of wedding vows by the groom] was not approved [by the kadi]. My dad was in tears – then he started again. Then signed. The minute it was signed, I felt relieved – all that tension. He came over, put the ring on; all fine. He was very relieved. Everything was really good. I was so happy on that day. Everything turned out fine.

Marriage and the Moral Imagination

After giving me a detailed account of the wedding ceremony and celebrations, and the second feast two months later at the house of her in-laws, as well as the couple's future plans for married life, Nadia returned to the theme of uncertainty. She spoke of her parents' relief that both she and her brother had married. Her sister's wedding was also imminent, so she and her siblings might all be married within one year. Her mother had hoped the wedding of her sister might have been combined with hers, but this had not transpired: 'My sister didn't want – not special', she said.

My husband's panic attacks have gone. He said, 'Let's forget all the bad memories'. It was the stress. I don't know what he was so stressed about. It turned out everything's a lot easier.

Nadia spoke about the pleasures of living and doing things together rather than by herself. Whether or not the anxieties of her betrothal might surface again later in her marriage, I had the sense that, for now at least, her life was happily resolved.

Unstable betrothals, as I have already noted, are not unusual in Malay marital negotiations. Others too spoke of betrothals that had not worked out, but their reflections were firmly in the past tense, processed in the light of subsequent experiences. The interviews with Nadia were exceptional in that, when I first met her, she was in the midst of a crisis, poised between uncertain outcomes. Present events threatened to overwhelm her, as suggested in the passage from Hisham Matar, and she was endeavouring to make sense of them. We saw in Chapter 4 how, when Rashidah reacted to her husband's infidelity and reflected on it, she did this in light of her experience of his earlier infidelity, viewing recent events through the lens of the past, and her marriage foundered. Sequences of events are thus connected together in recounting the course of a marriage or a betrothal, and judgements about past untoward occurrences may be amplified or diminished depending on what subsequently transpires.

6 Those Who Leave and Those Who Stay

The narrative of Maryam, whom I interviewed in her university office in 2018, is a case in point. After telling me about her extensive family, including ten siblings, the apparently happy marriage of her parents who were teachers and her upbringing on the east coast of Malaysia, Maryam turned to her own education. She had originally wanted to be an astronomer, and then an engineer, she said, but her mother had encouraged her to go into teaching because she thought it would be easier to combine with family life. In the end, Maryam had opted for a career in science.

I met someone at the beginning of my undergraduate studies. We graduated together. I was going for a Masters. We got engaged. I was going to marry in the semester break. His mother was opposed to me. She didn't want someone from Kelantan – she thought I would go back there. His father really liked me.

In spite of this, all seemed to be going well, and her fiancé had visited her family. But then,

One month before the marriage, [we] had prepared a lot. The gifts and decorations were bought. Cards [invitations] had been given out. His father passed away. His family asked to postpone, but my family opposed – it wouldn't look good. My mother got into a quarrel. My fiancé said, 'I don't want to continue'.

The engagement had been broken off and, not untypically, parental involvement was understood to have contributed to the breakdown. But there was an unexpected sequel here in the form of a different marriage:

My husband is the best friend of my [former] fiancé. He tried to help sort it out. He was in the car and saw me from the car.

My ex-fiancé tried to be out of the context. I went for a job interview in KL. The boss wanted me to be his second wife. I was very surprised. He was Jordanian not Malaysian. I met my ex-fiancé's friend – he proposed at the bus station. It was just a few months after the cancelled engagement. He went to Kelantan to meet my parents – I was at [names university]. My father really liked him. My father said he would have to allow me to finish

Marriage and the Moral Imagination

my PhD. My sister really likes him.... My mother told him to come for *merisek*. He came the next week! With his family. Merisek – is the engagement ceremony. I said I needed more time. I was at the back of the house, preparing something.

I wanted him to go through the *process* properly. The previous one didn't – just by phone call. It seemed ridiculous.... My mother said yes! She didn't even ask me! My husband is very patient. I didn't really accept him till *after* the marriage.

Maryam spoke about the various conditions that had been set as part of the marital negotiations – that she would be enabled to complete her PhD studies, abroad if necessary, and subsequently be allowed to work. In this account, which notably included a further and unsought-for marital proposition from an already-married man, we get a measure of the bruised feelings that follow in the wake of a broken engagement. Parents are often pivotal participants both in successful betrothal outcomes and in their failures. But here a marriage that, six years on, appeared stable had been built on the collapse of an earlier betrothal. It seemed likely from Maryam's account that the earlier engagement would continue to diminish in importance in hindsight: 'My husband listens to me a lot. But I'm thankful I married him, compared to my ex-fiancé', she told me.

In Maryam's case, a broken engagement was enfolded into a subsequent marital story. Here Matar's evocation of the way we are all 'historians of our own lives', endeavouring to retrospectively find coherence in difficult events, is palpable. Others might be less successful in this endeavour. The potential damage to personal and familial reputations of such a public reversal after wedding invitations have already been sent out, which figured in Nadia's and Maryam's accounts, is not to be underestimated. In all such cases, sensitivities run high and it was often difficult to know what had precipitated a breakdown, and whether or how it might become part of any future narrative or instead be passed over in silence.

6 Those Who Leave and Those Who Stay

The Middle Years: Staying Precariously

While unstable betrothals are a familiar feature of marital trajectories in Malaysia, and this seems particularly the case for Malay engagements, most people expect the subsequent years and the anticipated arrival of children to bring stability to marriage. As already noted, although divorce has historically been relatively easily accommodated in Malay culture and far from unusual, this is less the case for other ethnicities (and, in general, familial and communal pressures are exerted to ensure the stability of marriages and avoid the financial and emotional upheaval of divorce). This of course does not mean that marriages are necessarily happy. In several cases I knew of, long-term work commitments in different states of Malaysia, perhaps combined with grandparental care for children, resulted in a couple maintaining separate homes, with the wife living together with children and the husband visiting. Sometimes, I had the impression such arrangements were also a way to avoid divorce. Separate living arrangements, with all their attendant unbalanced responsibilities, may enable women to maintain some everyday autonomy in decision-making as well as the respectability and protection that marital status accords.

Ai Lun, a Chinese-Malaysian woman whom I had known for several years, spoke to me over lunch in a local café about her marriage. Beginning with her family background, she told me about her upbringing as one of four sisters in a working-class urban neighbourhood of Penang. Her father's parents had migrated to Penang from China and had divorced. Her maternal grandparents had been born in Penang; they 'also stayed separately'. 'Grandmother washed clothes for people.... It was very tough'. Her parents' marriage in the early 1970s 'was match-made'; it was 'a very simple celebration – they didn't earn a lot'. Ai Lun had completed high school and gone on to take an undergraduate degree in sciences in KL. She had been married for ten years and had dated for eleven years before that – from when she was 21. 'We knew each other for *many* years', she said.

As she told me, this was not exactly a conventional marriage.

Marriage and the Moral Imagination

To a lot of people, our marriage doesn't really look like marriage because we stay separately. He trained me to be very independent. Not that I don't want someone to rely on. But I need to protect my parents, my sister. If I want my husband to save me, I better get a policeman – would be quicker!

When I asked why they had waited for eleven years before marrying, Ai Lun told me,

I was not ready yet. I don't like too big a change in my life. My grandmother was still here. The four of us [sisters] were very close to my grandmother. I didn't want to leave her. She was very sad when she heard I was going to marry. She was happy when she learned I would live in two houses. My husband was not worried – he knows I'm a very responsible person.

I probed a little to understand the strains these arrangements might have involved. Ai Lun told me that her husband had not been surprised:

My mother-in-law more. She says, 'Your husband spoiled you. Gives you too much freedom'.
He pays for my gym course. I'm thankful to him – thanks to him, grow to a different lifestyle. Get satisfaction. Sometimes I feel sorry for him because I don't take care of him. I trained him to be very independent. Before marriage, I already told him, 'I don't plan to have a child'. At first, he thought I might change my mind. But also he doesn't want to boss me.

Notably, Ai Lun here reversed her earlier statement that it was her husband who had 'trained her to be independent', and this might suggest a mutuality of this trajectory of autonomy within marriage. Perhaps unsurprisingly, it was her mother-in-law who had objected most to their decisions – although when the latter had become terminally ill, in the absence of daughters, it was Ai Lun who had taken care of her. For the future, things looked somewhat uncertain. Her husband had recently taken a job in KL, and this seemed to have the potential to upset the delicate balance of this marital relationship: 'If we had kids, I told him he'd have to take care of them too'. He said, 'No. It's a woman's job'.

6 Those Who Leave and Those Who Stay

I told him I want us to be the most important for each other as we get older. But I'm not sure. Especially since he's working in KL. He doesn't come back very often. He has a father here on his own. It makes my mother angry. I have to look after him [her father-in-law]. He should. But I say don't get angry about what you can't change.

Although Ai Lun assured me that hers was not an unusual residence pattern among contemporary couples, and in Chapter 5 we encountered others who lived separately, it was unclear how happy she was.

Very normal – right now a lot of people stay separately. We are a selfish type of people. We don't want a lot of changes.
  Some people ask, 'Are you sure he hasn't met someone else?' But I don't have that kind of feeling. I don't want to cause problems with wrong perceptions.

I sensed that Ai Lun was uneasy about the latest phase of her marriage with her husband living far away, and it was difficult to tell how stable this arrangement was likely to prove for the future. A consistent theme in her account was her awareness of the opinions and judgements of family members – those of her grandmother, mother-in-law, her mother, and her husband as well as others. But more widely, there were numerous references to what 'some people', 'many people' or 'most people' thought or said. Referring to the fact that she didn't normally wear a wedding ring, Ai Lun concluded, 'That's why most people think I'm not married. I have a ring from him – a diamond one. I don't wear it every day'. Marriage, as a public enactment, is the subject of 'other people's' opinions. While for Ai Lun these might be experienced as pressures to adopt a more conventional conjugal lifestyle – which, so far, she had withstood – one might also note that she saw her marital relation as in keeping with changes to broader patterns of conjugality. And this suggests that, while individuals may feel constrained to accept the normative forms of married life, a contrary trend towards the adoption of less conventional solutions, and their wider acceptance, was also in play.

Marriage and the Moral Imagination

Although some couples may find a precarious balance in staying together separately, others may end up severing their ties. Here again, as the epigraph to this chapter from Matar intimates, it could be difficult to perceive the unfolding significance of a rift in relations within the timescale in which it occurred. Sometimes, it seemed to take many years to understand or process a separation. I had a lengthy and quite intense initial meeting with Mei Ling and her husband, Raymond, in a local Starbucks one Saturday evening in 2018. From early in our conversation, they stressed their 'untypicality' and it took me a while to get the measure of this. We briefly encountered this couple in Chapter 3. They were both in their late fifties, had been married for about twenty-five years and Mei Ling had described herself as belonging to three generations of 'strong women' who had been the main income earners in their families. The couple had no children, she said, 'by choice'. They had got to know each other through their church and gone out together for a couple of years in the late 1980s before Raymond had gone abroad for several years to study. They had married on his return to Penang, and the wedding for 550 guests had been planned and organised by Mei Ling. There were commonalities as well as differences in their backgrounds. His family were more educated than hers, but both had grandparents who migrated from China. Both families had experienced dislocation during the Second World War and Japanese occupation, both sets of parents having gone into hiding in rural areas. Raymond's father had been largely absent in his childhood and his parents had had 'a poor relationship', he said. His mother had been on the point of leaving her husband when she discovered that she was pregnant with Raymond: 'so I was the peace child', he stated.

Mei Ling and Raymond described how their marital expectations had been different. She believed in marital equality, was the main income earner and had grown up with 'a father at home, mother at work'. Raymond, on the other hand, said 'I was mothered, never fathered. I was the one who was mothered. That set the tone for how I expected to be treated'. At this point, Mei Ling interjected, 'We expected

6 Those Who Leave and Those Who Stay

differently. Head of family. His expectations were different'. While she put energy into the business, they drifted apart. And here we seemed to be approaching the heart of what they had come to relate. The choice not to have children had been hers, Mei Ling said: 'It was difficult to have children and the business'. Their communication suffered: 'At that time, in the drama period', she continued, 'we were not really talking. We separated for seven years and got back together last year'. This separation had come after eighteen years of marriage, and both agreed that a lot of adjustments had been necessary in order to reunite. Raymond said,

Our expectations have changed. Even now, there's a lot of adjustment. Now we work at it. I suspect we're not typical. We might have divorced. I wanted to divorce. She wouldn't. I didn't do much about it.

Mei Ling was more adamant: 'I don't believe in divorce. I decided to initiate. We kept in touch. My mum and sisters are Christians – they prayed'.

Raymond articulated his feelings about their lack of children and the gap this had left:

I do have regrets about children. Children give a husband and wife something in common. Help the marriage. When I was in my 30s, people said, 'you should be a father'. The road not travelled…

Mei Ling seemed less regretful, and both spoke warmly of relations with nieces and nephews and the children of these relatives whom they had been able to support. Mei Ling said, 'My nieces, I do things with them…. So, that I have no regrets about. We are very close – it's a taste of motherhood'. And Raymond, in a similar vein but shifting the generations, spoke of a great-nephew:

The children of my nephews – when they came back to Penang to visit my sister. I had a hand in my oldest great nephew learning to speak. He spent two months in Penang with his great uncle. Went from silence to unstoppable. So, that was a little glimpse of grandfatherhood.

Marriage and the Moral Imagination

Both spouses, when I asked, agreed that there was no one event, or set of events, that had caused their separation. Raymond said, 'non-communication is the cause of lots of problems', and Mei Ling too had mentioned how, when she was very preoccupied with her business, they hadn't really been talking. It seemed that the lack of children had in some way, temporarily, blocked the future of this marriage – at least until they had reunited and found a way forward. Mei Ling, looking back, drew a connection with the previous generations of her family:

In 1929 when my grandmother lost her husband, I'm impressed by how the aunties and uncles took care of each other. I want to be that kind of family member. I didn't have a university education. I worked hard. Could provide for my entire family. I lived out my dream as an elder sister though I failed as a wife. But this is a second chance for the rest of our lives.

In this bittersweet register, and as the historian not just of her own life but of her family's, she looked back to her grandmother's generation to explain her past decisions, present stance and her hopes for the future. Through such an elongated time-frame, which appeared to acknowledge that the disappointments might have been more difficult to bear for her husband than for herself, Mei Ling seemingly assimilated – for both of them – failures and successes, reversals, dreams and desires.

In a subsequent conversation, more than a year later, Mei Ling and Raymond related how their new life seemed to be going well. Each had involved themselves in independent pursuits – she in her work and her natal family, and he in athletics and various cultural activities. They were not planning to separate again and had 'adjusted their expectations'. It was their 'wrong expectations of each other' that had caused problems, they emphasised. Mei Ling talked about how she could write a book about the story of her marital reconciliation – although, practically minded, she would prefer to run workshops – and about the counselling she had given to friends who were on the point of divorce.

6 Those Who Leave and Those Who Stay

She had 'helped them stay together'. They agreed that what was important was companionship – not to find oneself alone when sick or in need. There was a sense here that expectations had been lowered. Raymond wryly commented that he was, 'a footnote in a story of marital expectations'.

The theme of expectations, which runs strongly through this marital account, seems at once obvious in relation to marriage and also suggestive. Expectations in these 'middle years', when experience has been accumulated, are framed and understood through hindsight; from the simultaneous vantage point of the present and the past, such expectations look towards the future. One might thus say that they occur in a 'past-future-imperfect' tense, enfolding memories and disappointments but also hopes. In other words, the register of expectations is one that reflects an endeavour to bring the past, present and future into a simultaneous alignment – with the risk that this will prove impossible or that hopes will be forestalled. Here Hisham Matar's depiction of the way 'indulgent optimism' is brought into alignment with experience through an effort to contain and organise an incoherent past is apt. This entanglement of tenses, and the vision it implies, may shift in older age when the possibilities of alternative futures begin to narrow (Carsten 2000; Das 2007; 2010; Gell 1992; Maqsood 2024). And here regret, evident in Raymond's comments, could be considered the temporal counterpoint to expectations.

The Late Years: Leaving Unexpectedly

Aisyah was a forceful and energetic woman in her sixties whom I had met on several occasions through a mutual friend, and who kindly agreed to talk to me about her marriage in the latter's company in 2018. She had been introduced to her future husband by colleagues at her place of work in the late 1970s.

Marriage and the Moral Imagination

We were allowed to go out – clubbing, cinema, everything. My parents accepted him; they liked him very much.

We married in 1980 – two years later. Malay style. Small – by their standards – because my father was sick by then. The *kenduri* [wedding feast] was in a community hall for weddings. The *berhinai* [henna night] and *akad nikah* [Muslim marriage ceremony] were in the house. The *belanja* ['wedding expenses' traditionally paid by the groom] was 2000, and a ring. Everything was standard.

Although Aisyah emphasised the conventional nature of these arrangements, it was also clear that she came from a privileged and quite wealthy background. Her husband had been from Kuala Lumpur and had grown up in different places: 'He was brought up everywhere. He lost his religion'. They had had three children, and Aisyah had not worked while they were growing up, but after about twenty years' of marriage, she had opened a small business.

Aisyah might reasonably have expected to be heading into a quiet and settled marital old age. But this was not to be:

The marriage went bad in 2011 to 2014. After 30 years. It was stressful – his job, I did business. Really working hard. I'm not sure if that was the cause of it or middle-aged crisis for men. He's always had a *notion* of the kampung [village] life. In the back of his mind, that he's a simple village guy. A fantasy. His father came from – but not really…

What had occurred was something in keeping with recent marital trends but unfamiliar to me from my earlier research in Malaysia in the 1980s – the formation of polygamous unions, particularly among middle-class or elite men (Nurul Muda 2021a; 2021b; Zeitzen 2018). Aisyah continued,

He met this girl in KL. He wanted to have a second marriage. He married her. I had to stay married to him because all the property was in our joint name. I smartly made him sign things over to me. He said, this is the life he was searching for – a village in Indonesia. Now he's always here. I'm still friends with him.

6 Those Who Leave and Those Who Stay

I already knew that Aisyah had had a difficult time coming to terms with her new circumstances, and she related how she had relied on friends for support. As in Ferrante's novel, at this critical juncture, female friendship, rather than the marital relationship, emerged into the spotlight of her narrative. Now a few years after the crisis point, things seemed to have resolved in a way that she (mainly) found satisfactory. This was partly to do with the way she had apparently outwitted her husband over the division of marital property:

I'm very clever. I made him sign at a Commissioner for Oaths, and only then asked for a divorce. I said, 'Have to do it in court'. The first divorce was a *jatuh talak* [a divorce through the husband's pronouncement of the Muslim divorce formula, which can subsequently be revoked]. Then I took him to court. The court was so good to me.

Aisyah related how the judge had taken her into a private chamber to find out what had caused this long-standing marriage to break down, whether she was sure about the divorce and whether she had enough property.

The judge just granted [the divorce]. I explained everything – that I'm 60 years old. The judge is very pro-women. The judge understands – at this age we know.

The favourable view that Aisyah had formed of the treatment of women in the Muslim divorce courts in Penang accords with that of Rashidah, recorded in Chapter 4, who had also found the court sympathetic to her claims.[2] But one might suspect this experience to have been predicated on

---

[2] See Peletz (2020b, Chapter 5) for an in-depth discussion of how women are getting 'more justice' from the syariah courts in Malaysia compared to the 1970s and 1980s. His detailed accounts of a *fasakh* divorce hearing and the broader significance of these for women (2020b, 194–204) are pertinent here. In contrast, however, Maznah Mohamad (2015; 2020) argues that, over recent decades, decisions taken in the syariah courts reflect the standardisation of Islam and adoption of less plural, more patriarchal interpretations, which has had a distinctly negative impact on women. See also Carla Jones (2023, 206) for a comparable Indonesian example.

the class and status of both these female divorce claimants. The granting of 'an official divorce', as she put it, through the court (in other words a termination via *fasakh*, the judicial voiding of a marriage contract or annulment, in contrast to a simple *jatuh talak*) had placed Aisyah in a stronger position:

> I notice he [her ex-husband] comes back to Penang quite often now. He wants to get back with me... I have an official divorce – if not, he can claim one quarter of my property. That's why the judge gave an official divorce.

There was no doubt that this sequence of events had been very difficult at the time for Aisyah to absorb – partly because of the public humiliation involved through her status and the longevity of her marriage. But in the end – and from a later vantage point – she clearly expressed the view that she had come out on top:

> I told him strictly, 'Don't *ever* ask me to marry you!' He's hoping. It will never work; we always fight. But after, I can go back to my own house. I can go out. I'm already *used* to not being together. I don't need to compromise any more. I don't think I can ever remarry. Unless the man understands I've got my own standing.
>
> I told my husband, 'The truth is, you are still in love with me. You mixed up sex (with her) and love with me'. Now he leaves her for one month. She's in her thirties, maybe 40. He's 66. Now he's finding out – he's bored.

Looking back, Aisyah articulated the ambivalence that underlay her experiences: on the one hand, her husband had had a previous episode of infidelity in her marriage – with the same woman – and she also had friends with similar experiences. On the other hand, 'it was a surprise', she said, 'because ours was a love marriage. He's a faithful guy, very Westernised – otherwise I wouldn't have married him'. So, what is encountered here as a 'surprise' can also be something that somehow one should have expected all along; or vice versa, events that, given the experiences of others, might be predictable, can nevertheless come, personally, as a shock. And such reassessments too are part of the retrospective reordering of events.

6 Those Who Leave and Those Who Stay

This kind of 'surprise' in late married life has effects not only for a spouse but also for the children of a marriage, and Aisyah had mentioned the anger of her children when they had found out about their father's infidelity. Amina, an unmarried woman in her mid-30s, whom I met in 2018 after she volunteered to be interviewed, spoke to me about the marriage of her parents. They both came from Penang-based families and had married in the early 1980s after a lengthy betrothal. Her father had had a government job in the Penang port; her mother had worked as a journalist. The wedding had been a 'very traditional Malay' one, but also 'modern': there had been two sets of wedding outfits, her father wore a suit, her mother had worn a white dress, but they had also worn traditional Malay costumes. 'They came from very different backgrounds', she said; her mother's side was Malay, her father's Jawi Peranakan (Malay-speaking Muslims of mixed Indian and Malay descent).

Father was very traditional. Mother was more of a free spirit. Father was more disciplinarian. Mother let us do what we wanted. She was artistic.

Here 'traditional', for Amina, did not connote the Malay values of gender complementarity and female autonomy with which I was familiar from the 1980s, but a more patriarchal disposition that was understood to be old-fashioned and traditional rather than modern. Amina also related that her mother had not adopted Muslim head covering until the mid-1990s (relatively late by Malaysian middle-class standards of that era), and her father had not been in favour of this – 'he was a bit modern'.

They were unhappy – different personalities, different expectations. There were external factors too – family members' involvement. Father's side were not very keen on mother because Jawi Peranakan regarded Malay as low class, and she was not fair my like paternal grandmother.

Amina recounted how her parents' divorce and the events of its aftermath had hit her unexpectedly. They had divorced after nearly twenty years of marriage:

199

Marriage and the Moral Imagination

The divorce came as a surprise. I had just finished SPM [national exams sat by all fifth formers in Malaysia] on the mainland, aged 17 going on 18. They don't talk about it. Maybe my mother thought, maybe don't need to look after. Father got custody of all the children – the youngest was 11. I was the one who got the letters. They were still together. I was shocked because it was normal for them to fight. I was angry at my mother because she didn't tell me.

Although Amina first said that she was 'unaffected' by the divorce, she quickly went on to relate how, 'personally, it's difficult'. It seemed that she had gradually lost confidence, and she judged that her own marital prospects had been negatively affected. A betrothal had been broken off some years earlier, and for this she blamed her father:

I had a boyfriend for three years. We met at work. I'm very confident at work, no problem. My traditional father played a part. We were planning to marry. Had *merisek* [rituals for betrothal] for *bertunang* [formal engagement]. There was miscommunication about *hantaran* [gifts specified for a wedding sent by each side] – father's lack of experience. My boyfriend was also adamant. Father was *wali* [bride's formal representative].

As we saw in the earlier section on disrupted betrothals, this kind of breakdown during the delicate process of marital negotiations is not unusual. Here the sticking point had been over the stipulations for gifts sent to and from the bride's family when it is customary that those from the groom's side should be of much higher value than those sent from the bride's side. But negotiating these matters requires delicacy as people are liable to take offence, and often it is more distant relatives who mediate the discussions.

Since her engagement had collapsed, friends had tried to introduce her to other possible suitors, but this had not worked out.

I would like someone passionate, kind, intelligent. I have a thing about smart boys. I would prefer someone of the same education levels. Because of my parents – my mother had to boost a male ego; she was confined. She had an offer to go to the UK to study. So, it's very important.

6 Those Who Leave and Those Who Stay

Amina told me that she would prefer to marry a Malay from 'a kampung [village] background', and in articulating this preference, it seemed she was aligning herself with her mother rather than her father. 'It's very important to me that we should be equal', she asserted. She also said that she would both like to have the option of working *and* the possibility of not working, so that she would not become like her married women friends who 'carry a double burden'.

They all work. So much is expected of them. Women should have the option of not working. Most of my friends – without the wife's income, the family would not survive.

We can begin to see how, in this story of marital expectations that have twice been disappointed in successive generations, further expectations and ideals are articulated for the future. These show the lessons from earlier experiences apparently being processed and absorbed. But this of course does not mean that there is necessarily a linear progression at work. Neither Amina herself, nor we as observers, can know at this point whether she will manage to avoid the pitfalls of her parents' marriage, encounter new ones or indeed whether she will marry at all – although she made clear that she was hoping to do so, and to have children. Such intergenerational family stories are, as we saw in Chapter 3, open-ended and unfinished.

Conclusion

How can we gather up the threads of these disparate marital stories? Although it might have been obvious in the Malaysian context to view these marriages primarily through a lens of ethnicity, I have tried to resist this possibility. While some facets of the events recounted are particular to ethnic origins, especially the unstable betrothals and the polygamous unions that are sometimes features of Malay Muslim marriage, this chapter highlights what can be learned from placing diverse accounts

Marriage and the Moral Imagination

side by side. Rather than attributing particular 'marital dispositions' to religion or ethnicity in a way that risks teleology, I have instead explored what marriage does more broadly – in terms that would be recognisable across ethnic, religious or national boundaries. To conclude, I bring together the themes of uncertainty and expectations that, beyond ethnic specificities, are common to the marriages we have encountered here – as well as being pertinent to marriage beyond Malaysia – and consider the multiple temporalities in which they occur.

Taking vantage points from different stages of marital life, we have begun and ended with accounts of broken betrothals as if to underline the complex, looping and long-term temporality these stories encompass. Rather than a delineation of stark antimonies between 'those who leave and those who stay', we can read these narratives as articulating the delicate balance of possibilities involved in either trajectory. Some protagonists, indeed, seem – like Lenu and Lila in Ferrante's novel – uncertainly poised between staying and leaving, anchored to a burdensome past that has become increasingly difficult to sustain. Disrupted beginnings have been one theme of this chapter. Expectations – looking forward to a marital future – have been another, but these are assessed and judged with the benefit of hindsight. We have encountered hopes and prayers looking forward, as well as retrospective relief and regret; each of these may be invested in the marital relation, in children, grandchildren or – in their absence – in nephews, nieces and great nephews. Chances (and second chances) substitute for surprises; shocks are recalibrated in hindsight as stories of mismatched expectations. As 'historians of their own lives', protagonists attempt to align or realign the past, present and future in order to judge what has gone wrong, what could have been done differently and what might yet be put right. Maqsood's attention to the coexistence of different temporalities in marital stories, following Das (2007; 2010), is apt here (see also Carsten et al. 2021), as is her observation that, 'The work of time provides possibilities to carve out individual and married futures, rewriting and crossing out older histories and

6 Those Who Leave and Those Who Stay

weaving new narratives of self-making and of bringing change in others' (Maqsood 2024, 68).

At the beginning of this chapter, I asked what does uncertainty, or what do encounters with the unexpected, do in a marriage? How are they absorbed? What are their effects? While we could understand disruptions to the smooth course of events in the shape of the untoward and unexpected as negative personal experiences, as in many of the accounts in this chapter, I am interested in whether we can also discern in them the seeds of some larger and more generative processes. Anand Pandian (2019) has suggested that the transformative possibilities of anthropology inhere in its encounters with the unexpected: 'An apprenticeship in anthropology is a lesson in accommodating the unknown'. And he asks, 'What happens when the ordinary course of thought and action is suspended by something unassimilable?' (2019, 66). In an unpredictable and sometimes risky experiment, anthropology sets up its students to confront the unexpected. The transformative possibilities of this encounter might be one source of the particular loyalty adherents often feel for their discipline. But as the marriage stories in this chapter show, for all of us, everyday life is liable to throw up confrontations with the unexpected whether they are deliberately sought out or not.

I suggest that, just as Pandian argues, the unexpected is transformative as a mode of anthropological learning, it is also so in everyday life. And we can see this through the manner in which the unexpected unfolds in the marriage stories presented here. Marriage is, necessarily, an intimate encounter with another. The process of assimilating the other – becoming known – occurs incrementally and is always incomplete. Sometimes, in this process, events or circumstances arise, seemingly out of the blue and contrary to earlier expectations – the 'surprise' articulated in many of these accounts. When Maryam's first betrothal broke down, she and her father put the knowledge gained to use by including stipulations asserting her right to work and to complete a PhD abroad into the negotiations and contract for her subsequent marriage to a different man.

Marriage and the Moral Imagination

The effects of Amina's parents' divorce and her own broken betrothal, similarly, can be traced in the values and expectations that she asserted would be important in any future marriage she might contract. Aisyah, whose marriage collapsed after thirty years, and whom I met on several occasions, seemed to be adjusting quite well to living alone and had come to value her newfound autonomy and her friends – although the circumstances in which this came about had been a shocking upheaval.[3] All of these adjustments in values were made through encounters with the unexpected, and they ricocheted outwards from the principal participants to their families and others – a father in Maryam's case, Amina's absorption of the impact of her parent's divorce, and the adult children and friends who gave support to Aisyah. We might imagine that these experiences could influence how those who participate in them will view analogous predicaments of relatives, friends or acquaintances in the future, perhaps enlarging the scope of their judgements and sympathy.

It is worth pausing over the way these are gendered stories: the uncertainties, surprises and shocks encountered here seem to be absorbed and accommodated by women more than by men. And this reflects the gendered hierarchies of marriage and the greater precariousness of women's position in marital relations and elsewhere – as has been noted for South Asian contexts (see, for example, Chaudhry 2021; Vatuk 2015). This was articulated in many accounts of marriage, and in the advice older women told me they had been given by their mothers – to marry a man who was more in love with them than they were with him – which opens this chapter. But beyond this, the prominence of women's accounts of precarity and uncertainty also suggests the centrality of women's experiences to the transformations that these unexpected events set in train, the adjustments and accommodations to living arrangements, property and values that were made. If families, friends and law courts can be

---

[3] Similarly, Azman (2011) notes the high value single Malay women place on their independence and autonomy.

6 Those Who Leave and Those Who Stay

sources of support, they are also part of this ongoing process of negotiation and transformation.

Returning to the theme of temporality, it is clear that all of the narratives presented in this chapter are captured at a particular moment in time, none of them can be seen as 'completed'. This was especially palpable in my encounter with Nadia – in the midst of a 'marital crisis' and uncertain, just a few weeks before her wedding, whether it would in fact go ahead. In the case of those whose weddings were abruptly called off after invitations had gone out, such uncertainty only became obvious (at least for others) in retrospect. And we could detect a similar indeterminacy in the accounts of independent living arrangements told by spouses who seemed precariously poised between remaining together and separating, staying and leaving. But this is the case too in the narratives that take a longer view, such as that of Mei Ling and Raymond who had separated for seven years but had managed to reunite, or of Aisyah who spoke ambivalently of the pleasure of her post-marital independence but also of her former husband's continued attempts to get back together with her.

Across these marital accounts, the juncture of the present affords a condensed glimpse of uncertainty, distilled and in process. As the quote from Hisham Matar in the epigraph to this chapter eloquently asserts, those who trace their own marriages, as 'historians of their own lives', do so through the mechanisms of time. Those I spoke to looked back to the past, sometimes across generations, and simultaneously forward to unknown futures, to make sense of their experiences and relationships. And I often had the sense that the conversations and interviews recorded here provided a welcome opportunity for such relational ethical reflection in which I too participated. Memoirists make this terrain their own, and it is no accident that the turbulence of twentieth-century history has yielded an efflorescence of autobiographical family accounts. But as Matar reminds us, there is also an ongoing and everyday internal dialogue to which we are all subject, and which makes up our imaginative and creative lives.

Marriage and the Moral Imagination

Time-frames, which may be narrow in the pressure of current events, expand when these events are viewed retrospectively. In the present, events can seem overwhelming and outcomes are unknown; through the lens of retrospection, time enables an order to be imposed. Mei-Ling took a specific year, 1929, when her grandmother had unexpectedly been widowed at a young age, as a narrative origin point. Many, like her, spoke of 'expectations' that had been misaligned or unfulfilled. Mei-Ling's husband, Raymond, as well as referring to 'the path not taken', memorably described himself as a 'footnote in a story of marital expectations'. I have suggested that the register of expectations, evoked in the past tense, simultaneously records memories, fears and hopes, dreams and desires – a past-future-imperfect that attempts to bring the multiple tenses of experience into alignment. Narratives reconfigure the past, present and future in order to judge what has gone wrong, what could have been done differently and what might yet be put right. Attachments and detachments in the marriages considered here are revealed as not only those of kinship and relatedness but also of temporality itself.

If time is the medium, or vector, of these processes of consideration and absorption, their subject matter and focus is relatedness in both its intimate and more public forms. The adjustments and accommodations recorded here – to values as well as to practical arrangements – are not standpoints adopted publicly with some major project of change to marriage in view. On the whole, these are understated modifications in everyday life that nevertheless have the capacity to ripple out gradually from individual marriages to friends, relatives and communities.[4] When Ai Lun spoke of the unconventional nature of her marriage, and how, 'To a lot of people, our marriage doesn't really look like marriage because we stay separately', she was expressing both the hold of

---

[4] See also Carla Jones's detailed account of an activist's 'aberrant' marriage in Indonesia as 'a quiet but radical expression of hope' (2023, 201).

6 Those Who Leave and Those Who Stay

conformist values and the space that marriage can provide to do things differently. The numerous references to 'other people' in her account reflected her consciousness of the public nature of marriage, but the absent wedding ring, and the diamond one that she chose only occasionally to wear, were material signs of her determination to maintain her autonomy and do things in her own way. How this might resolve itself in the future was unclear. Marriage provides a mask of conventionality – to some extent at least accommodating unorthodox arrangements. But Ai Lun also noted how separate living arrangements for married couples were becoming a more common pattern. Encounters with the unexpected, and the shocks of surprise and uncertainty through which they are gradually assimilated, can thus generate wider transformative possibilities in their aftermath – as we will explore more fully in Chapter 7.

SEVEN

Imagining Conjugal Futures

The Personal and the Political

At the beginning of her pioneering feminist study of five literary marriages in Victorian Britain, *Parallel Lives*, Phyllis Rose (2020 [1984]) lays out her central argument:

> I believe marriage to be the primary political experience in which most of us engage as adults, and so I am interested in the management of power between men and women in that microcosmic relationship. (Rose 2020, 4)

Although she takes power as the primary and revealing axis of conjugality, imagination is no less a key to her understanding of the marriages she describes. As Sheila Heti states in her perceptive introduction to this work, 'Rose's point seems to be, *Imagination is the glue*' (Heti 2020, xiii, original italics). These formulations frame the current chapter not so much in the sense that I focus on the dynamics of power within individual conjugal relationships (all the chapters of this book touch on that theme), but in the broader perception that it is through its imaginative possibilities in conjunction with the dynamics of power that marriage forms a 'primary political experience'. This is both the case for individual marriages, as Rose describes, and in the way that marriage is at the same time a productive imaginative terrain for considering the ethical ground on which wider gendered relationships should be based.

One of Rose's case studies is the partnership between the novelist George Eliot and George Henry Lewes, a relation that endured for

7 Imagining Conjugal Futures

twenty-four years from 1854 until the latter's death in 1878. This was, famously, a union of exceptional devotion, a marriage of minds in which Lewes provided Eliot with protection from any external criticism (including by careful oversight and selection from reviews of her work or letters from her publishers) and unmitigated encouragement of her writing. Temperamentally, they seem to have been opposites – while Eliot was prone to being gloomy, anxious and highly sensitive to any criticism of her work, Lewes was of a cheerful, optimistic disposition. Protectiveness, on his part, and mutual devotion were the fabric of their union. As Rose puts it, 'They were the perfect married couple. Only – they weren't married' (2020, 24).[1] This was not because of a political stance against marriage, as she explains, but because Lewes was unable to marry. His wife, Agnes Lewes, had had a long-term affair with Thornton Leigh Hunt (who was also married), by whom she had borne three children at the time that Lewes and Marian Evans (Eliot) eloped on their 'honeymoon' abroad. While one child would have given Lewes legal grounds for divorce on the basis of adultery, further children removed this possibility – on the basis that failure to lodge a complaint at the first pregnancy legally constituted condonement of adultery. George Henry and Agnes clearly had radical and non-traditional views about marriage, and he continued to support her and her children until his death (Rose 2020, 222–23).

Because their union was so far outside the bounds of Victorian morals, law and convention, Eliot and Lewes lived an exceptionally isolated and quiet life with very few visitors. And this afforded Eliot the perfect conditions for her work. A question that Rose asks of their relation is, 'how much did their happiness depend upon the irregularity of their

---

[1] Clare Carlisle (2024, xvi–xvii) inserts some caveats into Rose's portrayal of this relationship in the preface to her philosophical exploration of George Eliot's life, reminding us of the ambiguities of conjugality, the difficulty of grasping the dynamics of any intimate relationship from the outside and of how Rose's argument suits the period of second-wave feminism in which it was written.

Marriage and the Moral Imagination

union?' (Rose 2020, 242). And she concludes that these circumstances – as well as the unusual and harmonious dynamics of power between them – were in fact central to the success and happiness of their conjugality. But as Rose notes, 'For Marian Evans ... falling in love with a man who could not marry her was a test case in personal ethics at the profoundest level' (Rose 2020, 231). It is clear that law, religion and ethics in relation to marriage not only preoccupied Mrs Lewes – as Marian Evans referred to herself and preferred to be known after 1854 – but these are also central themes of Eliot's novels. Ethical imagination and sympathetic tolerance are at the heart of George Eliot's work and of her life. Rose writes, 'To say that George Eliot was the child of the extraordinarily happy union of Marian Evans and George Henry Lewes is more than wordplay' (Rose 2020, 228). The moral construction of the central relation in her life against the grain of convention – but certainly without disregard of it – allowed and extended her imaginative capacities and the extraordinary perceptiveness about human relations in her writing, enabling her to become 'Britain's voice of morality' (Rose 2020, 243) against the force of law and conventional religion.

In a more everyday register, the theme of moral and imaginative continuities between intimate familial life and the assertion of more political stances runs through this chapter. Bringing together ethics and imagination as I do here is not intended to delineate a bounded terrain or to suggest an essentialised essence for either. On the contrary, as discussed in the Introduction, we have observed how the ethical, following Das (2018a), is part of 'the ordinary', and threaded through everyday life. Through its relational nature, kinship is a particularly thick terrain of ethical evaluations and judgements (see Faubion 2001; McKinley 2001). By the same measure (and as Eliot's novels amply demonstrate), it requires imaginative engagement to understand, gauge and evaluate the behaviour and motives of others, or to plan one's own and others' relational futures. Anthropologists have explored how new and/or challenging aspects of kinship bring out such imaginative possibilities especially

7 Imagining Conjugal Futures

starkly. Thus Marilyn Strathern (1992), among others, has elucidated the imaginative potential and impetus of reproductive technologies, while Rayna Rapp and Faye Ginsburg (2001) have written of the ways in which disability may initiate a reimagination of kinship. In both cases, reimagining is also an ethical process in the sense that it entails consideration of the rights and wrongs of present and prospective relations. In this context, Ginsburg and Rapp cite Lauren Berlant:

To rethink intimacy is to appraise how we have been and how we live and how we might imagine lives that make more sense than the ones we are living. (L. Berlant 1998, 286, cited in Rapp and Ginsburg 2001, 537)

I draw parallels here between the way Ginsburg and Rapp consider disability and kinship, or Strathern discusses reproductive futures, and marriage – which involves incorporating a new person (and sometimes their relatives) into a family. Marriage has engaging with the new and rethinking the old built into it. In this sense, like other aspects of kinship, it is a creative endeavour – which can of course simultaneously be a conservative one (Magee 2021). This apparent conservatism may be what lies behind the tendency among anthropologists and sociologists to ignore the innovative and creative aspects of marriage. Crucially, what interests Strathern about the consideration and absorption of assisted reproductive technologies, and Ginsburg and Rapp in the entailments of disability in kinship, is the way they also take place in and through public culture. Rapp and Ginsburg discuss an 'expanded domain of "public intimacy" linked to disability' (2001, 537), which occurs partly through electronic media. Such media sites are both sources of information and of imaginative play that 'help to create a new social landscape' (2001, 551). As we have already seen in Chapter 2, and I pursue further here, marriage is a crucial – yet ordinary – axis bridging intimate family life with wider public discourse and institutions.

Harnessing imagination and ethical engagement in a discussion of marriage is thus a way to focus on what marriage does – the way that it

Marriage and the Moral Imagination

expands the possibilities of intimacy and also creates 'new social landscapes'. Following Sheila Heti's insight (which some may find counterintuitive), I suggest that what imagination glues in marriage are not only the internal aspects of an intimate relationship but also relations between family life and wider social horizons and institutions. And this is not exactly to conjure marriage as a 'technology of the imagination', in the sense of Sneath, Holbraad and Pederson (2009), which would seem a reductive and instrumentalist move here, but perhaps nevertheless a way to illuminate 'the processes by which imaginative effects are engendered' (Sneath, Holbraad and Pedersen 2009, 11). Marriage might be one of many such processes, bound into the everyday and the ordinary, but with a capacity to emerge at particular junctures as not 'ordinary' at all.

In Chapter 6, we saw how new kinds of marital uncertainties, experienced in the changing social contexts of Penang, have intertwined with older forms of marital instability to shift the contours of conjugal landscapes. For many people, marriage is no-more an assured route to security in old age today than it was in the past – and quite possibly less so. Non-marriage and later marriage are rising trends in Malaysia, across Asia, and in many other parts of the world (see, for example, Chiu 2023; Davidson and Hannaford 2023; Jones 2005; 2009; 2021; Jones, Hull and Maznah 2015). This suggests new visions of conjugality within individual perceptions and in wider social imaginaries. To speak of 'non-marriage' in fact begs certain questions. To what extent is non-marriage a transient situation arising out of personal circumstances, and to what extent is it an explicit stance? It is unclear what ethical assessments might result in non-marriage, or how non-marriage – like marriage – could constitute a political experience. If imagination is the glue of marriage, what might have shifted (or become differently glued) to encourage more people not to marry? To probe the conjunctions of the intimate and the political, in the sections that follow, I draw on interviews with women who have

7 Imagining Conjugal Futures

remained single past the usual age for marrying to understand how their trajectories and their imagination of marriage have been shaped through familial experiences. I go on in the later part of this chapter to discuss interviews with those who have engaged in broader social struggles that aim to remould gender and marital relations in light of their ethical understandings and the imaginative possibilities they have considered.

Chapters 3–6 have illuminated the way that marriage is a terrain for ethical judgements and evaluations that are made by individuals, within and between relationships, communities and ethnicities. These evaluations are relational – they are judgements about, and between, relations; they are also judgements that shift over time as people evaluate marriage in different periods and epochs. They occur in past, present and future tense – sometimes simultaneously so (Carsten et al. 2021). Evaluations at the same time help to delineate what is past, what is present and what might be hoped for in the future. They thus also shape time, separating eras and generations or establishing continuities between them.[2] Participants in marriages, and in such judgements, engage in ethical assessments that are at once temporal, relational, intimate and political. Exploring the views of those activists or organisers whose everyday work concerns marriage is not only intended to provide a glimpse of a variety of privileged expert opinions – although it may do that. These participants are situated in the midst of their social worlds and have myriad engagements with local communities and cultures. Here Carla Jones's depiction of middle-class political activists in Indonesia as 'figures of modernity' like career women (Jones 2023, 208; Barker et al. 2014) is pertinent. I thus treat these conversations and statements ethnographically as resonating with the contexts through which they have emerged.

---

[2] I am very grateful to Koreen Reece for her suggestions to elucidate and expand the discussion here and elsewhere in this chapter.

213

Marriage and the Moral Imagination

Placing conversations with community organisers or activists side by side with those who are unmarried, as I do here, is intended not to mark a sharp distinction between categories of participants but, on the contrary, to see what convergences or continuities we can discern in their different perspectives. What kinds of marital futures do these divergent actors imagine and describe? How might currently non-normative conjugal forms gain traction – or not – in Malaysia or elsewhere? How is marriage likely to transform in the future – or to transform the future? While in some respects, as we see in what follows, the answers to these questions may depend on the position from which people speak, and on the experiences their positions encapsulate, the aspirational potential of marriage and its wider public resonances also suggest the possibility of transcending individual experience to imagine new – and newly ethical – possibilities. In this way, the ethical and imaginative scope of marriage transforms and is itself transformative.

It is not necessarily straightforward or obvious to trace how ethical judgements about marriage travel beyond spouses and families into wider communities. But this process is especially palpable for marriages between local, religious or ethnic communities or when marriages break down – in other words, at 'stress points' in the fabric of conjugality. The move from intimate relational contexts to wider imaginative assessments is accessible in the stances taken by activists, lawyers and others who are closely concerned with cases that condense such stress points and contestations, and with the broader social issues arising from marriage. I show how their work, rather than constituting a separate sphere of activity marked off from kinship and family, is broadly continuous with these spheres. It derives and draws inspiration from the kinds of intimate familial experiences and judgements that are threaded through such narratives as I have presented in Chapters 3–6. Reflecting on and speaking about marriage, I suggest, is always in this sense political and imaginative work in the way that Phyllis Rose describes.

7 Imagining Conjugal Futures

Polygyny Refracted

I met Alicia in early 2019 near her office in a local educational institution. She was in her thirties, unveiled and articulate in perfect English. Recounting her background, she told me about periods spent outside Malaysia, which she had enjoyed, as a child at school when her father worked abroad and then later pursuing her university studies. Subsequently, she had taught in school and then in tertiary education, which she preferred. Her parents, she told me, had married in the 1980s. Both were from towns in northern Malaysia. Theirs was not an arranged marriage, but they had had 'a traditional Malay wedding'.

As with some other interviewees, after a time, it became clear that Alicia had a particular story she wanted to recount:

I thought everything was normal till a revelation a few years ago. My father was mostly away. My mum raised us single-handedly. So, I was alone a lot – she was at work…. The age gaps [with my sisters] are quite big. I remember not seeing my father a lot. We've not really had conversations – till now.

… My mother had a very short temper. It was very difficult for her. Still now, she brings up issues from the past. We thought we had a normal life. We found out. We found out he had a second wife for 10 years now and he even has a son. [We] found out a couple of years ago. There was a big conflict in the family when we found out he'd been married for eight years.

We idolised him. We thought he was busy working when he was away. Our half brother – when we found out, he was a couple of months old. We always knew when we were growing up he wanted a son. His ultimate dream. My parents, they wanted a son.

The shock of discovering her father's second marriage after it had already existed for many years was palpable in Alicia's modes of expression, repetitions and in the emotional tenor of her words. Like the narrative of Aisyah, whom we met in Chapter 6, her account made clear how adult children can become embroiled in the story of their parents' divorce and how difficult it is to remain neutral. As Alicia said, 'it's hard to be in the middle'.

Marriage and the Moral Imagination

My mother goes back and forth about divorce. He told her he would divorce his second wife. I asked my mother why she doesn't divorce him. My mother suspected. She never told us. It was not the first time. There were other affairs. It was very difficult for me, finding out about it. My second sister found out. My two older sisters took it quite hard. They wanted to confront my father. Me and my younger sister wanted to avoid him.

We don't want to know what my half brother looks like. But we do have contact with my father. He lives with my mother now. But goes off to her for one or two nights. It's a cycle – he goes off, and mum gets in touch. I live in Penang – it's better – I feel conflicted. I don't want to take sides. My mother says she can't believe it – at her age, 60, after all the sacrifices. Whenever he goes away, she's restless. 'To be with his friends', he says. I sense he longs for his other family. I feel for him.

After touching in somewhat muted terms on the marriages of her sisters, Alicia went on to speak of her own single status:

I was in a relation. I was put off marriage; became wary towards men. Malay men can legally take more wives. They can do it secretly. It terrifies me. I feel the current system doesn't protect women.

In spite of her reservations, we don't know whether Alicia might eventually marry or not. It would seem a stretch to say that she has adopted a strong stance against marriage. What is clear is that her narrative connects her reservations to what had transpired in her parents' marriage – her imaginative horizon, by her account, has been shaped by her experience and perceptions of her parents' marriage. In this sense, at the time of the interview at least, Alicia's intergenerational experience of marriage seemed to exercise a constraint that limited or overshadowed the imagination of new or different ways of doing marriage. As she told me,

I find it difficult to want to get married. In terms of what happened. I'm a bit similar to my mother. I'm a bit afraid. My mother understands. She always tells me not to rush. Most of my friends are already married. Some have three children already.

7 Imagining Conjugal Futures

While experience here limited the possibility of imagining alternative marital scenarios, it did allow Alicia to expand the possibilities of living alone. As she recognised, her own situation had its attractions, and these seemed to be growing on her: 'I live alone. I love it! It's getting too comfortable'.

In the longer term, Alicia expected her parents to remain in the situation they were in, with her father maintaining two marriages. She had confronted her father, she told me, and she was sure that he would neither leave her mother nor his second wife.

I think they will stay married. I think [my mother] will never leave him. Nor him her. He won't leave his second wife either. He really loves her.

In the closing section of Chapter 6 we encountered Amina, also in her mid-thirties, who spoke about how her parents' divorce had impacted her own marital prospects, disrupting a betrothal. Alicia's narrative thus echoes aspects of Amina's, but it expresses more directly the possibility that the shocks of divorce or polygyny can reverberate in the next generation in the formation of a choice to remain single.

Delaying Marriage, Staying Single

Alicia clearly articulated how remaining single (or unexpectedly becoming single in the case of Aisyah, whom we met in Chapter 6) could turn out to have its attractions despite normative expectations to be married. After decades spent as part of a couple, this could come as a surprise. As Aisyah had put it, 'I'm already used to not being together. I don't need to compromise any more. I don't think I can ever remarry'. Such independence, for these two women of different generations, was constructed through financial autonomy and living alone – a prospect not open to, or necessarily desired by, all. Most of the single people I knew in Penang lived with other family members.

Marriage and the Moral Imagination

I met Farah through a local history event we both attended. She worked in local government and was in her mid-forties when I interviewed her in 2018. She had been born and brought up in Penang, she told me, and had been raised with her siblings by a single mother. Farah lived together with her mother and younger sister. She articulated an open-minded set of attitudes that was reflected in her multicultural friendships and which she attributed to her mother's similar stance and 'respect for other religions'.

My childhood was filled with compassion. Whenever someone came to my mum for help, she helped a lot of people. She cooked and gave to neighbours – it was a Chinese neighbourhood. Not for money; she believed in giving.

This comment came towards the close of our conversation after she had spent time telling me about her family background and her own attitude to marriage.

Farah's parents had married in the early 1970s. Her father was from a large sibling group and came from a mixed Indian Muslim and Malay background on his mother's side, and Pakistani on his father's side. Her mother had been born into a Hindu family on the mainland and was brought up on a plantation. Her mother's mother had converted to Islam along with Farah's mother. Farah described her parents' wedding as 'Pakistani style'. After their marriage, her parents had lived with her father's extended family in urban Penang:

All my father's siblings lived in one house. Very Indian – a family house. They would cook and eat together. Some had their own small dwellings. My mother talks about it because the rest were not accepting of her. She was only loved by the main leader of the house – my father's older brother. He was a strict disciplinarian, but not so strict with her. He passed away a long time ago.

As Farah's description indicated, this kind of extended family household with married siblings co-residing is a minority residential form

7 Imagining Conjugal Futures

in Malaysia.[3] Relations became difficult, and her parents had separated after a few years; an official divorce had taken longer. 'It was hard for my mother but she was quite strong'.

> My mum moved out. There was some fight between the ladies of the house. She moved to a friend's house.... The friend became our nanny, she took care of us. She was paid. I was only four years old. My brother was five, and she was pregnant with my sister. It was very difficult.

Neither of her parents had remarried; her mother had brought up the children with limited help and there had been little contact with her father. When I asked Farah why her parents had separated, she said,

> It has to do with the whole family thing – a very Indian thing, family living. It's good and bad. You do not get your space unless a lot of land separates the houses.

Through her childhood, Farah moved around different areas of Penang depending on her mother's employment. For herself, education had seemed more important than marriage:

> I'm not married. I never thought of marriage. I'm more of a book person. Only I graduated with a degree in my family. I concentrate on my job. I'm not opposed to marriage. I get pressure from family members – some tried to match-make me. They respect my decisions. They're not really pushing me into marriage. One mind set – came to study. I did have a good guy friend – but I didn't think...

Her voice trailed off here.

Notably, Farah was more than ten years older than Alicia. In her mid-forties, it was perhaps more likely (though still by no means certain) that she would remain unmarried. She mentioned an older sibling who

---

[3] The 'traditional' rural Malay preference was for a period of residence with the bride's parents after marriage (and/or alternation between the two parental households), followed by setting up a couple's independent household (Carsten 1997).

Marriage and the Moral Imagination

had married at a young age and a younger one who was likely to become engaged soon. When I asked about her own expectations for the future, she told me,

My expectations came to a full-stop. Thinking about marriage. If I came across a good friend, I would marry. All these years I've been alone and very independent. Unless you find someone really compatible…

The majority of my friends are not married. For some, they had failures in relationships. Some found the wrong guy.

Here again, one could not say that Farah had adopted a strong stance against marriage as such. Rather, her own single status seemed to have arisen out of her circumstances, and, like Alicia, she endeavoured to make sense of it in terms of her own familial and other experiences. Reflectively, like others whom I interviewed, Farah placed this trajectory in a broader social context where not marrying had emerged as a recent possibility: 'It's a growing trend', she said, while observing that this was less true of her Malay friends than of others.

Most of my friends from college are married to each other. One or two girls and guys are not married. It's different from my parents' generation. Some married at 15; almost all were married by 24. Their parents got them married by match-maker.

Like other research participants who were also keen observers of their own society, Farah attributed these changes in the first place to education:

Education is the reason: my mum made sure we got all the education. My cousins' children are also educated. That means delays, or being less likely to marry. My parents' generation complain.

While some of her friends went out a lot and had boyfriends, her own disposition, like that of her close friends, leaned more towards staying at home.

And then there were the issues of work and independence – again, ones we have met in Chapters 3–6. When I asked how she saw the future, Farah said,

7 Imagining Conjugal Futures

Difficult to predict but I would like not to be alone. Maybe in the Pakistani clan, if you're opinionated, hot-headed, it may put off guys. In my family, the Pakistani part, wives stay at home. I would like to stay working – not to get a wage, but social work, voluntary.

Here, interestingly, employment is explicitly distinguished from paid employment, an acknowledgement that, in a conservative community, the former might be more acceptable after marriage than the latter. Education and employment were clearly to the fore in Farah's consideration of the ways in which marriage was different today from the recent past and the ways this might affect her own future. Not far behind, however, was the issue of children.

On the one hand, as Farah perceived, children could be considered the primary reason to marry. On the other, as she also understood, this too might be changing:

I come from a mixed background. My mum's family, some are Catholics, Christians on the other side. I've seen them being married and divorced. It's kind of complicated. You have to get into marriage for a purpose. That's why I've held back. If you want to have children…

Now my friends, I see perceptions of marriage – which used to be primarily for children – different, as a partner, friend; equal partners, live-in partners. So, children are not so much the centre.

Thus, one effect of this shift from marriage, primarily, in order to have children to conjugality based more around companionship, equality and intimacy was perceived to be the decentring of reproduction. Some of her friends were having children in their mid- to late forties. 'My friends, most are having children late. Now, as soon as you get married, you leave the house'. The effects of these changes could be mixed. As Farah viewed things,

[The] Young generation now have less empathy. Before, people feel for the older generation. They grew up with grandparents. So, don't feel for them. Now the new generation is more into technology – robots.

Marriage and the Moral Imagination

Here Farah placed herself in a middle generation with values derived from an older one that were different from those of today's young people. A dystopian vision of a world in which caring might be undertaken by robots, and the ethics of connection and compassion were on the decline, contrasted with the values in which Farah had been brought up by her mother. The interview concluded with a paean to Penang's multiculturalism and the values of respect for other traditions on which it rested. Expounding on the many different kinds of weddings that she was accustomed to attending, Farah attributed this to her mother's attitudes in her childhood:

My mother was very open-minded. She knew we'd always have our roots, would respect other religions. And also our Christian relatives. There would be separate catering, and no beef on the first day of Hari Raya, and a separate vegetarian dish for vegetarians. I had that opportunity – quite Penang. Penang is so multi-cultural!

One interesting feature of this interview is the way that it shifted from recounting a personal trajectory to reflecting on historical changes and a broader social context. And we might contrast this with Alicia's quite raw discussion of her father's polygynous marriage and her understanding of its implications articulated within the uncertainties of Malay marriage. Farah's narrative moved from her own and her parents' experiences, first to the Pakistani background of her paternal grandfather, then to the stresses of 'Indian' residential patterns and then to education, employment, reproduction and the broader values of empathy, compassion and caring that she situated between communities and religions. Notably, she described herself as coming from a 'mixed background'. This suggestively links her familial experience of social differences to an expansion of imaginative horizons. It also recalls the mixed ethnic backgrounds of the arts activists in Sumit Mandal's (2001) study, which I noted in the Introduction to this book. Social difference can lead to an enlargement of imaginative possibilities, and imagination also enables connections to transcend social differences. At various points in the interview she had mentioned the marital experiences of her friends, specifically alluding to Malay, Indian and Chinese friendships, and to marriages within and beyond these boundaries, including to a man in the UK and to a 'Mid East guy'. In this account, a 'happy and difficult' childhood in urban Penang under conditions of some precarity is understood to have encouraged relations across communal lines, and to have fostered the value of compassion.

The point here is not simply to draw utopian lessons about the social relations of Penang from Farah's narrative. There were allusions to difficulties and pressures associated both with the circumstances of her upbringing and with her single status, which would have been difficult to ignore. She mentioned such tensions at various points, including when describing attending the weddings of younger relatives. On such occasions, the talk of family members who blamed her mother for Farah's unmarried status could become irksome. What seems important, however, is the way reflections and judgements move from personal backgrounds and involvements to the wider social and historical settings in which they are placed. Not only was this account rendered in a strongly ethical register – with positive and negative evaluations of behaviour and circumstances clearly expressed – but we can also see how imagination provides a creative glue beyond marriage itself to close together intimate and wider social or political worlds. Pursuing the theme of ethical work in communities, in the next section these links between ethics and imagination emerge more clearly.

From Intimate Experience to Community-organising

Many of those I interviewed or knew in Penang were active in their communities, taking part in heritage, artistic, environmental, religious or charitable projects of different kinds. I might learn of these involvements incidentally during a conversation or interview or because it was the path through which I met some of those who became research participants. Some of these activities related directly to marriage and their own personal experience. Amelia, whom we encountered at the beginning of Chapter 3, told me about the marital counselling work she did through her church, and Mei Ling who we met in Chapter 6, who had separated from her husband Raymond for seven years and then reunited, also spoke about marital advice that she had given to friends and workshops she might organise. Others were active in Penang's state government or civil society women's development organisations that focused on a broad range of gendered issues, including education, livelihoods and domestic violence. One could describe these kinds of engagements as 'ethical endeavours' in the sense that they were motivated by concerns to improve the conditions of people's lives or alleviate social ills, and they often arose directly from personal or familial experience. In this sense, they expressed an imaginative expansion from personal experience to broader social horizons.

I met Malika in a popular and busy café near her workplace one lunch hour early in 2019. She described herself as a 'community organiser rather than an activist', explaining the difference in this way: 'Activism focuses more on external relations, outwards. For me, the focus is on internal relations'. Our conversation was partly about the current political moment in Malaysia, which seemed precariously poised between political reform and a more conservative retrenchment. As she observed of the government,

They're trying to secure the Malay/Muslim vote – the new coalition. The optimistic mood is on the decline. In general, the government promised a lot, but they're not doing the reforms they promised.

This was a fairly widespread view that I heard repeatedly from reformist-minded observers and those moving in academic and activist circles at the time. I had originally contacted Malika with the intention of learning

7 Imagining Conjugal Futures

about developments in the area of LGBTQ rights – a highly sensitive topic – but in fact, our conversation moved between this and Malika's own personal background and trajectory (potentially no less sensitive) in interesting ways.

Born in Penang, a period studying abroad as an undergraduate had been instrumental in opening Malika's eyes to the politics of gender. Returning to her local university, she had felt very isolated: 'I came back ... and came out. I was very alone. I started working. There were no groups to join, so I thought, "I will do it myself"'. She described how she had 'started a small group' based in Penang. Although KL had its attractions with its larger LGBTQ community, 'I'm an island girl. I always felt a kinship with Penang'. She had started posting events online.

I wanted a space for people to comment; 'sober spaces' (no alcohol) – bring a dish; connect with people. Started a potluck, every week – to discuss. Four to five people, then 25, then it shrank – people moved away to KL.

Malika described how they had gone on to help organise a 'mini-festival on rights' with a local NGO with a focus on community building, and then a further one:

A whole day of workshops – talking about relationships in the community, long-term commitments, not knowing how to manage risks, social security, sickness – when a partner has no say. The workshops were really interesting. What does it mean to have a healthy relationship? There's lots of 'don't ask, don't tell'. Lots of husbands marry and are gay. Why? And who resists pressure? Who is the victim here? The wives. It leads to friction within the community. Men say they have to. Women say, 'you don't'. Why do men cave in more than women? Men have more freedom and more social mobility – definitely, there's an imbalance.

In spite of her downbeat assessment of political developments in Malaysia, Malika seemed more optimistic about the long-term prospects for gay rights.

Marriage and the Moral Imagination

For me, it's predictable. With the advent of the internet, the younger generation are pushing for more liberalisation. Even Malays. [Those who are] urban, progressive. But there's a lot of silence. The loudest voices are traditionalists, nationalists.

In the meantime, she thought the government would be caught between its more progressive leanings and these 'traditionalist' elements: 'They're trying to court both sides – the liberal progressives and nationalist Muslims'.

After some further conversation about the recent elections of 2018, current politics and likely future developments in Malaysia, Malika told me more about her own personal story. What she understood to be unusual was the support she had received from her mother, to which she gave due recognition:

My mother was always very supportive. I came out to my mother ... Father was less so. I wrote him a letter – which he's never referred to. Most women are more accepting than men. Because masculinity for men – they want sons to be masculine. My experience in Malaysia is very, very rare – to have supportive parent(s).

As Malika recounted, for her mother, this support was inseparable from concerns about the political risks entailed in her daughter's involvements:

My mother was very worried when I got involved in activism – worried about me getting arrested. Mum came to the workshop about healthy relationships. A lot of people were very happy that a supportive parent was there. One woman came with a nine-year old child. Someone said, 'You're a good parent, to bring a child'.

Here we get a sense not just of how personal experience through having a child who comes out may have an impact on parental attitudes to sexuality, leading to less conservative views, but also how this may lead to further community engagements. Significantly, the gendered nature of kin support as well as the perceived importance of masculinity to male personhood suggests this is more likely to occur between and through female relatives than male ones.

When I asked Malika about the possibility of same-sex marriage in the future in Malaysia, or whether marriage abroad might offer any alternative to that, she replied,

Marriage abroad has no legal standing here. My mum asks, 'Will you marry?' 'Will you have children?' Can't adopt here. For her, family means blood. Can't marry here. Commitment ceremonies – people still use the term 'marriage'. The organising is very hush-hush. I've never been to one. Can be in a hotel. Could be a very LGBT family – the hotel owners. Or people just say, 'It's a party'. People can call and complain. So far, the ones I've heard of, there's not been much backlash. Except one Chinese one towards a Chinese newspaper, which published a positive article. Nationalist fundamentalists got hold of it. There was a backlash. In terms of going abroad – lots can't afford that. Unless you elope – if you want a small ceremony. The options in Southeast Asia are not many. The nearest is Taiwan.

This response indicated the unlikeliness of same-sex marriage becoming a realistic prospect in Malaysia for the foreseeable future. But it also suggested that, in the familial context, its possibilities were not beyond the bounds of what could be articulated. Malika mentioned that one of her aunts had told other relatives in a cell phone text message that she was 'hoping for a "wedding"', accompanying this with photos of 'a very feminine one'. Beyond this, however, Malika saw the local activist scene as reflecting the conservatism of the wider context in Malaysia:

Their focus is on heterosexual marriage. They don't have systems to help trans people. They're not proactive. They know people who have knowledge; they don't want to open up within. So, they could support; they worry about losing their funding. Why not have bisexual or trans women? – They only have heterosexual women. Why not under the radar? It's the culture within them. In general, it's very trans/homophobic. They're not willing to be more inclusive.

Marriage and the Moral Imagination

In Malika's view, this conservatism was partly due to the age structure of development and feminist organisations in which positions of authority tended to be taken by older women. But beyond this, as she noted and we saw in Chapter 2, there were undoubtedly severe political constraints on the activities of such organisations (see Maznah 2020; Peletz 2023).

Malika made acute observations on oppositions between progressives versus traditionalists, a younger generation versus an older one and the gendered nature of attitudes and behaviour. In terms of gender, fathers were seen as likely to be less supportive and progressive towards gay offspring than mothers, and gay men were more likely to 'hide' in heterosexual marriages causing their wives to become victims of their attempts to conceal (Boellstorff 1999). But what is also striking here is how family ties may both reinforce and undercut these binaries. In her own family, as Malika related, women in a senior generation – her mother and an aunt – not only backed the non-normative stance of their younger relative, but they also took this progressive position into public or semi-public contexts. As she indicated, this was highly unusual. More commonly, gay and bisexual people experience considerable pressure from their families to conform to heterosexual norms and are likely never to come out to their parents or to do so only in veiled terms that can be bypassed or ignored. But as in other accounts of marriage in this book, and as is evident in Phyllis Rose's account of George Eliot's union with George Henry Lewes, the 'exceptional' may nevertheless be indicative of points of pressure to social norms or changes that might alter conjugal possibilities in the future.

Legislative Reform and the Public Sphere

My conversation with Malika was a pointed reminder of the entwinement of personal experiences of intimacy with political life – whether at the local, community level, that of larger-scale activism or in terms of national politics in Malaysia. Whereas discussions of marriage in anthropological literature, with some notable exceptions (see, for example, Mody 2008), tend to focus on one or other of these arenas, all of them figured strongly in Malika's account. This rendering 'from the margins' is particularly suggestive of the myriad interconnections at play in the transforming landscape of marriage and conjugality. Carla Jones's (2023) perceptive rendition of the surprising marriage of Dita, an activist friend, in Indonesia (which bears many cultural similarities with Malaysia) provides a telling example here. Jones describes how Dita, brought up in a middle-class family in Yogyakarta, by parents who participated in an earlier generation of activism in the 1990s, first married a fellow student when she was in her twenties, but when she discovered his infidelity while she was pregnant, her parents immediately filed for divorce in a religious court on her behalf, and in due course she was awarded custody of her daughter. Instead of retiring to a life of single motherhood, Dita proceeded to further education, including a master's degree in Europe and further postgraduate study in the US, while her parents and other members of her family supported her by looking after her daughter. Returning to Indonesia, she took up again an involvement in activist politics and, at the age of thirty-nine and more than fifteen years after her divorce, on forming a special bond with a fellow activist, embarked on a second marriage, having resisted such a possibility on previous occasions. The question that Jones poses is why did she do so? The answer, she suggests, lies in the kinds of intimacy and care generated through activism in Indonesia, and the new kinds of companionate marriage that result, encompassing alternative visions of the future (see also Freeman 2020). Dita's second 'aberrant marriage' was not a conventional one – it was based not on being a 'normal wife', or simply setting up a home together, but on shared political commitments, with Dita continuing her professional life as an activist, and she and her husband moving between three dispersed marital locations.

Marriage and the Moral Imagination

Several elements of Dita's story echo those presented here. First, the importance of parental and other family support during and in the aftermath of divorce is crucial (Jones 2023, 200), and also recalls the circumstances of Rashidah discussed in Chapter 4. Second, it is worth noting the transmission of political ideals or social stances from one generation to the next – another feature that marks some of the marital stories I became familiar with. And third, the continuities between Dita's personal life and her political activism echo those of several of the protagonists in this chapter, including Malika. While marriage in Jones's account could be a 'political act of optimism' (2023, 210), the narratives in this chapter (as well as Dita's story) show how it can also furnish negative models that propel protagonists towards activism. As discussed in Chapter 2, I interviewed a number of lawyers and activists whose work directly concerned marriage. The questions I put to them were directed at eliciting perspectives on legal and political changes and how these might affect marriage rather than on their own intimate experiences. Nevertheless, even here, and after the fact as it were, when I looked back through my notes, I could find traces of the personal threaded through these conversations.

An interview with Sakina, a staff member of a Muslim feminist activist organisation in 2019, ranged over the many obvious areas that impinged directly on marriage – current political developments, a proposed Gender Equality Act, child marriage, a recent women's march in Kuala Lumpur, LGBT rights, the Islamic legal framework governing marriage and inheritance, religious conversion, polygyny and domestic violence – among other issues.[4] Echoing Malika's views of activist organisations, as Sakina saw things, it seemed unlikely that LGBT rights would be the new government's first priority for reform:

---

[4] For accounts of Muslim feminist activism in Malaysia – particularly Sisters in Islam – and the backlashes against such movements, see Lee (2010); Liow (2009); Moustafa (2018); Norani (2005); Norani et al. (2008); Peletz (2020b, 21–25, 222–23; 2023).

7 Imagining Conjugal Futures

Which area might be first for reform? Not LGBT – just to be given constitutional rights; non-discrimination, freedom from persecution. Not demanding to be recognised as separate sexuality, or same-sex marriage. We're aware they're not ready. The government is worried that the question will be brought up in relation to gender equality even. They're worried that they may be seen as acknowledging that LGBT exists.

If new laws surrounding same-sex relations were not on the immediate horizon, possibly gender equality for women might be the first of these issues for legislative reform: 'we hope it will move', she said. But even this was unlikely to be the new government's top priority: 'Politicians just concentrate on how to maintain power; getting a two-thirds majority, winning the next election – it's very worrying', she said. Discussing the contradictory tensions between Islamic conservatism, as manifested in recent events in the east coast state of Kelantan (see Chapter 2), and a more progressive agenda for women's rights, in a context of rapidly shifting political alignments, Sakina speculated,

How things will develop? I don't know. There's a view that the Malays' Islamic culture is under threat…Things are really shifting. But it's a change that had to happen. It couldn't have stayed in the situation we were in before. There's more speaking out; checks and balances… There's a concern that it will go to violence. The Islamic fundamentalists promote violence. That's a real worry.

From the perspective of her organisation, there was a disjuncture for Muslim women between their situation at home and at work.

Looking at the division between private and public space, a lot of women we talk to feel very disempowered at home; empowered at work. They feel they have rights at work. At home there's a different view of rights. They see the differences but don't see it as a right to be treated equally. We're at a crossroads where women feel they have a right to be equal. The issue of obedience and submission has become very central to marriage. It's an issue of how they're taught and what.

Marriage and the Moral Imagination

While (non-Muslim) Malika viewed the younger generation as a progressive hope, in Sakina's view, among Muslims, the younger generation was a regressive force:

The younger generation are very different on religion. Very rules-bound, different, on halal and haram… they won't leave it to their own judgement.

This understanding, that a younger generation of Muslims was more conservative than their seniors, accords with scholarly accounts of the changing nature of Islamic jurisdictions and legal institutions in Malaysia over the past several decades (see Maznah 2020; Peletz 2020b; 2023). The resulting growing divergence between Muslims and non-Muslims is replicated for Muslims in this scenario by oppositions between home and work, women and men:

We know women who aren't able to study. Their husbands say, 'Your place is at home'. Women are getting more empowered. But men are not moving in the same direction. It's not always their fault. They are thinking 'Islam requires me to have authority'. Very few Malay men are househusbands.

The disjuncture between home and work, depicted as being experienced particularly acutely by Muslim women, expressed a growing divergence between the latter and their non-Muslim contemporaries. We might pause here, however, to note that, indirectly, we have in fact encountered Malay househusbands earlier in this book, for example, the husband of Dr Hasnah in Chapter 3 and of Wahidah in Chapter 5. Although quite probably rare, there seem to be some men who take such non-normative positions in their own marriages. Sakina concluded, switching gears to her own life, 'It starts with the family. I have two children – a girl and a boy. It's a work in progress'. She went on to note the difficulties she had encountered in educating her children in the Malaysian state school system, which takes a conservative line on gender issues when it comes to Muslim school students. Here Sakina echoed the views of other reformist-minded Muslims (as well as non-Muslims) I met – including

7 Imagining Conjugal Futures

Alicia whose account begins this chapter who had found school teaching particularly constraining – who saw the education system as a main inculcator of a retrogressive version of Islam and patriarchal values and an obstacle to reform.

I omitted to ask Sakina much about her own personal history; it seemed beyond the bounds of how this interview had been set up. But placing her account side by side with that of Malika, we can find both echoes and divergences between them. Both spoke from a feminist standpoint; both painted the current political picture in Malaysia in broadly similar terms. One was a non-Muslim, the other Muslim; one was unmarried and a self-declared lesbian, the other had children and did not spontaneously mention her own marriage. But crucially, both drew connections between their own experiences and the wider public sphere, and beyond what goes on in houses and families, to the politics of Malaysia.

I interviewed another experienced organiser in a different civil society activist group a few weeks after my meeting with Sakina. When I asked Sharon about what she saw as the most important issues surrounding marriage, she began, 'From my point of view, [it is] the differences in personal laws – Muslim and not-Muslim – with quite different implications'. Briefly referring to other issues, the 'multiple burdens' affecting women, including family, childcare and labour force participation, she noted that, in Penang particularly, issues of class and ethnicity were important. Both of these were associated with further divergences, for example, age at marriage, although she noted that the stigma of later marriage had been gradually receding in recent times. But this was less the case for Malays, Sharon asserted. The strict penalties for intimacy between members of the opposite sex who are not married to each other (khalwat) in Muslim law meant that Muslims were likely to marry younger to avoid this (see Chapters 5 and 6). In her view, this in turn led to a higher divorce rate and less stigma for divorce.

Marriage and the Moral Imagination

The big division for marriage is between Muslims and non-Muslims, and conversion is necessary. It's hugely problematic, and flows into everything, for example, treatment of corpses – how to bury. There are socio-legal implications.

In Sharon's articulation, these difficulties were likely to be compounded if there were also class differences between spouses. This observation seemed to draw partly on her own familial experiences as she followed it up by stating,

My family has quite a few mixed marriages. But both [partners are] Catholic – Indian-Chinese, so there's less gap around religion. Two married Germans [in the] older generation, less happy. Education level also influences attitudes.

From here, she went on to speak of other issues, including child marriage and the problems of instituting reform because of the regulation of syariah law by states in Malaysia's federal system. Like others I spoke to in 2019, Sharon was not optimistic about the prospects for reform under the current government:

[We're] very baffled and disappointed by the new government. The PM set out a directive against child marriage. Selangor and Penang are following it but not the other states. Syariah law is under state jurisdiction. They tiptoe around Malay-Muslim sensibilities. They're worried about losing their votes. I am wondering if it makes much of a difference – if the half-measures they're doing will satisfy anyone.

With fractures beginning to appear in the new government, there were, in her view,

A lot of concerns for the future. Not sure how far we're getting with Malay Muslims. Two by-elections have been lost. We've not gotten out of the race rut. The election win [in 2018] was only because of Mahathir. Attitudes are changing slowly.

7 Imagining Conjugal Futures

While she perceived Chinese attitudes to marriage as focused on the economic and more pragmatic, with views on cohabitation 'loosening', Sharon suggested that Malays were becoming more conservative:

There are very few women who have their hair uncovered. Women talk about 'permissive' or 'supportive' husbands who 'give permission'.

The perceptions Sharon articulated could in some ways be broadly aligned with those of Sakina and Malika, although the concerns were focused a little differently. Notably, there had been little mention of same-sex equality or gay rights until towards the end of our conversation, when she stated,

There's a huge backlash on LGBT coming. The Minister of Religion is a former PAS person. And he threatened organisers of the Women's March for sedition because of their support for LGBT. LGBT is a peripheral issue for lots of people.

This understanding, which could be seen as echoing the majority view in Malaysia, was, however, followed up with a reference to a recent performance for a prize at a literary festival in George Town:

The participant who won was a young Indian gay guy, who spoke about his first kiss. He got a lot of support from the audience. And a Malay girl with a very bold piece. Young people's attitudes are changing. Travel and technology changes social relations among the young.

Sharon's comments here on the linked issues of marriage, the current political situation and the prospects for gender equality legislation seemed to focus on two oppositions in particular – that between Muslims and non-Muslims and between heterosexual and same-sex relations. Both of these were seen as intractable, and this might partly be because of the entanglements between them. Discussion of marriage in her articulations, led directly to the distinction between Muslims and non-Muslims, which, as we saw in Chapter 5, is the single most salient difference when it comes to mixed marriages. Interestingly, class here is seen as amplifying other distinctions rather than constituting a fundamental line of fracture, and here Sharon drew on her own familial experiences. Because of the categorical requirement of conversion for non-Muslims who marry Muslims, ethnicity is perceived through the lens of religion, but Islam is salient to a different degree than other religions. As Sharon commented, this issue 'flows into everything'.

As Sharon saw things, while non-Muslims were becoming more liberal in their attitudes to cohabitation and sexuality, Muslims were moving in the opposite direction and becoming more conservative. The differences between Muslims and non-Muslims thus encompassed other attitudes and distinctions, including perceptions about LGBTQ rights. Exactly as Malika had suggested was the case, these were seen as quite peripheral to mainstream concerns, politically risky and thus off-limits for many civil society or activist organisations.

Cutting across this rather monolithic view of the likely limits and obstructions to liberalisation, however, as with Malika and Sakina, there was, for Sharon, a chink of possible light afforded by differences between generations. Young people were understood to be changing more than their elders, and this was partly a matter of the new experiences afforded by travel and technology. This generational shift might yet have the momentum to upend any simple narrative about gender relations in Malaysia.

Conclusion

This chapter has problematised a too-easily assumed boundary between the personal and the political. Feminists have long understood that the personal is political. But the question here is how is it so? We began with experiences of difficult marital scenarios in a parental generation, which apparently seep into the attitudes of adult offspring making them hesitant or reluctant to marry. In line with current trends in Malaysia and elsewhere, increasingly, marriages may be delayed or avoided altogether.

7 Imagining Conjugal Futures

Here, 'non-marriage' hovers suggestively between being a transitory phase in a personal biography and a more political stance. This is also a gendered story that connects to the changing educational and employment opportunities for women discussed in Chapters 1 and 3, and it is indicative that the narratives presented here have been those of women. If marriages are fundamentally gendered relations of power and also an imaginative terrain of possibility, it might not be surprising to find that the work of reimagining their ethical contours over recent decades has primarily been undertaken by those who have been historically less empowered – women.[5]

Parallel with the suggestive ways in which we have observed the experiences of one generation refracted in those of the subsequent one, we have also seen how familial stories flow into community activities and organisations, and into national movements for change. Those who become involved in counselling, community organising or activism are often motivated by their personal or familial experiences. The accounts they give of marriage or gendered relations draw on their personal lives. This is not to suggest in any simple or facile way that the family is the crucible of wider politics. I did not explicitly set out to question professional representatives of civil society organisations about their personal lives, but I was struck nonetheless by how they drew on these experiences in their answers to my broader questions about marriage or the current political context in Malaysia. This echoes Doreen Lee's account of how Indonesian political activism 'bridges public and private domains, and individual and collective memories' (2016, 3). The personal, for those I interviewed, was part of the material through which judgements, evaluations and social imaginaries of the future were drawn and extrapolated.

---

[5] See Carla Jones (2004) for a pertinent discussion of the toll of 'emotion work' undertaken by middle-class Javanese wives and maids in Yogyakarta as part of their domestic labour.

Marriage and the Moral Imagination

In Penang, the circles in which people moved could be tightly drawn. Some of those whom I interviewed about their marriages turned out to volunteer for community or civil society organisations that worked and campaigned for women's development or political change on gender issues. Some took a courageous and public stance to promote the transformation of gendered relations. When marriages broke down, some, like Rashidah whom we met in Chapter 4, contacted such organisations for advice about their rights under Muslim law. Thus, the avenues of communication between personal experience and overt political struggle were open and potentially expansive.

These entangled trajectories of personal, familial, communal and national life touch on gender relations, marital rights, child marriage, conversion, polygyny, divorce and LGBTQ rights – among other issues – all of which, as we saw in Chapter 2, are matters of intense public concern in Malaysia. Significantly, they are highly amenable to being framed in moral terms; often it seems impossible to avoid doing so. We observed in Chapter 2 how such issues surfaced conspicuously at a moment of unprecedented political change in 2018–19. During this period, one might say that the future of marriage appeared more than usually a matter for public debate – as it was at the time that George Eliot wrote her novels when Victorian Britain became so preoccupied with the 'marriage question'. To put this another way, marriage was a locus that condensed the moral and the political as perceived through different ethnic, religious, gendered or communal lenses.

At the beginning of this chapter, I cited Phyllis Rose's (2020) work on five exceptional British nineteenth-century literary marriages, including that of George Eliot, and Sheila Heti's apt summary of her insights: 'imagination is the glue' (Heti 2020, xiii). Bringing together imagination and ethical or moral evaluation, not as bounded or exceptional processes, but as woven through experiences of marriage and conjugality, has allowed us to cast marriage in a particular light. To see it as a process that inherently involves the absorption of the new, and with a consequent potential

7 Imagining Conjugal Futures

for innovation, focuses our attention on the creative and transformative potential of marriage. We have observed how social differences may expand the imaginative capacities of marriage and also how transformation may not necessarily correlate with generations in a linear fashion. In Chapter 3, we saw that generations may nevertheless provide a way to understand and mark changes to conjugality. Imagination and ethical engagement, working through the terrain of everyday experience, bind the two protagonists of a marriage just as they bind the personal to the wider social landscape, sometimes spilling over into community organising or political activism. And here it is worth noting how negative experiences of marriage, as in the case of Dita described by Carla Jones (2023), in one's own or in a previous generation, may exert a special emotional power in reformulating ethical visions of marriage.

What the future of marriage might hold could be articulated through a number of familiar and sometimes mutually reinforcing binaries from the Malaysian social landscape: between Muslims and non-Muslims, traditionalists and progressives, Malays and non-Malays, old and young, home and work, rural and urban, men and women and heterosexual and LGBTQ relations. The overlapping or cross-cutting intersections between the conventional juxtapositions of Malaysian sociality seemed to intimate that, while for some, gender relations were moving in a direction of greater equality, for a large section of the population, the reverse might be the case. The disturbing nature of this second trajectory inhered both in the seemingly retrograde direction of unfolding political developments as seen from a feminist or liberal standpoint and in the manner in which it countered the ethical reimagination of marriage and gendered relations on which this was based. It thus challenged assumptions about the linear and progressive forward march of history – as is the case in other parts of the world too.

Imagination may have disruptive effects. Complicating, and perhaps destabilising, understandings of where current developments might lead, we have encountered suggestive exceptions to normative patterns. As well as increasing trends towards delayed marriage or non-marriage among Muslims and non-Muslims, we have accounts of Malay house-husbands and a mother and an aunt publicly supporting the non-normative sexuality of their younger relative. Carla Jones's nuanced depiction of a female activist's marital trajectory in Indonesia as 'a quiet but radical expression of hope' (Jones 2023, 201) that 'could also expand the boundaries of "normal" to include novel forms of family' (2023, 210) is suggestive here. In terms of social attitudes, perhaps the least determined of the oppositions articulated in this chapter might be that between an older and a younger generation. The young have an enhanced capacity to trigger novel and unpredicted social scenarios, upending the plans and visions of their parents. These unstable qualities extend the possibilities and attributes of youth as a category, making it a 'social shifter', in Deborah Durham's (2004) evocative phrase.[6] Here too, negative experiences might exercise a propulsive force. In such unanticipated and evolving scripts, prompted by the stimulus of their offspring and the emotional and material investments of parenthood, occasionally, members of an older generation may find themselves taking stances they could hardly have foreseen. Differences between old and young, parents and adult children, can thus sometimes double-back or be erased in surprising ways. Here imagination may be harnessed retrospectively to reassess earlier moral standpoints and judgements so that paths of transformation are not simply linear or unidirectional. Through their uncertain intersections with the categorical distinctions of wider social life, generational discontinuities can thus precipitate new and unexpected turns in the established scripts of marriage.

---

[6] As Durham points out in the context of her material on Botswana, understanding what 'youth' represents means unpicking the space of youth within a wider social imaginary. 'In arguing over the space of youth, people argue over the nature of their social lives, bringing together historical shifts and new projects, to address issues of power, personhood, and moral agency' (Durham 2004, 601). One could say something quite similar here for marriage.

Conclusion

'There is something dazzling about marriage – that leap into the open-endedness of another human being. It is difficult to look directly at it, difficult to think that thought'. Thus begins Clare Carlisle's own dazzling philosophical enquiry into the life of George Eliot, *The Marriage Question: George Eliot's Double Life*. Where Carlisle comments that 'marriage is rarely treated as a philosophical question' (2024, xi), we might say that, although marriage has been an anthropological question seemingly forever, anthropologists have often somehow failed to do it justice. Concentrating on its structural and social correlates, they have tended to lose sight of its most obvious, personal attributes – failing to keep the familial and intimate facets of marriage in view beside the structural patterns. They have thus struggled to convey how it is in the conjunction of broader, social and historical norms with personal, intimate qualities that marriage becomes a unique and startling institution – a creative, ethical, imaginative and transformative endeavour, as well as a conventional and conservative one. Transformative and conservative aspects of marriage are in continuous tension, layered through time and generations as they are lived by families and communities and forged too in the crucible of religious, legal and state institutions.

I have found it impossible to convey what marriage is without reference to specifics – the specifics of time, people and place – in this case,

Marriage and the Moral Imagination

Penang, through the eyes and words of those who live there. This of course is a classic anthropological dilemma: how to trace the broad contours and questions while simultaneously paying adequate attention to locally distinctive phenomena. Or, to reverse the problem, how to do justice to the minutiae of familial and communal experience while not losing sight of the wider, underlying questions. Because of its very nature as at once a most intimate, personal and structured social phenomenon, marriage somehow makes this tension palpable.

In Chapter 1, I sketched what might have seemed a far-fetched analogy between marriage and anthropology. It hinged on the idea of both as close-up encounters with difference or with the unexpected. Both anthropological encounters and marital ones thicken – or break – with time. One becomes a different self in marriage – and in long-term fieldwork. Anthropologists, like spouses, may struggle against the constraints of their situation or with the conventions and ethics of how their encounters should be lived. Immersion in an unfamiliar social world for research, like marriage, can sometimes feel suffocating. One may struggle to find ways to translate one's own experience in a culturally appropriate and authentic manner to those one meets during fieldwork, aiming for something close to the 'truth'. This too has its parallels in marriage where spouses are continually faced with the difficulties of knowing, imagining or understanding each other's thoughts, feelings and experiences. How then to render the other's experience adequately, how to avoid telling untruths? This is the subject of many novels (George Eliot's *Middlemarch* among them), as is the notorious difficulty of knowing or understanding a marriage from the outside. The ethical quandaries, as well as the imaginative challenges, of marriage and anthropology seem, in the end, to have much in common. I find they have drawn me in through the writing of this book.

What do the narratives I have presented in this book, given at particular historical moments and from particular standpoints, tell us about what marriage does, the processes it enfolds and their wider

Conclusion

implications? In the Introduction, I referred to two women, Lydia and Haryath, whose 'marital accounts' seemed to resonate with the themes in this book. Lydia's story brought together the most intimate aspects of marriage and family life with the geopolitical events of the Cold War and the Malayan Emergency, which precipitated her father's arrival in late-colonial Malaya as part of his national service. Rather than assuming that personal and familial life is simply encompassed and dominated by the state, I referred to McKinnon and Cannell's (2013a) argument that the apparent subordination of kinship to politics is an effect of persuasive ideologies of modernity. In actuality, kinship and marriage have a propensity to exceed and sometimes to evade the controlling measures of the state (Carsten et al. 2021; Lambek 2013).

Marriage is at once a widespread and a culturally and historically specific phenomenon, and this is part of its broad sociological interest. Marriages take place in history and in local cultural contexts even as they may participate in, or buck, global trends. These characteristics are reflected in the accounts given in this book. What makes the marriages depicted here seem especially Malaysian or – to focus more locally – particular to Penang? What do they tell us, not only about these locales, but about marriage in other places? The conjunction of languages, ethnicities and familial migration histories in Haryath and Lydia's accounts is telling. In Chapter 1, I outlined how the history of Penang has resulted in a remarkably diverse population in terms of its historical antecedents and ethnic, linguistic and religious composition. To a social scientist concerned with processes of cultural separation and mixing – social transformation in other terms – Penang could be seen as a veritable laboratory of such interactions (see Carsten 2019a). But these are also ubiquitous global processes. Marriage is perhaps one of the most obvious and familiar ways in which a constant simultaneous movement of demographic incorporation and differentiation occurs. It requires its principal protagonists, their family members and communities, to make accommodations and adjustments to new elements introduced into their worlds. The results of these changes may be small and gradual and, from the perspectives of the main actors, of personal rather than political significance.

We have gained some insight into how individual marriages are experienced and absorbed by spouses and by their families. We have also acquired a sense of how marriage reverberates down the generations of families and into larger communities – once again, these are both widespread and particular phenomena. Lydia's recital instantiated how vividly people may recall the marriages of their parents and grandparents and how marriage in one generation between those of very different backgrounds set a course for further cosmopolitan exchange. As Haryath made clear by indicating the unhappy marriage of her sister, and as we have explored at various points, the marriages of relatives continue to constitute reference points and models, negative as well as positive, for relational behaviour sometimes long after the death of these ancestors. More immediately, the accounts of marital uncertainties and instability in Chapters 6 and 7 show how the adult children of unhappy or unsatisfactory marriages form their own attitudes and adjust their behaviour in the light of their experiences growing up. All of these are experiences that readers will be familiar with from their own lives or those of others they have witnessed.

Marital accommodations occur in the slipstream of other kinds of change. A tension between ever more sumptuous wedding celebrations and a critique of these as 'wasteful' or immoral was clearly articulated by many of those I spoke to and often seen as part of changing marriage patterns between generations. While one woman described hiring a horse-drawn carriage for her daughter's wedding, red carpets in driveways, drones taking photographs and a banquet with many hundreds of guests, others recalled their own much more modest occasions. Often, the extravagant celebrations of younger family members were heavily criticised by their older relatives. As Haryath told me:

Conclusion

I don't agree with spending a lot for weddings – it's a *waste*. Nowadays, the nieces and nephews spend very lavishly. There's a party for the engagement, a party at registration – a second one, *and* a temple marriage – to invite the whole community. [They] do *all* the great ones in Bollywood style.

There were many such comments articulated in varying religious or ethnic registers. They are echoed in accounts in the global media around the world that lament the increased materialism and cost of 'showy weddings' – at the same time as glamorizing them. The entanglements of class, wealth, ethnicity, generation, religion and morality here speak to the ways in which different 'marital topics' seemed impossible to separate as they ineluctably bled into each other. It is no surprise, then, to find that the personal, the political and the ethical merge in marriage, and that each of these aspects has the capacity to ineluctably generate others.

The most remarked-upon transformations, articulated by those to whom I listened, were changes in education and employment patterns for women, which again are threaded through the circumstances of Lydia and Haryath's families. These changes were seen as fundamentally affecting relations between husbands and wives over the course of recent decades, rendering women more independent and autonomous and reducing, for some at least, the patriarchal tenor of familial life. The lives of women such as Anna and Rashidah, portrayed in Chapter 4, who were of different generations, ethnicities and religions, reflect these expanding opportunities for women, and the changes in conjugality that accompanied them. They resonate with accounts from other parts of the world showing how new opportunities for women correlate with changes to conjugality (see, for example, Collier 2020; Davidson and Hannaford 2023). While marriage, crucially, was not the launchpad for the new kinds of lives forged by Anna or Rashidah – having embarked on successful careers before marrying – they both married foreigners, and their marital pathways, while conventional in some respects, also diverged in significant ways from those of their parents and familial backgrounds. We see here the plasticity and mutability of conjugal forms – marriage as contributing to, and the expression of, wider changes, but also how it may simultaneously reveal the limits of change.

Such 'modernising' tendencies are broadly in line with changes in many parts of the globe. Their conjunction in contemporary Malaysia with the rise of a more conservative Islam is interpreted, by some people at least, as limiting the possibilities open to women and expanding patriarchal expectations of family life. Different forms that modernity may take thus disrupt any simplistic reading of the progressive march of history and may impinge on women in unforeseen ways. As discussed in Chapter 2, the issue of 'child marriage' could be read by the colonial and post-colonial state, and in public discourse, as simultaneously 'immodern' (Lambek 2013) and as an attack on Islam in Malaysia. In such a potential clash of different visions of progress, there is opportunity for misunderstanding, discord and political strife. On a smaller and more local scale, and in the ebb and flow of processes of mixing and separation of ethnic, linguistic, religious and cultural elements in marriage that are described in Chapter 6, the differences least easy to accommodate in marriage are those between Muslim and non-Muslim spouses. Because of the way Islam in Malaysia is ethnically, legally and politically privileged as the majority religion of Malays, the requirement for non-Muslims who marry Muslims to convert, the ban on apostasy for Muslims, and the everyday effects of strictures over bodily and culinary practices in Islam, the prospect of marriage to a Muslim is likely to generate anxiety and concern in the parents and wider family of a non-Muslim spouse. While some families manage to accommodate these tensions relatively smoothly, in others, familial strains are still palpable many years after such a wedding has occurred. But the tensions and ambiguities of religious difference in relation to marriage are hardly restricted to Malaysia – the recent history of Northern Ireland, to take one example, shows how difficult it is for intimate relations to bridge the deep fractures of sectarian politics.

How these stories develop is embedded in histories of colonialism, migration and communal relations in Malaysia, as they are elsewhere.

Conclusion

These were evident in the circumstances that brought Lydia's and Haryath's antecedents to Malaya from China and India, respectively. They are thus part of national narratives and global flows as well as a more local 'Penang story' with its particularly dense landscape of cultural, religious and ethnic pluralism. Ethnographies are situated not just in localities but also in their own historical moments. The accounts of marriage highlighted here were collected at an exceptional juncture in Malaysian political life. The period 2018–19 was, for many, a time of unparalleled hope and expectation of political change, and this was probably especially true of Penang as a long-standing base of political opposition. The upsurge of open discussion and creative cultural events in George Town described in Chapter 2 seemed to express this heady atmosphere. It is hard to judge in what ways the more intimate accounts of marriage I recorded were directly inflected by the politics of the moment, and perhaps this is beside the point. In one way, we could view this simply as 'background' to conversations about marriage. But if we understand marriage to be a coming together of the intimate with the political, then there were clear indications in the directions conversations took that those I spoke to were reflecting not just on histories of marriage from their own experiences, but also on the past, present and possible futures of Malaysia. While the particular history of these political tensions may be specifically Malaysian, the broader contours of how gender relations and marriage refract such concerns, coalescing around moments of political change, are familiar too from other parts of the world. To take just one example, Fintan O'Toole's *We Don't Know Ourselves: A Personal History of Ireland Since 1958* (2021) is a wonderful and clear-eyed evocation of how deeply religion and politics may impregnate intimate gendered and familial relations and also shows how resistance to the entwined power of Church and state in Ireland has been generated through personal and familial lives.

In the accounts I listened to in Penang, reflections that alluded to the intersection of politics with intimate relations could be woven through

Marriage and the Moral Imagination

discussions about changing norms of conjugal relations over several generations of one family. They could be articulated in unusually outspoken debate – about a notorious case of religious conversion and subsequent abduction of a child or about LGBTQ rights. But they could also appear as unexpected offshoots of a conversation about marriage – an apparently chance reference to participation in (as opposed to avoidance of) the patriotic gestures expected for Merdeka (National) Day celebrations. Some recapitulations of history remained obscure or hidden, as with the two cases of child marriage discussed in Chapter 2, separated by many decades, but emerging at equally critical moments in the unfolding saga of the nation. Sometimes, conversations about marriage provided an entry point for understanding how families had been impacted by wider geopolitical events – the Japanese occupation of Malaya in World War Two or the Malayan 'Emergency' of 1948–60, as in Lydia's father's case. On other occasions, a national commemoration or anniversary sparked heart-stopping personal accounts of what had occurred during the widespread civil unrest of May 1969 – when proving oneself a Muslim – or not – could have been a matter of life or death. Such stories are not easily told, and, despite my familiarity with Malaysia over four decades, I was unused to hearing them. But of course the idea that families may, wittingly or not, silently pass over the personal impact of traumatic political events is all too familiar from twentieth-century European history as elsewhere.

Peaceful political turnarounds after many decades of government dominated by one political party or alliance of parties, as occurred in the Malaysian elections of 2018, are rare and might be expected to be followed by reversals. This has certainly been the case in Malaysia in the months and years since May 2018. The swift demise of the new government elected in 2018 was accompanied by widespread disillusion and disappointment, already prefigured in conversations and events I recorded early in 2019. What all of these conversations make evident is that marriage provided a lens through which national and local histories, as well as familial and personal ones, could be grasped and understood. This way of absorbing and accommodating change is not particular to Malaysia and is familiar from other parts of the world (see, for example, Chiu 2023). The 'cesurae' (Feuchtwang 2005) or 'critical events' (Das 1995) that mark History with a capital H are, for most people, experienced, remembered and made sense of through their own personal and familial lives (Carsten 2007).

But this book also shows something beyond this: the way that families themselves make history through marriage in a deeper and more gradual sense. Partly because of the small scale and gradual nature of familial change and because the everyday is, by definition, usually experienced as ordinary rather than momentous, we are unused to thinking of families as producing history in their everyday lives (see Carsten 1997; Gow 1991). It is politicians and activists who appropriate that terrain, co-opting the rhetorics of authority and power and taking responsibility and credit for political transformation. If we turn these apparently persuasive optics of modernity around, however, we can begin to see other processes at work.

Taking marriage as a 'vital conjuncture' (Johnson-Hanks 2002), we see how, through its continual introduction of new elements into familial life, it is in fact a fulcrum of change. This kind of change is a long, slow, incremental process without obvious direction or end points, and it is masked by the conventional forms of marriage. Adherence to continuity and convention is most apparent in the attention paid to the minutiae of wedding rituals and to material objects – both of which, as we saw in Chapter 4, are often sources of particular tension when a marriage is being organised or dissolved. A deceptive cloak of conformity thus belies the nature of marriage as a transformative institution (see Carsten et al. 2021) – a tension that Haryath vividly articulated when she spoke of 'running red lights' in her seemingly conventional marriage. Perhaps it should be no surprise that wedding rituals may be elaborated or expanded at times when marriage, as a relation and an institution, is perceived to be unstable, declining or evolving in uncertain or contradictory directions. But in times of upheaval as well as in political stasis, weddings may also provide a way to express or create change. Around the world, in the stoppages to social life of the COVID-19 pandemic, the deprivation of being unable to hold weddings was keenly expressed.

In the Introduction and in Chapter 7, I took up Phyllis Rose's (2020 [1983]) insights about marriage as an imaginative endeavour together with recent anthropological work on 'ordinary ethics' (Lambek 2010b) and discussions of the nature of the 'ordinary' (Das 2020). Bringing together ethics and imagination to understand the larger processes at work in marriage illuminates how, as they take place within singular lives, marriages are the subject of ethical reflection that is always comparative and occurs in a temporal flow. What is the import of such imaginative and ethical endeavour? In *Life and Words*, Veena Das considers 'the work of time' (2007, 79) in marriages that take place in the aftermath of extreme communal violence. A marriage enacted in the shadow of the violence of the Indian Partition silently enfolds the relational consequences of shattered lives in terms of honour and shame without being explicitly articulated. And the repercussions of this may be passed down the generations in subsequent marriages (Das 2007, 79–94). Time here,

is an agent that 'works' on relationships – allowing them to be reinterpreted, rewritten, sometimes overwritten – as different social actors struggle to author stories in which collectivities are created or recreated. (Das 2007, 87)

Das's subject is the enactment and absorption of violence in the everyday, and

the pattern that occurs with different variations in the weave of Punjabi life – in the interior of families and kinship groups. (Das 2007, 87)

Her attentiveness to time is pertinent here, as is her exploration of 'the experimentation with different voices and the different modalities in which narratives of families develop' (Das 2007, 87).

Conclusion

If time 'works' on relationships, as Das suggests, we might also ask how relationships 'work' on time (see Maqsood 2024): How do marriages allow the reconfiguration and reabsorption of time? In Lydia and Haryath's accounts and in the narratives of others reproduced in this book, we have seen how prospective marriages are assessed in the light of others that have gone before as well as current exemplars of 'good' or 'bad' marriages that loom large in actors' experience. These marriages were not lived in the kind of profound and violent communal rupture depicted by Das – although the backdrop in some cases, of the Japanese occupation of Malaya, the subsequent Emergency and Independence, was political upheaval of geopolitical scale. But, whatever the context, judgements about marital relations are inherently and simultaneously both ethical (in the sense that they entail comparative evaluations and preferences) and imaginative in that they are attempts to envision preferred or improved marital forms and scenarios and enter the life worlds of others. Their more modulated effects on ordinary lives are no less significant in terms of their conventional and exceptional aspects than those enacted under conditions of national fracture.

In Chapter 3, we encountered a woman whose sister had died suddenly in childhood, and who reflected on this through the prism of her parents' unhappy marriage and her own, and who considered the ethical possibility that it would be better, in terms of breaking the cycle of misery, if her children were not to marry. Some people, no doubt, do not think too deeply about, or are unused to articulating, how they would like their own conjugal relations or those of their children to evolve over the course of a marital life. But many people do give these matters at least fleeting or more consistent and overt attention. Clearly, many conventional assumptions are built into how marriages are solemnised and the forms that conjugal relations should take. But equally, in the course of this book, we have seen how people reflect on these matters as part of considering their own or their parents' or grandparents' life stories, or those of other consociates. In so doing, as Lydia's and Haryath's accounts revealed, they rearrange the elements of their own and others' lives, speculating on how things might have been different, or how they might yet be done differently.

In one way, such reflection is unexceptional – so much so that anthropologists have perhaps paid less attention than they should have to its implications. But this kind of comparative, ethical and imaginative endeavour, which is threaded through ordinary, everyday lives, can also be the crucible of more explicit political or community engagement. This was evident in the stories of some of the female activists recounted in Chapter 7 who have taken their own personal or familial experiences into the wider community to provide marital counselling so as to improve conjugal relations or to fight for gender equality or LGBTQ rights. In these ways, experiences of marriage can precipitate political or communal commitments and activist engagement. The fact that women were particularly prominent in such forms of activism is an outcome of the unequal, gendered relations of power that are embedded in marriage and family life as well as the changing economic and educational opportunities available to women in recent decades.

The small, everyday processes described here are thus at once 'ordinary' and 'exceptional'. They show how the ordinary can give rise to the exceptional and, conversely, how what is exceptional at one moment – such as an illicit or outlawed form of relationship – can, over time, perhaps over generations, come to be accepted and re-enfolded into a newly expanded form of the ordinary. However slow and incremental these forms of social change may be, they may, finally, precipitate new legal enactments that bring statutes into line with what is no longer anathema to parents or wider families, but instead have become acceptable, newly liveable kinds of relations.

This does not of course mean that change necessarily takes progressive forms. In Malaysia, as in many other parts of the world, liberalising measures have occurred at the same time as illiberal reforms. And it is unclear how these tensions will play out in the future. While many

Conclusion

middle-class families may become more accepting of LGBTQ relations in the near future, others seem unlikely to do so. Whether the attitudes of a broadly more liberal, middle-class, urban, multi-ethnic youth will prevail over the forces of conservative Islam is unknowable and perhaps one of the most crucial questions to the future of Malaysian politics. The results of the elections of 2018 suggested one kind of answer to this question, but unfolding events since then make any certain prognosis doubtful to say the least. Nor is Malaysia an unusual exception in this regard. In the US too, to take just one example, the presumed forward march of increasing liberalisation of personal and gendered relations has in recent years been put in question.

Political moments – like the lives of research participants – can only be captured midstream or in hindsight – without knowledge at the time of what will happen next. We have seen how marriage was a topic that afforded opportunities for a kind of imaginative 'time travel' in assessing life courses and relationships in the past, present and future (Carsten et al. 2021, 31; Shryock 2013). For those who were narrating conjugal relations in the present, there was always a sense of the incompleteness, the unfinished nature, of these accounts. Some narratives seemed to come to a halt at an arbitrary point where the question of what would happen next was left unresolved. A planned wedding, for which invitations had been sent out, subsequently turned out not to have occurred; a marital story later revealed a previously 'hidden' family member, shedding a quite different light on a family trajectory over generations. Seduced by this sense of the unfinished, and in search of sequelae, I often wished for further interviews and follow-up conversations. One small effect of the profound disruption introduced by the COVID-19 pandemic in 2020 was the forced recognition that completeness here was a mirage. If marriage involves expansions and contractions of patterns laid down in childhood – as well as some surprising divergences from those patterns – these are, by nature, contingent, ongoing and unfinished processes. What was striking about the

Marriage and the Moral Imagination

articulacy of Lydia and Haryath, and of others to whom I listened, was how engaged they were in reflecting on the comparative textures of conjugality over time. Attending to the implications of this engagement means considering how the ordinary and the everyday are embedded in history, how they can give rise to the exceptional and how they produce social transformation. This is why it matters to listen closely to 'the music of what happens'.[1]

---

[1] This is the closing phrase of Seamus Heaney's poem, 'Song', published in his collection *Field Work* (1979), a volume that accompanied me on my first rural fieldwork in Malaysia.

Bibliography

Abdul Rahman Embong. 2018. 'Ethnicity and Class: Divides and Dissent in Malaysian Studies'. *Southeast Asian Studies* 7 (3): 281–307.
Abeyasekera, Asha L. 2021. *Making the Right Choice: Narratives of Marriage in Sri Lanka*. New Brunswick, NJ: Rutgers University Press.
Ahmad Fauzi Abdul Hamid, and Zawawi Ibrahim. 2017. 'The Governance of Religious Diversity in Malaysia: Islam in a Secular State or Secularism in an Islamic State?' In *The Problem of Religious Diversity: European Challenges, Asian Approaches*, edited by Anna Triandafyllidou and Tariq Modood, 169–203. Edinburgh: Edinburgh University Press.
Anderson, Edward. 2015. '"Neo-Hindutva": The Asia House M. F. Husain Campaign and the Mainstreaming of Hindu Nationalist Rhetoric in Britain'. *Contemporary South Asia* 23 (1): 45–66.
Andrikopoulos, Apostolos, and Jan W. Duyvendak, eds. 2020. 'Migration, Mobility and the Dynamics of Kinship: New Barriers, New Assemblages'. *Ethnography* 21 (3): 299–318.
Aw, Tash. 2021. *Strangers on a Pier: Portrait of a Family*. London: 4th Estate.
Azman Azwan Azmawati. 2011. '"I Am Not Alone": Managing Singleness-Exploring Single Malay Muslim Women's Voices in Malaysia'. *Forum, Komunikasi* 9 (1): 1–16.
Barker, Joshua, Erik Harms, and Johan A. Lindquist, eds. 2014. *Figures of Southeast Asian Modernity*. Honolulu, HI: University of Hawaii Press.
Baxstrom, Richard. 2008. *Houses in Motion: The Experience of Place and the Problem of Belief in Urban Malaysia*. Stanford, CA: Stanford University Press.
Berlant, Lauren. 1998. 'Intimacy: A Special Issue'. *Critical Inquiry* 24 (2): 281–88.
Berlant, Lauren G. 2011. *Cruel Optimism*. Durham, NC: Duke University Press.
Blackwood, Evelyn. 2005. 'Wedding Bell Blues: Marriage, Missing Men, and Matrifocal Follies'. *American Ethnologist* 32 (1): 3–19.

Bibliography

Boellstorff, Tom. 1999. 'The Perfect Path: Gay Men, Marriage, Indonesia'. *GLQ: A Journal of Lesbian and Gay Studies* 5 (4): 475–509.
    2007. 'When Marriage Falls: Queer Coincidences in Straight Time'. *GLQ: A Journal of Lesbian and Gay Studies* 13 (2): 227–48.
Bonney, Rollin. 1971. *Kedah, 1771–1812; the Search for Security and Independence*. Kuala Lumpur: Oxford University Press.
Borneman, John. 1996. 'Until Death Do Us Part: Marriage/Death in Anthropological Discourse'. *American Ethnologist* 23 (2): 215–35.
    1997. 'Caring and Being Cared for: Displacing Marriage, Kinship, Gender and Sexuality'. *International Social Science Journal* 49 (154): 573–84.
Bouquet, Mary. 2001. 'Making Kinship, with an Old Reproductive Technology'. In *Relative Values: Reconfiguring Kinship Studies*, edited by Sarah Franklin and Susan McKinnon, 85–115. Durham, NC: Duke University Press.
Bourdieu, Pierre. 1977. *Outline of a Theory of Practice*. Cambridge Studies in Social Anthropology 16. Cambridge: University Press.
    1987. 'The Force of Law: Toward a Sociology of the Juridicial Field'. *The Hastings Law Journal* 38 (5): 805–53.
    2008. *The Bachelor's Ball: The Crisis of Peasant Society in Béarn*. Cambridge: Polity Press.
Brettell, Caroline B. 2017. 'Marriage and Migration'. *Annual Review of Anthropology* 46 (1): 81–97.
Bruner, Jerome S. 1987. 'Life as Narrative'. *Social Research* 54 (1): 11–32.
    1990. *Acts of Meaning*. The Jerusalem-Harvard Lectures. Cambridge, MA: Harvard University Press.
Buch, Elana D. 2018. *Inequalities of Aging: Paradoxes of Independence in American Home Care*. New York: New York University Press.
Butler, Judith. 2002. 'Is Kinship Always Already Heterosexual?' *Differences (Bloomington, Ind.)* 13 (1): 14–44.
Carlisle, Clare. 2024. *The Marriage Question: George Eliot's Double Life*. Milton Keynes: Penguin Random House.
Carsten, Janet. 1995. 'The Politics of Forgetting: Migration, Kinship and Memory on the Periphery of the Southeast Asian State'. *The Journal of the Royal Anthropological Institute* (NS) 1 (2): 317–35.
    1997. *The Heat of the Hearth: The Process of Kinship in a Malay Fishing Community*. Oxford: Clarendon Press.
    2000. '"Knowing Where You've Come from": Ruptures and Continuities of Time and Kinship in Narratives of Adoption Reunions'. *The Journal of the Royal Anthropological Institute* 6 (4): 687–703.
    2004. *After Kinship*. New Departures in Anthropology. Cambridge, UK: Cambridge University Press.

ed. 2007. *Ghosts of Memory: Essays on Remembrance and Relatedness*. Malden, MA: Blackwell.

2012. 'Fieldwork since the 1980s: Total Immersion and Its Discontents'. In *The SAGE Handbook of Social Anthropology*, edited by Richard Fardon, Olivia Harris, Trevor H. J. Marchand, Mark Nuttall, Veronica Strang, and Richard A. Wilson, 2: 7–20. London: SAGE.

2019a. *Blood Work: Life and Laboratories in Penang*. The Lewis Henry Morgan Lectures. Durham, NC: Duke University Press.

2019b. 'The Stuff of Kinship'. In *The Cambridge Handbook of Kinship*, edited by Sandra Bamford, 133–50. Cambridge: Cambridge University Press.

Carsten, Janet, Hsiao-Chiao Chiu, Siobhan Magee, Eirini Papadaki, and Koreen M. Reece, eds. 2021. *Marriage in Past, Present and Future Tense*. London: UCL Press.

Cashin, Sheryll. 2017. *Loving: Interracial Intimacy in America and the Threat to White Supremacy*. Boston, MA: Beacon Press.

Charsley, Katharine. 2012. *Transnational Marriage New Perspectives from Europe and Beyond*. New York: Routledge.

Charsley, Katharine, and Alison Shaw. 2006. 'South Asian Transnational Marriages in Comparative Perspective'. *Global Networks* 6 (4): 331–44.

Chaudhry, Shruti. 2021. *Moving for Marriage Inequalities, Intimacy, and Women's Lives in Rural North India*. Albany, NY: State University of New York Press.

Chee, Heng Leng, Gavin W. Jones, and Maznah Mohamad. 2009. 'Muslim-Non-Muslim Marriage, Rights and the State in Southeast Asia'. In *Muslim-Non-Muslim Marriage: Political and Cultural Contestations in Southeast Asia*, edited by Gavin W. Jones, Chee Heng Leng, and Maznah Mohamad, 1–30. Singapore: ISEAS-Yusof Ishak Institute.

Chiu, Hsiao-Chiao. 2023. *Visions of Marriage: Politics and Family on Kinmen, 1920–2020*. New York: Berghahn Books.

Clark-Decès, Isabelle. 2014. *The Right Spouse: Preferential Marriages in Tamil Nadu*. Stanford, CA: Stanford University Press.

Cole, Jennifer, and Lynn M. Thomas, eds. 2009. *Love in Africa*. Chicago, IL: The University of Chicago Press.

Collier, Jane Fishburne. 2020. *From Duty to Desire: Remaking Families in a Spanish Village*. Princeton, NJ: Princeton University Press.

Constable, Nicole. 2003. *Romance on a Global Stage: Pen Pals, Virtual Ethnography, and 'Mail Order' Marriages*. Berkeley, CA: University of California Press.

2010. *Cross-Border Marriages: Gender and Mobility in Transnational Asia*. Philadelphia, PA: University of Pennsylvania Press.

Bibliography

2015. 'Migrant Motherhood, "Failed Migration", and the Gendered Risks of Precarious Labour'. *Trans-Regional and -National Studies of Southeast Asia* 3 (1): 135–51.

Cruz, Resto. 2020. 'Siblingship beyond Siblings? Cousins and the Shadows of Social Mobility in the Central Philippines'. *The Journal of the Royal Anthropological Institute* 26 (2): 321–42.

Das, Veena. 1995. *Critical Events: An Anthropological Perspective on Contemporary India*. Delhi: Oxford University Press.

⸺ 2007. *Life and Words: Violence and the Descent into the Ordinary*. Berkeley, CA: University of California Press.

⸺ 2010. 'Engaging the Life of the Other: Love and Everyday Life'. In *Ordinary Ethics: Anthropology, Language, and Action*, edited by Michael Lambek, 376–99. New York: Fordham University Press.

⸺ 2018a. 'Ethics, Self-Knowledge, and Life Taken as a Whole'. *HAU Journal of Ethnographic Theory* 8 (3): 537–49.

⸺ 2018b. 'On Singularity and the Event: Further Reflections on the Ordinary'. In *Recovering the Human Subject: Freedom, Creativity and Decision*, edited by James Laidlaw, Barbara Bodenhorn, and Martin Holbraad, 53–73. Cambridge: Cambridge University Press.

⸺ 2020. *Textures of the Ordinary: Doing Anthropology after Wittgenstein*. New York: Fordham University Press.

Davidson, Joanna, and Dinah Hannaford, eds. 2023. *Opting Out: Women Messing with Marriage around the World*. Politics of Marriage and Gender: Global Issues in Local Contexts Series. New Brunswick, NJ: Rutgers University Press.

Day, Sophie. 2018. 'An Experiment in Story-telling: Reassembling the House in Ladakh'. *Social Anthropology* 26 (1): 88–102.

⸺ 2023. *Rendering Houses in Ladakh: Personal Relations with Home Structures*. London: Routledge.

De Waal, Edmund. 2011. *The Hare with Amber Eyes: A Hidden Inheritance*. London: Chatto & Windus.

Djamour, Judith. 1965. *Malay Kinship and Marriage in Singapore*. 2nd ed. London: Athlone Press.

Donner, Henrike. 2002. 'One's Own Marriage': Love Marriages in a Calcutta Neighbourhood'. *South Asia Research* 22 (1): 79–94.

⸺ 2016. 'Doing It Our Way: Love and Marriage in Kolkata Middle-Class Families'. *Modern Asian Studies* 50 (4): 1147–189.

Durham, Deborah. 2004. 'Disappearing Youth: Youth as a Social Shifter in Botswana'. *American Ethnologist* 31 (4): 589–605.

Bibliography

Empson, Rebecca. 2007. 'Enlivened Memories: Recalling Absence and Loss in Mongolia'. In *Ghosts of Memory: Essays on Remembrance and Relatedness*, edited by Janet Carsten, 58–82. Oxford, UK: Blackwell Publishing Ltd.

Evans-Pritchard, E. E. 1951. *Kinship and Marriage among the Nuer*. Oxford: Clarendon Press.

Faubion, James D., ed. 2001. *The Ethics of Kinship: Ethnographic Inquiries*. Lanham, MD: Rowman & Littlefield.

Ferrante, Elena. 2014. *Those Who Leave and Those Who Stay. Book Three of the Neapolitan Novels*. Translated by Ann Goldstein. New York: Europa Editions.

Feuchtwang, Stephan. 2005. 'Mythical Moments in National and Other Family Histories'. *History Workshop Journal* 59 (1): 179–93.

Firth, Rosemary. 1966. *Housekeeping among Malay Peasants*. London: Athlone Press.

Foong, Andrew L. S., and Eliza J. Y. Teoh. 2022. 'Multiethnic Intergenerational Perspectives on Interethnic Marriages in Peninsular Malaysia: The Challenge of Ethno-religionist Identity'. *International Social Science Journal* 72 (244): 403–22.

Fortes, Meyer. 1949. *The Web of Kinship among the Tallensi: The Second Part of an Analysis of the Social Structure of a Trans-Volta Tribe*. Oosterhout: Anthropological Publications.

Franklin, Sarah. 1997. *Embodied Progress: A Cultural Account of Assisted Conception*. London: Routledge.

Franklin, Sarah, and Susan McKinnon, eds. 2001. *Relative Values: Reconfiguring Kinship Studies*. Durham, NC: Duke University Press.

Freeman, Carla. 2020. 'Feeling Neoliberal'. *Feminist Anthropology* 1 (1): 71–88.

Fuller, C. J., and Haripriya Narasimhan. 2008. 'Companionate Marriage in India: The Changing Marriage System in a Middle-Class Brahman Subcaste'. *The Journal of the Royal Anthropological Institute* 14 (4): 736–54.

Gell, Alfred. 1992. *The Anthropology of Time: Cultural Constructions of Temporal Maps and Images*. Explorations in Anthropology. Oxford: Berg Publishers.

Giddens, Anthony. 1992. *The Transformation of Intimacy: Sexuality, Love and Eroticism in Modern Societies*. Cambridge: Polity Press.

Goh, Beng-Lan. 2002. 'Rethinking Modernity: State, Ethnicity, and Class in the Forging of a Modern Urban Malaysia'. In *Local Cultures and the 'New Asia': The State, Culture, and Capitalism in Southeast Asia*, edited by C. J. W.-L. Wee, 184–216. Singapore: Institute of Southeast Asian Studies.

——— 2018. *Modern Dreams: An Inquiry into Power, Cultural Production, and the Cityscape in Contemporary Urban Penang, Malaysia*. Ithaca, NY: Cornell University Press.

Bibliography

Gow, Peter. 1991. *Of Mixed Blood: Kinship and History in Peruvian Amazonia*. Oxford Studies in Social and Cultural Anthropology. Oxford: Clarendon Press.

Gupta, Charu. 2016. 'Allegories of "Love Jihad" and Ghar Vāpasī: Interlocking the Socio-Religious with the Political'. *Archiv Orientální* 84 (2): 291–316.

Hansen, Thomas Blom. 1999. *The Saffron Wave: Democracy and Hindu Nationalism in Modern India*. Princeton, NJ: Princeton University Press.

Harper, Tim, and Sunil S. Amrith. 2012. 'Sites of Asian Interaction: An Introduction'. *Modern Asian Studies* 46 (2): 249–57.

Heti, Sheila. 2020. 'Introduction'. In *Phyllis Rose, Parallel Lives: Five Victorian Marriages*, 2nd ed., ix–xvi. London: Daunt Books.

Hirsch, Jennifer S., and Holly Wardlow, eds. 2006. *Modern Loves: The Anthropology of Romantic Courtship and Companionate Marriage*. Ann Arbor: University of Michigan Press.

Hirschman, Charles. 1986. 'The Making of Race in Colonial Malaya: Political Economy and Racial Ideology'. *Sociological Forum* 1 (2): 330–61.

——— 1987. 'The Meaning and Measurement of Ethnicity in Malaysia: An Analysis of Census Classifications'. *The Journal of Asian Studies* 46 (3): 555–82.

Holst, Frederik. 2012. *Ethnicization and Identity Construction in Malaysia*. Abingdon: Routledge.

Humphrey, Caroline. 2018. 'Reassembling Individual Subjects: Events and Decisions in Troubled Times'. In *Recovering the Human Subject*, edited by James Laidlaw, Barbara Bodenhorn, and Martin Holbraad, 24–50. Cambridge: Cambridge University Press.

Hussin Nordin. 2005. 'Malay Press and Malay Politics: The Hertogh Riots in Singapore'. *Asia Europe Journal* 3 (4): 561–75.

Inhorn, Marcia C., and Nancy J. Smith-Hefner, eds. 2020. *Waithood: Gender, Education, and Global Delays in Marriage and Childbearing*. New York: Berghahn Books.

Jamieson, Lynn. 1998. *Intimacy: Personal Relationships in Modern Societies*. Cambridge: Polity Press.

Jamilah Ariffin. 1994. *Women & Development in Malaysia*. Rev. ed. Petaling Jaya: Pelanduk.

Jenkins, Gwynn. 2008. *Contested Space: Cultural Heritage and Identity Reconstructions: Conservation Strategies within a Developing Asian City*. Zurich: LIT Verlag Münster.

——— 2019. *Contested Space Revisited: George Town, Penang, before and after UNESCO World Heritage Listing*. Penang: Areca Books.

Johnson-Hanks, Jennifer. 2002. 'On the Limits of Life Stages in Ethnography: Toward a Theory of Vital Conjunctures'. *American Anthropologist* 104 (3): 865–80.

Bibliography

Jones, Carla. 2004. 'Whose Stress? Emotion Work in Middle-Class Javanese Homes'. *Ethnos* 69 (4): 509-28.
Jones, Carla. 2023. 'Not a Normal Wife: Marrying Activism and Aberrance in Indonesia'. In *Opting Out*, edited by Joanna Davidson and Dinah Hannaford, 199-212. Ithaca, NY: Rutgers University Press.
Jones, Gavin W. 1981. 'Malay Marriage and Divorce in Peninsular Malaysia: Three Decades of Change'. *Population and Development Review* 7 (2): 255-78.
Jones, Gavin W. 1994. *Marriage and Divorce in Islamic South-East Asia*. Singapore: Oxford University Press.
   2005. 'The "Flight From Marriage" in South-East and East Asia'. *Journal of Comparative Family Studies* 36 (1): 93-119.
   2007. 'Delayed Marriage and Very Low Fertility in Pacific Asia'. *Population and Development Review* 33 (3): 453-78.
   2009. 'Women, Marriage and Family in Southeast Asia'. In *Gender Trends in Southeast Asia*, edited by Theresa W. Devasahayam, 12-30. Singapore: Institute of Southeast Asian Studies.
   2021. 'Divorce in Malaysia: Historical Trends and Contemporary Issues'. *Institutions and Economies* 13 (4): 35-60.
Jones, Gavin W., Terence H. Hull, and Maznah Mohamad, eds. 2015. *Changing Marriage Patterns in Southeast Asia*. London and New York: Routledge.
Jones, Gavin W., and Tan Poo Chang. 1990. 'Malay Divorce in Peninsular Malaysia: The Near-disappearance of an Institution'. *Asian Journal of Social Science* 18 (1): 85-114.
Jones, Gavin W., and Tey Nai Peng. 2021. 'The Changing Marriage Institution in Malaysia'. *Institutions and Economies* 13 (4): 1-3.
Kahn, Joel S. 1992. 'Class, Ethnicity and Diversity: Some Remarks on Malay Culture in Malaysia'. In *Fragmented Visions: Culture and Politics in Contemporary Malaysia*, edited by Joel S. Kahn and Francis Loh Kok Wah, 158-78. Honolulu, HI: University of Hawaii Press.
   2006. *Other Malays: Nationalism and Cosmopolitanism in the Modern Malay World*. Singapore: NUS Press.
Kahn, Joel S., and Francis Loh Kok Wah, eds. 1992. *Fragmented Vision: Culture and Politics in Contemporary Malaysia*. Sydney: Allen and Unwin, Asian Studies Association of Australia.
Kahn, Susan Martha. 2000. *Reproducing Jews: A Cultural Account of Assisted Conception in Israel*. Durham, NC: Duke University Press.
Karim, Wazir-Jahan. 1992. *Women and Culture: Between Malay Adat and Islam*. Boulder, CO: Westview Press.
   1995. *Male and Female in Developing Southeast Asia*. Oxford: Berg Publishers.
   2021. 'In Body and Spirit: Redefining Gender Complementarity in Muslim Southeast Asia'. In *Discourses, Agency and Identity in Malaysia*, edited by

Bibliography

Zawawi Ibrahim, Victor T. King, and Gareth Richards, 105–25. Singapore: Springer Singapore.

Keane, Webb. 2024. *Animals, Robots, Gods: Adventures in the Moral Imagination*. Milton Keynes: Allen Lane.

Kessler, Clive S. 1992. 'Archaism and Modernity: Contemporary Malay Political Culture'. In *Fragmented Visions: Culture and Politics in Contemporary Malaysia*, edited by Joel S. Kahn and Francis Loh Kok Wah, 133–57. Sydney: Asian Studies Association of Australia.

Khoo, Salma Nasution. 2007. *Streets of George Town, Penang*. 4th ed. Penang: Areca Books.

King, Victor T. 2021. 'Culture and Identity on the Move: Malaysian Nationhood in Southeast Asia'. In *Discourses, Agency and Identity in Malaysia*, edited by Zawawi Ibrahim, Gareth Richards, and Victor T. King, 23–57. Singapore: Springer Singapore.

King, Victor T., Gareth Richards, and Zawawi Ibrahim. 2021. 'Introduction'. In *Discourses, Agency and Identity in Malaysia*, edited by Gareth Richards, Victor T. King, and Zawawi Ibrahim, 1–19. Singapore: Springer Singapore.

Kowalski, Julia. 2024. 'Adjustment Problems: Ambivalence and Moral Imagination in North Indian Kinship'. In *Difficult Attachments: Anxieties of Kinship and Care*, edited by Kathryn E. Goldfarb and Sandra Bamford, 182–192. New Brunswick, NJ: Rutgers University Press.

Laffan, Michael Francis. 2022. *Under Empire: Muslim Lives and Loyalties Across the Indian Ocean World, 1775–1945*. Columbia Studies in International and Global History. New York: Columbia University Press.

Laidlaw, James. 2002. 'For an Anthropology of Ethics and Freedom'. *The Journal of the Royal Anthropological Institute* (NS) 8 (2): 311–32.

Lambek, Michael. 2010a. 'Introduction'. In *Ordinary Ethics Anthropology, Language, and Action*, edited by Michael Lambek, 1–36. New York: Fordham University Press.

——— ed. 2010b. *Ordinary Ethics: Anthropology, Language, and Action*. New York: Fordham University Press.

——— 2010c. 'Towards an Ethics of the Act'. In *Ordinary Ethics: Anthropology, Language, and Action*, edited by Michael Lambek, 39–63. New York: Fordham University Press.

——— 2011. 'Kinship as Gift and Theft: Acts of Succession in Mayotte and Ancient Israel'. *American Ethnologist* 38 (1): 2–16.

——— 2013. 'Kinship, Modernity, and the Immodern'. In *Vital Relations: Modernity and the Persistent Life of Kinship*, edited by Susan McKinnon and Fenella Cannell, 241–60. Santa Fe, NM: School for Advanced Research Press.

Lee, Doreen. 2016. *Activist Archives: Youth Culture and the Political Past in Indonesia*. Durham, NC: Duke University Press.

Bibliography

Lee, Julian C. H. 2010. *Islamization and Activism in Malaysia*. Singapore: Institute of Southeast Asian Studies.

Lee, Molly N. N. 2014. 'Educational Reforms in Malaysia: Towards Equity, Quality and Efficiency'. In *Routledge Handbook of Contemporary Malaysia*, edited by Meredith L. Weiss, 302–11. London: Routledge.

Leow, Rachel. 2016. *Taming Babel: Language in the Making of Malaysia*. Cambridge: Cambridge University Press.

Lévi-Strauss, Claude. 1969. *The Elementary Structures of Kinship*. Revised edition. Boston, MA: Beacon Press.

Lewis, Su Lin. 2016. *Cities in Motion: Urban Life and Cosmopolitanism in Southeast Asia, 1920–1940*. Cambridge: Cambridge University Press.

Lindenberg, Jolanda. 2009. 'Interethnic Marriages and Conversion to Islam in Kota Bharu'. In *Muslim-Non-Muslim Marriage: Political and Cultural Contestations in Southeast Asia*, edited by Gavin W. Jones, Chee Heng Leng, and Maznah Mohamad, 219–52. Singapore: ISEAS–Yusof Ishak Institute.

Liow, Joseph Chinyong. 2009. *Piety and Politics: Islamism in Contemporary Malaysia*. Oxford: Oxford University Press.

Livingston, Julie. 2005. *Debility and the Moral Imagination in Botswana*. Bloomington: Indiana University Press.

MacIntyre, Alasdair C. 2013. *After Virtue: A Study in Moral Theory*. 3rd ed. London: Bloomsbury.

Magee, Siobhan. 2021. '"You Can Learn to Do It Right, or You Can Learn to Do It Wrong": Marriage Counselling, Togetherness and Creative Conservatism in Lynchburg, Virginia'. In *Marriage in Past, Present and Future Tense*, edited by Janet Carsten, Eirini Papadaki, Koreen M. Reece, and Hsiao-Chiao Chiu, 54–75. London: UCL Press.

——— 2025. 'Getting Your Ducks in a Row: Marriage, Protection, and Love without Regret in Virginia'. *Cultural Anthropology* 40 (2): 301–27.

Majumdar, Rochona. 2009. *Marriage and Modernity Family Values in Colonial Bengal*. Durham, NC: Duke University Press.

Mandal, Sumit K. 2001. 'Whither the Cultural Bases of Political Community in Malaysia?' In *The Politics of Multiculturalism: Pluralism and Citizenship in Malaysia, Singapore, and Indonesia*, edited by Robert W. Hefner, 141–64. Honolulu, HI: University of Hawaii Press.

Manickam, Sandra Khor. 2015. *Taming the Wild: Aborigines and Racial Knowledge in Colonial Malaya*. Singapore: NUS Press.

Maqsood, Ammara. 2021. 'Love as Understanding Marriage, Aspiration, and the Joint Family in Middle-Class Pakistan'. *American Ethnologist* 48 (1): 93–104.

Bibliography

2024. 'The Work of Time: Personhood, Agency, and the Negotiation of Difference in Married Life in Urban Pakistan'. *The Journal of the Royal Anthropological Institute* 30 (1): 58–74.

Matar, Hisham. 2019. *A Month in Siena*. Milton Keynes: Viking.

Mattingly, Cheryl. 2014. *Moral Laboratories: Family Peril and the Struggle for a Good Life*. Berkeley, CA: University of California Press.

Maunaguru, Sidharthan. 2019. *Marrying for a Future: Transnational Sri Lankan Tamil Marriages in the Shadow of War*. Seattle: University of Washington Press.

Maznah Mohamad. 2010a. 'Making Majority, Undoing Family: Law, Religion and the Islamization of the State in Malaysia'. *Economy and Society* 39 (3): 360–84.

2010b. 'The Ascendance of Bureaucratic Islam and the Secularization of the Sharia in Malaysia'. *Pacific Affairs* 83 (3): 505–24.

2013. 'Legal-Bureaucratic Islam in Malaysia: Homogenizing and Ring-Fencing the Muslim Subject'. In *Encountering Islam: The Politics of Religious Identities in Southeast Asia*, edited by Hui Yew-Foong, 103–32. Singapore: Institute of Southeast Asian Studies.

2015. 'Gender Battles and the Syariah: Translating Islamic Marital Law into Everyday Practice in Malaysia'. In *Changing Marriage Patterns in Southeast Asia*, edited by Gavin W. Jones, Terence H. Hull and Maznah Mohamad, 171–84. London and New York: Routledge.

2020. *The Divine Bureaucracy and Disenchantment of Social Life: A Study of Bureaucratic Islam in Malaysia*. Singapore: Springer Singapore.

Maznah Mohamad, Zarizana Abdul Aziz, and Chin Oy Sim. 2009. 'Private Lives, Public Contention: Muslim-Non-Muslim Family Disputes in Malaysia'. In *Muslim-Non-Muslim Marriage: Political and Cultural Contestations in Southeast Asia*, edited by Gavin W. Jones, Chee Heng Leng, and Maznah Mohamad, 59–101. Singapore: ISEAS–Yusof Ishak Institute.

McKinley, Robert. 2001. 'The Philosophy of Kinship: A Reply to Schneider's Critique of the Study of Kinship'. In *The Cultural Analysis of Kinship: The Legacy of David M. Schneider*, edited by Richard Feinberg and Martin Oppenheimer, 131–66. Urbana: University of Illinois Press.

McKinnon, Susan. 2013. 'Kinship within and beyond the "Movement of Progressive Societies"'. In *Vital Relations: Modernity and the Persistent Life of Kinship*, edited by Susan McKinnon and Fenella Cannell, 39–62. Santa Fe: School for Advanced Research Press.

2019. 'Cousin Marriage, Hierarchy, and Heredity: Contestations over Domestic and National Body Politics in 19th-Century America'. *Journal of the British Academy* 7: 61–88.

Bibliography

McKinnon, Susan, and Fenella Cannell. 2013a. 'The Difference Kinship Makes'. In *Vital Relations: Modernity and the Persistent Life of Kinship*, edited by Susan McKinnon and Fenella Cannell, 3–38. Santa Fe: School of American Research.
    eds. 2013b. *Vital Relations: Modernity and the Persistent Life of Kinship*. Santa Fe: School for Advanced Research Press.
Milner, Anthony C. 2008. *The Malays*. Oxford: Wiley-Blackwell.
Milner, Anthony, and Helen Ting. 2018. 'Race and Its Competing Paradigms: A Historical Review'. In *Transforming Malaysia: Dominant and Competing Paradigms*, edited by Abdul Rahman Embong, Anthony Milner, and Tham Siew Yean, 18–58. Singapore: ISEAS–Yusof Ishak Institute Singapore.
Mody, Perveez. 2008. *The Intimate State: Love-Marriage and the Law in Delhi*. New Delhi: Routledge.
    2022. 'Intimacy and the Politics of Love'. *Annual Review of Anthropology* 51 (1): 271–88.
Moustafa, Tamir. 2018. *Constituting Religion: Islam, Liberal Rights, and the Malaysian State*. Cambridge Studies in Law and Society. Cambridge: Cambridge University Press.
Nagaraj, Shyamala. 2009. 'Intermarriage in Malaysia'. *Malaysian Journal of Economic Studies* 46 (1): 75–92.
Nagata, Judith A. 1976. 'Kinship and Social Mobility among the Malays'. *Man* 11 (3): 400–9.
Ng, Cecilia, Maznah Mohamad, and tan beng hui. 2006. *Feminism and the Women's Movement in Malaysia: An Unsung (r)Evolution*. London: Routledge.
Nielsen, Kenneth Bo, and Alf Gunvald Nilsen. 2021. 'Love Jihad and the Governance of Gender and Intimacy in Hindu Nationalist Statecraft'. *Religions* 12: 1068.
Nonini, Donald Macon. 2015. *Getting By: Class and State Formation among Chinese in Malaysia*. Ithaca, NY: Cornell University Press.
Norani Othman, ed. 2005. *Muslim Women and the Challenge of Islamic Extremism*. Kuala Lumpur: Sisters in Islam.
    2008. 'Religion, Citizenship Rights and Gender Justice: Women, Islamization and the Shari'a in Malaysia since the 1980s'. In *Sharing the Nation: Faith, Difference, Power and the State 50 Years after Merdeka*, edited by Norani Othman, Mavis Puthucheary, and Clive Kessler, 29–58. Petaling Jaya: Strategic Information and Research Development Centre.
Norani Othman, Mavis Puthucheary, and Clive S. Kessler, eds. 2008. *Sharing the Nation: Faith, Difference, Power, and the State 50 Years after Merdeka*. Petaling Jaya: Strategic Information and Research Development Centre.

Bibliography

Norani Othman, Zainah Anwar, and Zaitun Mohamed Kasim. 2005. 'Malaysia: Islamization, Muslim Politics and State Authoritarianism'. In *Muslim Women and the Challenge of Islamic Extremism*, edited by Norani Othman, 78–108. Kuala Lumpur: Sisters in Islam.

Nurul Huda Mohd Razif. 2020. 'Intimacy Under Surveillance: Illicit Sexuality, Moral Policing, and the State in Contemporary Malaysia'. *Hawwa* 18 (2–3): 325–56.

⸻ 2021a. 'Chasing Fate Fortune in the Borderland: Cross-Border Marriage Migration at the Malaysian-Thai Frontier'. *Archipel* 102: 155–86.

⸻ 2021b. 'Nikah Express: Malay Polygyny and Marriage-Making at the Malaysian-Thai Border'. *Asian Studies Review* 45 (4): 635–55.

⸻ 2022. 'Between Intention and Implementation: Recent Legal Reforms on Child Marriage in Contemporary Malaysia'. *Journal of Legal Anthropology* 6 (1): 1–23.

Ochs, Elinor, and Lisa Capps. 1996. 'Narrating the Self'. *Annual Review of Anthropology* 25 (1): 19–43.

⸻ 2001. *Living Narrative: Creating Lives in Everyday Storytelling*. Cambridge, MA: Harvard University Press.

Ong, Aihwa, and Michael G. Peletz, eds. 1995. *Bewitching Women, Pious Men: Gender and Body Politics in Southeast Asia*. Berkeley, CA: University of California Press.

Osella, Caroline. 2012. 'Desires under Reform: Contemporary Reconfigurations of Family, Marriage, Love and Gendering in a Transnational South Indian Matrilineal Muslim Community'. *Culture and Religion* 13 (2): 241–64.

O'Toole, Fintan. 2021. *We Don't Know Ourselves: A Personal History of Ireland since 1958*. London: Bloomsbury Publishing.

Padilla, Mark, Jennifer S. Hirsch, Miguel Munoz-Laboy, Robert Sember, and Richard G. Parker, eds. 2007. *Love and Globalization: Transformations of Intimacy in the Contemporary World*. Nashville, TN: Vanderbilt University Press.

Pandian, Anand. 2019. *A Possible Anthropology: Methods for Uneasy Times*. Durham, NC: Duke University Press.

Parry, Jonathan P. 2020. *Classes of Labour Work and Life in a Central Indian Steel Town*. London: Routledge.

Peletz, Michael G. 1996. *Reason and Passion: Representations of Gender in a Malay Society*. Berkeley: University of California Press.

⸻ 2002. *Islamic Modern: Religious Courts and Cultural Politics in Malaysia*. Princeton, NJ: Princeton University Press.

⸻ 2009. *Gender Pluralism: Southeast Asia since Early Modern Times*. New York: Routledge.

⸻ 2020a. 'Neoliberalism and the Punitive Turn in Southeast Asia and beyond: Implications for Gender, Sexuality, and Graduated Pluralism'. *Journal of the Royal Anthropological Institute* 26 (3): 612–32.

Bibliography

2020b. *Sharia Transformations: Cultural Politics and the Rebranding of an Islamic Judiciary*. Berkeley, CA: University of California Press.

2023. 'Companionate Marriage and Contested Masculinity in Late-Modern Malaysia: Ambivalences, Anxieties, and Vulnerabilities'. *Journal of Anthropological Research* 79 (2): 201–27.

Pue, Giok Hun, and Nidzam Sulaiman. 2013. '"Choose One!": Challenges of Inter-Ethnic Marriages in Malaysia'. *Asian Social Science* 9 (17): 269–78.

Qureshi, Kaveri. 2016. *Marital Breakdown among British Asians: Conjugality, Legal Pluralism and New Kinship*. London: Palgrave Macmillan.

2019. *Chronic Illness in a Pakistani Labour Diaspora*. Durham, NC: Carolina Academic Press.

Radcliffe-Brown, A. R., and Daryll Forde, eds. 1950. *African Systems of Kinship and Marriage*. London: Oxford University Press.

Rapp, Rayna, and Faye Ginsburg. 2001. 'Enabling Disability: Rewriting Kinship, Reimagining Citizenship'. *Public Culture* 13 (3): 533–56.

Reece, Koreen M. 2023. 'Telling Families, Telling AIDS: Narratives of Crisis in Botswana'. *Ethnos* 88 (5): 972–93.

Rose, Phyllis. 2020. *Parallel Lives: Five Victorian Marriages*. 2nd ed. London: Daunt Books.

Rumsey, Alan. 2010. 'Ethics, Language, and Human Sociality'. In *Ordinary Ethics: Anthropology, Language, and Action*, edited by Michael Lambek, 105–22. New York: Fordham University Press.

Shafak, Elif. 2021. *The Island of Missing Trees*. London: Viking.

Shamsul, A. B. 1996. 'Debating about Identity in Malaysia: A Discourse Analysis'. *Japanese Journal of Southeast Asian Studies* 34 (3): 476–99.

Shamsul, A. B., and S. M. Athi. 2014. 'Ethnicity and Identity Formation: Colonial Knowledge, Colonial Structures and Transition'. In *Routledge Handbook of Contemporary Malaysia*, edited by Meredith L. Weiss, 267–78. London: Routledge.

Shree, Geetanjali. 2021. *Tomb of Sand*. Translated by Daisy Rockwell. London: Tilted Axis Press.

Shryock, Andrew. 2013. 'It's This, Not That: How Marshall Sahlins Solves Kinship'. *HAU: Journal of Ethnographic Theory* 3 (2): 271–79.

Smith-Hefner, Nancy Joan. 2019. *Islamizing Intimacies: Youth, Sexuality, and Gender in Contemporary Indonesia*. Honolulu, HI: University of Hawaii Press.

Sneath, David, Martin Holbraad, and Morten Axel Pedersen. 2009. 'Technologies of the Imagination: An Introduction'. *Ethnos* 74 (1): 5–30.

Stoler, Ann Laura. 1995. *Race and the Education of Desire: Foucault's History of Sexuality and the Colonial Order of Things*. Durham, NC: Duke University Press.

Bibliography

2010. *Carnal Knowledge and Imperial Power: Race and the Intimate in Colonial Rule*. Berkeley, CA: University of California Press.

Strathern, Marilyn. 1992. *After Nature: English Kinship in the Late Twentieth Century*. The Lewis Henry Morgan Lectures 1989. Cambridge: Cambridge University Press.

Tagliacozzo, Eric. 2013. *The Longest Journey: Southeast Asians and the Pilgrimage to Mecca*. Oxford: Oxford University Press.

tan beng hui and Cecilia Ng. 2014. 'Filling in the Gaps: The Pursuit of Gender Equality in Malaysia'. In *Routledge Handbook of Contemporary Malaysia*, edited by Meredith L. Weiss, 347–60. London: Routledge.

Tan, Lee Ooi. 2024. 'Interracial Marriages Getting Popular in Malaysia: Government Support Would Be Welcomed'. *Penang Institute Issues: Analysing Penang, Malaysia and the Region* (blog). 10 July 2024. https://penanginstitute.org/publications/issues/interracial-marriages-getting-popular-in-malaysia-government-support-would-be-welcomed/.

Tan, Liok Ee. 2009. 'Conjunctures, Confluences, Contestations: A Perspective on Penang History'. In *Penang and Its Region: The Story of an Asian Entrepôt*, edited by Yeoh Seng Guan, Loh Wei Leng, Khoo Salma Nasution, and Neil Khor, 7–29. Singapore: NUS Press.

Taylor, Charles. 1989. *Sources of the Self the Making of the Modern Identity*. Cambridge, MA: Harvard University Press.

Tey, Nai Peng. 2015. 'Understanding Marriage and Divorce Trends in Peninsular Malaysia'. In *Changing Marriage Patterns in Southeast Asia*, edited by Gavin W. Jones, Terence H. Hull, and Maznah Mohamad, 137–55. London and NY: Routledge.

2021. 'The Changing Spousal Differentials in Socio-Demographic Characteristics in Malaysia'. *Institutions and Economies*, 13 (4): 121–51.

Thambapillay, Sridevi. 2020. 'The 2017 Amendments to the Law Reform (Marriage and Divorce) Act 1976: A Milestone or a Stone's Throw in the Development of Malaysian Family Law?' *IIUM Law Journal* 28 (2): 449–79.

Thambiah, Shanthi. 2012. 'Between Malay Kinship and Islamic Marriages: Negotiating Polygamy from Past to Present in Malaysia'. In *The Family in Flux in Southeast Asia: Institution, Ideology, Practice*, edited by Yoko Hyami, 145–62. Chiang Mai: Kyoto University Press.

Thelen, Tatjana, and Erdmute Alber, eds. 2018. *Reconnecting State and Kinship*. Philadelphia, PA: University of Pennsylvania Press.

Thompson, Charis. 2005. *Making Parents: The Ontological Choreography of Reproductive Technologies*. Cambridge, MA: MIT Press.

Bibliography

Thompson, Eric C. 2003. 'Malay Male Migrants: Negotiating Contested Identities in Malaysia'. *American Ethnologist* 30 (3): 418–38.

——— 2007. *Unsettling Absences: Urbanism in Rural Malaysia*. Singapore: NUS Press.

Trautmann, Thomas, John Mitani, and Gillian Feeley-Harnik. 2011. 'Deep Kinship'. In *Deep History: The Architecture of Past and Present*, edited by Andrew Shryock and Daniel Lord Smail, 160–88. Berkeley, CA: University of California Press.

Vatuk, Sylvia. 2015. 'What Can Divorce Stories Tell Us about Muslim Marriage in India?' In *Conjugality Unbound: Sexual Economics, State Regulation and the Marital Form in India*, edited by Srimati Basu and Lucinda Ramberg, 190–216. New Delhi: Women Unlimited, an associate of Kali for Women.

Walker, Kirsty. 2012. 'Intimate Interactions: Eurasian Family Histories in Colonial Penang'. *Modern Asian Studies* 46 (2): 303–29.

Willford, Andrew C. 2006. *Cage of Freedom: Tamil Identity and the Ethnic Fetish in Malaysia*. Ann Arbor, MI: University of Michigan Press.

——— 2014. *Tamils and the Haunting of Justice: History and Recognition in Malaysia's Plantations*. Honolulu, HI: University of Hawaii Press.

Williams, Susan. 2007. *Colour Bar: The Triumph of Seretse Khama and His Nation*. London: Penguin.

Wu, Jialin Christina. 2017. 'Private Lives, Public Spheres: Contesting Child Marriage at the Age of Independence in British Malaya, 1950'. *Gender & History* 29 (3): 658–74.

Yan, Yunxiang. 2003. *Private Life under Socialism: Love, Intimacy, and Family Change in a Chinese Village, 1949–1999*. Stanford, CA: Stanford University Press.

Yanagisako, Sylvia Junko, and Carol Delaney. 1995. 'Naturalizing Power'. In *Naturalizing Power: Essays in Feminist Cultural Analysis*, edited by Sylvia Yanagisako and Carol Delaney, 1–22. New York: Routledge.

Yeoh, Seng Guan. 2014a. 'The Great Transformation: Urbanisation and Urbanism in Malaysia'. In *Routledge Handbook of Contemporary Malaysia*, edited by Meredith L. Weiss, 249–60. London: Routledge.

Yeoh, Seng Guan, ed. 2014b. *The Other Kuala Lumpur*. Oxford: Routledge.

——— 2019. 'Domesticating Anthropology in West Malaysia'. In *Southeast Asian Anthropologies: National Traditions and Transnational Practices*, edited by Eric C. Thompson and Vineeta Sinha, 141–68. Singapore: NUS Press.

Yeoh, Seng Guan, Loh Wei Leng, Khoo Salma Nasution, and Neil Khor, eds. 2009. *Penang and Its Region: The Story of an Asian Entrepôt*. Singapore: NUS Press.

Bibliography

Yeung, Wei-Jun Jean. 2022. *Demographic and Family Transition in Southeast Asia.* Cham: Springer Nature.
Yeung, Wei-Jun Jean, and Gavin W. Jones. 2024. 'Emerging Dimensions of Marriage in Asia'. *Journal of Family Issues* 45 (5): NP1–8.
Zeitzen, Miriam Koktvedgaard. 2018. *Elite Malay Polygamy: Wives, Wealth and Woes in Malaysia*, New York and Oxford: Berghahn Books.
Zigon, Jarrett. 2021. 'How Is It between Us? Relational Ethics and Transcendence'. *The Journal of the Royal Anthropological Institute* 27 (2): 384–401.

Index

Page number followed by n refers to footnotes.

Abeyasekera, Asha, 11, 13–14, 21, 25
abuse, 3, 4, 68n10, 76, 79. *See also* domestic violence
   sexual, 58, 77, 88
activism
   anti-child marriage, 69
   arts, 222
   as bridging public and private domains, 237
   feminist, 82, 85, 121
   LGBTQ rights, 2, 56, 60–61, 64, 88
   and non-marriage, 27
   and personal experience, 21, 208–40, 252
adat (custom), 38n9, 109n4
adultery, 131, 136, 209, 216
agency, 13, 32n3, 123, 240n6
akad nikah, 169, 185, 196
altruism, 16
ancestor worship, 158
annulment, 136n5, 198
anthropology
   as analogous to marriage, 24, 28, 46, 52, 174
   changes in, 29–30, 35–36
   of ethics, 4, 15–18
   and imaginative empathy, 40
   of kinship/relatedness, 2
   of marriage, 9–13, 93, 175
   narrative conventions of, 49
   and the unexpected, 203
anti-miscegenation laws, 145
apartheid, 72, 75, 145
arranged marriages, 102–4, 111, 114–15, 126, 154
   complex reality of, 93–94
art, 61, 111, 159, 222
autonomy
   as customary value for Malay women, 107, 199
   in doing fieldwork, 43
   and family relationships, 150
   and living arrangements, 189, 204, 207, 217
   and paid employment, 114, 117, 161
   in spouse selection, 94, 96

Baba-Nyonya, 45, 91
Bahasa Malaysia, 32, 32n3, 151n3. *See also* Malay, language
bangsa (race, ethnicity), 32n3
Barisan Nasional, 51, 52, 78
belanja kahwin (marriage expenses), 130, 196
Berlant, Lauren, 40, 135, 211
bersanding (wedding enthronement), 31

271

Index

bertunang (betrothal), 200
betrothal. *See also* engagement
    customs, 31, 50, 169
    instability of, 26, 180, 183–89, 200, 202
blood, 10, 42–43, 145, 151, 173, 227
Bollywood, 113, 144, 245
Botswana, 14n4, 49n16, 72, 74–75
boundaries
    of historically formed communities, 175
    marriage across, 17, 32, 167
    between Muslims and non-Muslims, 165, 168, 173
    normative, 143, 153, 176, 240
    relative permeability/salience of, 26, 147–48, 152–56
Bouquet, Mary, 135
Bourdieu, Pierre, 7, 12, 144
British Empire, 32, 51, 72, 73–74
Buddhism, 98–100, 159
Bumiputera, 33, 45
businesses
    family, 111, 113–14
    operated by women, 97–98, 129, 193–94, 196

caning, 86–87, 89
Cannell, Fenella, 9, 12, 54, 88, 243
Cantonese community, 32n4, 91–92, 165
care, 17, 20, 101, 229
career women, 138, 213
Carlisle, Clare, 209n1, 241
Catholics, 120, 129, 153, 156, 221, 234
Chandra Muzaffar, 67–68
change
    across generations, 92–96, 104, 114, 171, 235
    and continuity, 6–8
    gender differences in attitude toward, 102
    imagination and possibilities for, 14
    limits of, 246
    marriage as generating, 2–3, 120
    slow/incremental, 17, 249, 252
    in women's education and employment opportunities, 22, 245
Chettiars, 102, 147
child marriage, 68–74, 83, 89, 230, 234, 248
    colonial/post-colonial politics of, 246
    as topic of public concern, 87–90, 238
childcare, 107, 155, 219, 233
children, 160, 167, 189, 192–94
    conversion of, 64–67, 148
    custody of, 79, 81, 82
    education of, 107, 232
    of mixed marriages, 158–59
China, 44, 97, 100, 116, 189
Chinese language, 32n4
    Hokkien, 32, 101, 159
    schools, 153
Chinese-Malaysians, 5, 34, 43, 45, 159
    attitudes toward divorce, 181
    attitudes toward marriage, 235
Chiu, Hsiao-Chiao, 47, 212, 249
choice
    of career, 100
    of marriage rites, 168
    to not have children, 97, 192
    of spouse, 10–11, 139, 181
    to remain single, 217
    versus arrangement binary, 13, 93–95, 96, 117
Christianity, 92, 126, 170–71, 193, 221, 222
cities, 36, 43, 45. *See also* urbanisation
civil courts, 64–65, 81–83
civil law, 33, 59, 68, 80, 157
civil society, 37, 56, 83, 121, 224, 236–38
Clark-Decès, Isabelle, 12, 94
class. *See also* middle-class; middle-classification; working-class
    marriage across differences in, 166, 199, 234
    in Penang, 45, 147
    and wedding ceremonies, 172, 245
cleaning, 77, 98, 101, 125, 133
clothing, 132, 134, 157

Index

cohabitation, 79, 130, 139, 235, 236
Cold War, 8, 243
Collier, Jane, 11, 12, 93, 141
Colombo, 13
colonialism
    and anthropology, 36
    in family histories, 45, 126, 243, 246
    and history of Penang, 43
    as origin of dual court system, 33
    policing of interracial marriage under, 8, 74, 145, 173
commensality, 31, 166
communication, 98, 154, 193, 194
community organising, 214, 224, 233, 237, 239
companionate marriage, 58, 136n5, 229
comparative labour, 141, 152
comparison
    across generations, 93, 123
    and ethical imagination, 110, 141
        and possibilities for change, 14
    and judgements, 118
compassion, 218, 222
compromise, 4, 15, 80, 83, 198, 217
conformity, 9, 18, 122–23, 139
    deceptive, 25, 120, 249
conjugality
    changes in, 24, 191, 221, 245
    as encounter with the other, 19
    and ethical judgements, 15
    and gendered power dynamics, 208, 210
    importance of intergenerational ties alongside, 166
    new forms of, 142, 212, 229
conservatism, 2, 57, 211, 227, 231
    creative, 118
constitution, Malaysian, 149, 176
continuity
    and change, 2, 14, 25, 105
    in kinship, 12, 93
    and reproduction of ethnic communities, 32
    in wedding rituals, 249

conventionality, 2, 6, 25
conversion, religious
    of children, 24, 64–66, 148
    legal implications of, 56, 148–50
    requirement for non-Muslims marrying Muslims, 26, 166, 234, 236
    as topic of public concern, 88, 238
cooking, 129, 132, 174, 176, 218
    and division of household tasks, 98, 102, 161–62
    and ethnic differences, 165
    and family life, 97, 218
    moral associations of, 165
    for weddings, 31
cosmopolitanism, 45, 93, 244
counselling, 19n10, 109, 194, 224, 237, 252
    Islamic pre-marital courses, 181
courts. *See also* civil courts; Federal Court; syariah courts
    civil, 81–83
    federal, 64
cousin marriage, 35, 75n21
cousins, 35, 75n21, 124
COVID-19, 1, 29–30, 52–53, 250, 253
creativity, 2–3, 8, 205, 211. *See also* innovation
Cruz, Resto, 123n1, 124
custody
    disputes involving conversion, 56, 63–65, 88, 157, 176
    and women's legal rights, 67, 79, 82
customs, 33, 41, 102, 130, 159, 200
    wedding, 154, 168–70, 172

Das, Veena
    on agency, 140
    on history, 249
    on the ordinary/everyday, 16–18, 122–23, 132, 136, 141, 210
    on time, 202, 250–51
death, 99, 137
delayed marriage, 11, 220, 236, 240
democracy, 84–86

Index

difference
  accomodation/negotiation of, 147, 150, 173
  anthropology as encounter with, 29, 52, 242
  and continuity in kinship, 7
  as expanding imaginative horizons, 222, 239
  incorporation/suppression of, 174
  marriage as encounter with, 8
disability, 22, 77, 211
divine bureaucracy, 181
divorce
  cases involving conversion to Islam, 66
  impact on adult children, 199–200, 203–4, 215, 217
  Indira Gandhi's, 64, 148, 176
  rates, 1, 37n8, 180–81, 233
  separate living arrangements as alternative to, 189
  support from family following, 106, 229
  Victorian debates on, 9
  and women's legal rights, 63, 78–83, 136, 197–98
domaining effects, 54, 88
domestic labour, 107, 126, 174, 237n5
domestic violence, 55, 67, 78, 88, 137
  activism, 75, 81–82, 224
door gifts, 184
dowry, 132, 170
dress, 35, 87, 160, 163
  wedding, 134, 171, 185, 199
Durham, Deborah, 240
Dutch East Indies, 71

East India Company, 44
education, 170, 187, 194, 222, 224
  and delayed marriage, 219–21
  Islamic, 44
  levels of spouses, 200, 234
  Malaysian state school system, 233
  tertiary, 111, 229
  women's increased opportunities for, 181, 237, 245
elections, 2018, 52, 57, 78, 84, 226, 253
Eliot, George, 20, 209, 228, 238, 241–42
elopement, 26, 172, 176, 209, 227
empathy, 14n4, 40, 46, 53, 110, 221–23
employment
  changes in women's, 11, 104, 118, 152, 221, 245
  shift to urban, 93
Empson, Rebecca, 135
endogamy, 7, 35, 144, 151
engagement, 180, 182, 184, 189, 200, 245. *See also* betrothal
English language
  press, 72
  schools, 159
  and transethnic Malaysian identity, 154
ethical, the, 13, 16, 21, 23, 122, 245
ethical endeavours, 224, 252
ethical engagement, 40, 118, 211, 239
ethical imagination, 9, 13–14, 27, 118, 210, 239–40. *See also* moral imagination
ethical work, 5, 16, 18, 152, 223. *See also* moral labour
ethics, ordinary, 15n5, 19, 23, 250
ethnicity, 24, 26, 31–34, 201
  links with religion and law, 55, 62, 88, 236
ethnography, 24, 58, 123, 180, 247
everyday, the
  and ethics, 15–16, 121–24, 141–42, 210
  and history, 249–52, 254
  and new forms of social relations, 123, 132, 212
everyday ethics, 15n5. *See also* ordinary ethics
everyday life, 123, 132, 203, 206
exogamy, 7, 144–45
expectations
  of kinship, 16
  marital, 21, 179, 194–95, 201–2, 206

Index

normative, 16, 139, 217
patriarchal, 246

family life, 7, 12, 211, 243, 246
fasakh (annulment of marriage), 136n5, 197n2, 198. *See also* divorce
Faubion, James, 16, 210
feasts, 31, 169, 184, 186, 196
Federal Court, 33, 64, 66–68
feminism, 109, 209n1, 233, 236
  second-wave, 36
feminist
  activism, 75, 82, 121, 230
  movement, 37
  organisations, 228
  scholarship, 10, 19, 181, 208
fertility, 1, 37n8, 146
fieldwork, 24, 29–53, 174, 242
food, 31, 35, 161, 169
  and ethnic/religious boundaries, 155, 160, 165–66
foreigners, 130, 138, 139
From Duty to Desire, 11, 93
future, the, 195, 214, 238, 252

Gandhi, Indira, 64, 65–66, 148, 176
gender complementarity, 38n9, 39, 95, 109n4, 199
gender equality, 121, 230, 235, 252
gender relations
  anthropological study of, 10
  contradictory trends in, 37, 39, 84, 121, 239
  feminist ideals of, 21, 23, 109
  generational shifts in, 22, 236
  heightened salience of, at times of political change, 24, 57–58, 63, 87–90, 238, 247
  Islam and, 165
  in Malay kinship, 39
generations
  comparative reflections on marriages across, 5–6, 19, 123
  continuity and change across, 2, 7, 91–118, 239, 240
  fractures between, 226
George Town, 41–43, 47, 78, 170
  cultural life, 51, 58, 76, 235, 247
  diversity of population, 44
George Town Festival, 56, 57, 59, 67, 75, 86
gifts, 132, 170, 172, 183–84, 187, 200
Ginsburg, Faye, 22, 211
grandchildren, 102, 166–67, 182, 202
grandparents, 65, 94, 155, 167, 192
Gujarat, 111
Gujaratis, 113

Hajj, 44
Hakka, 32n4, 101, 147
halal, 161–162, 165
hantaran (formal marriage gifts), 200
head covering, 128, 163, 199. *See also* Hijab; *tudung* (head covering, veil); veiling
Hertogh, Maria, 71–74
Heti, Sheila, 208, 212, 238
hierarchy
  based on age and generation, 39, 95
  gender, 95, 204
Hijab, 65. *See also* head covering; *tudung* (head covering, veil); veiling
Hinduism, 111
Hindu-Muslim marriages, 17, 145
Hindus, 56, 64, 145, 149, 218
Hindutva, 145
history, 25, 95, 116, 243, 246–50, 254
  of intermarriage, 148
Hokkien, 32, 32n4, 101, 159, 165
homemaking, 129, 133, 140, 156, 176
homosexuality, 70
hope, 19, 29, 179, 182, 195, 240
hospitality, 35
househusbands, 97, 107, 232, 240
houses, 131–35, 156
  renovation of, 184
housewives, 82, 101, 113, 129, 161

275

Index

human rights, 67
humour, 76–78, 88, 154
hybridity, 30, 45, 152n3, 159

imagination
  and community involvement, 224, 239–40
  ethical/moral, 14, 25, 27, 40, 210–13, 250
  and marriage, 19–23, 208–14, 216–17, 242
  and social difference, 222–23
  and time, 178–79
imaginative labour/work
  comparison as, 110, 141
  creating narratives as, 95, 214
  and encounter with difference, 22
  marriage as, 3–5, 7, 19
incest, 7, 58, 88
Independence (national)
  and conflicts around marriage, 24, 71, 73, 74–75
  Malaysian, 44, 51, 251
independence (personal)
  after separation/divorce, 194, 205, 217–20
  within marriage, 92, 95, 161
  and women's employment, 110, 114, 117, 220, 245
India, 44, 89, 102, 111, 113, 145
  marriage in, 25, 72, 182
Indian Malaysians, 32, 127, 144, 147, 181, 222
  Catholic, 125, 234
  Muslim, 33, 45, 218
Indian Partition, 250
indigeneity, 33
Indonesia, 113, 196
  marriage in, 89, 136, 145, 197n2, 206n4, 240
infidelity, 5, 142, 163, 186, 198, 199, 229
in-laws, 6, 14, 144, 162–63, 170, 186
innovation, 2–3, 122–25, 171, 211, 239

instability, 178, 180, 182, 250
inter-ethnic marriage, 37n8, 148, 150n2. *See also* mixed marriages
intergenerational relations, 110, 166–67
interracial marriage, 8, 55, 72, 89, 145
intimacy
  egalitarian, 11, 93, 109, 221
  everyday, 50
  modern political salience of, 11
  new possibilities for, 22, 211–12
  and political activism, 228–29
  regulation of, 145–46, 233
  in unequal relationships, 182
Ireland, 247
Islam
  conservative, 27, 37–40, 230–33, 253
  conversion to, 153, 156–60, 167, 218, 236
  privileged legal status of, 26, 163–65, 246
  reformist, 67
Islamic courts. *See* syariah courts
Islamic law (syariah)
  and civil legal system, 234–35
  and legal age of marriage, 69
  and Muslim engagements/marriages, 180–81
  status of women in, 60, 63, 82, 136
  trend toward punitive interpretations of, 88

jatuh talak (pronouncement of divorce), 197, 198. *See also* divorce
Java, 71, 229, 237n5
Jawi Peranakan, 45, 147, 199
Jones, Carla, 229, 239–40
judgements, 14–16, 124, 140–41, 213–14, 251
Justice for Sisters, 87

Kadi, 81, 185
Kahn, Susan Martha, 146
Karim, Wazir-Jahan, 37–40, 107, 162
karma, 98–100
Keane, Webb, 17

Index

Kelantan, 74, 106, 113, 187
  2018 child marriage case in, 56, 68–69
kenduri kahwin (wedding feast), 31, 169, 183. *See also* feasts
Kerala, 119–20, 125, 153, 154
Kessler, Clive, 26, 32, 33n6, 165
keturunan (descent), 32n3
Khama, Seretse, 72, 74
kin marriage, 12, 94
kinship
  anthropological study of, 10–11
  and associative power of objects, 135
  as balancing continuity and difference, 7–8, 144
  Chinese and Indian (patrilineal), 95
  Dravidian, 12
  and ethics, 16, 122
  Jewish, 146
  Malay (bilateral), 31, 38–40, 151, 158, 162
  political salience of, 22, 243
  reimagining of, 210–11
  and social mobility, 124
Kuala Lumpur, 120, 130, 140, 167
  Women's Day march, 84–85, 89

labour force, 95, 117, 139, 175, 181, 233
Lahore, 182
Lambek, Michael, 16–17, 18, 88, 243, 246, 250
Langkawi
  author's fieldwork in, 24, 30, 34–35, 42, 50, 174
  marriage in, 39, 126, 151, 172, 180
law
  age of marriage, 68–70
  anti-miscegenation, 145
  civil, 59, 80
  for conversion, 65
  dual system of, 33, 157, 234
  family, 37, 81
  Islamic. *See* Islamic law

Law Reform (Marriage and Divorce) Act 1976, 79
lawyers, 59, 64–66, 78–84, 136, 230
Lee, Doreen, 237
Leow, Rachel, 32n3, 33n6, 50n17, 151, 151–2n3, 173
lesbians, 86, 233
Lévi-Strauss, Claude, 7, 10, 93, 144
Lewes, George Henry, 209, 228
LGBTQ rights, 55, 61, 225, 238, 248, 252
  cleavages over, 63, 87
  conservative Muslim opposition to, 23, 236
  public debate over, 56
liberalisation, 87, 136n5, 226, 236, 253
liberals, 108, 159, 226
life course, 115, 118, 122, 153, 253
  normative, 131, 139
living arrangements, 27, 154–55, 189, 204–5, 207, 217
looping effects, 114, 117, 202
love, 11–12, 18, 91, 178, 217
  advice on, 109, 116, 160, 162, 204
  marriages, 94, 103, 140, 198
  versus arrangement binary, 13, 93
Loving v. Virginia, 89, 145

Magee, Siobhan, 47, 55–56
Mahathir Mohamad, 51, 60
Mahkamah Kadi (Islamic court), 80
Malay
  divorce, 189
  ethnicity, 31, 33, 151
  language, 32, 34, 71, 113, 199. *See also* Bahasa Malaysia
  marriage, 26, 38, 50, 95, 144
  religion, 33
Malayan Emergency, 8, 243, 248, 251
Mandal, Sumit, 50n17, 154, 159, 159n7, 222
Maqsood, Ammara, 8, 18, 182
Marina Mahathir, 60, 62
marriage(s). *See also* arranged marriages; child marriage; companionate

277

Index

marriage(s) (cont.)
    marriage; cousin marriage; delayed marriage; inter-ethnic marriage; interracial marriage; kin marriage; love, marriages; mixed marriages; polygamy/polygyny; same-sex marriage; weddings
  to foreigners, 138, 139, 245
  gendered power dynamics of, 80, 92, 208–10, 252
  happy/successful, 80, 103, 104, 156
  intergenerational experiences of, 216
  as mask of conformity, 122, 207
  and modernity, 74, 93, 109
  Muslim, 33, 80, 164, 180, 201, 233
  and the nation, 24, 75, 152
  progressive account of, 95
  question, 9, 238, 241
  role of families in, 175
  as site of creativity, 2, 25, 211
  as site of encounter with difference, 8, 46, 52, 203, 242
  unhappy/unsuccessful, 5, 99, 199, 244, 251
  Victorian, 9, 19–20, 208–10, 238
masculinity, 58, 68n10, 181, 226
Matar, Hisham, 178–79, 186, 192, 195, 205
matchmakers, 91, 189, 220
materialism, 16, 245
Mattingly, Cheryl, 13n3, 16, 20, 23, 94
Maznah Mohamad, 32n2, 33n5, 37, 87, 149, 181
McKinley, Robert, 16, 210
McKinnon, Susan, 12, 54, 75n21, 243
media, 56–58, 66, 68–69, 148, 164
memoirs, 32n4, 132, 205
Merdeka (National) Day, 56, 248
merisek (rituals for betrothal), 188, 200. *See also* betrothal; engagement
middle years, 180, 195
middle-class, 50, 95, 141, 171, 196
  attitudes on social issues, 23, 37, 121, 253

middle-classification, 33
migration
  family histories of, 100, 111, 189, 192, 243, 246
  within Malay world, 151
  for marriage, 116, 182
  to Penang, 44
mixed marriages, 26, 142, 152–53, 169, 173, 234
  Muslim/non-Muslim, 157, 159, 236
mixing, 144–48, 150–51, 153, 173, 177
  perceived increase in, 174, 176
  and separation, 243, 246
  stalled/partial, 156, 171
modernity
  continued political salience of kinship/marriage in, 11–12, 54
  critique of simplistic narratives of, 93, 109, 117, 246, 249
  marriage as ambivalent symbol of, 74
Mody, Perveez, 11, 13, 25, 140, 145, 176
moral imagination, 19n10, 21, 25, 28, 40. *See also* ethical imagination
moral laboratories, 16, 21
moral labour, 3–5, 7, 18. *See also* ethical work
moral panic, 58, 88
morality, 56, 59, 94, 210
motherhood, 42, 193, 218, 229
Mujahid Yusof, 60–62, 69, 85
multiculturalism, 222

narratives, 20–21, 48–49, 205–6
natal family, 140, 171, 194
nation, the, 24, 63, 74–75, 152, 248
nationalists, 226, 227
neighbourhoods, 34, 91, 101, 133, 189, 218
Netherlands, 71, 73
NGOs, 69, 75, 81, 83, 87, 225
non-marriage, 27, 141, 212, 237
  rates of, 1, 11, 240
Norhayati Kaprawi, 63

278

novels, 132, 179, 210, 242
Nyonya, 45, 91

objects, 17, 122, 125, 132–36, 141, 142
optimism, 178, 195, 230
  cruel, 40, 52, 135
  political, 51, 57, 80, 83–84
ordinary, the, 16–18, 46, 122, 210–12, 252, 254
ordinary ethics, 15n5, 16–17, 19, 23, 250
other, the, 17, 203
O'Toole, Fintan, 247

paedophilia, 88
Pakatan Harapan (Alliance of Hope), 51–52
Pakistan, 18
Pakistanis, 218, 221, 222
Pandian, Anand, 29, 182, 203
Papadaki, Eirini, 47, 71n16
parenting, 22, 165
parents
  anxiety about non-Muslim child's marriage to a Muslim partner, 158–60, 164, 166, 246
  coming out to, 5, 228
  impact of divorce of, 199, 215, 217
  involvement in betrothals, 185, 188
  reflections on marriages of, 113, 115, 116, 137–38
  relations with adult children, 162, 166–68, 175
patriarchy
  perception of, as traditional, 39, 199
  and trend toward a more conservative Islam, 32n2, 39, 96, 121, 246
Peletz, Michael, 58, 88, 136, 149
Penang
  change, 43
  diversity of population, 44, 147, 175, 222
  history, 44, 243
Peranakan, 45, 91
photographs, 48, 126, 133, 135, 244

plantations, 120, 125–26, 133, 155, 218
plays, 75–78
pluralism, 20, 63, 247
police, 64, 82, 134, 190
political change
  debates around marriage at times of, 55, 75, 87, 238, 247
  hope for, after 2018 election, 74
  marriage as site of, 9, 27, 51, 120
polygamy/polygyny, 39, 70, 74, 88, 230, 238
poverty, 16, 34, 126, 181
pragmatism, 162–63, 167, 235
precarity, 204, 223
pregnancy, 98, 129, 131, 209, 219, 229
present, the, 178–79, 186, 194–95, 205–6, 253
privatisation, 11
progressives, 67, 74, 226, 228, 239
property, 7, 9, 12, 204
  division during divorce, 82, 133–35, 196–98

race, 32, 45, 55, 173. *See also bangsa* (race, ethnicity); ethnicity
Rapp, Rayna, 22, 211
Reece, Koreen M., 18n8, 47, 49n16, 143, 213n2
Regina Ibrahim, 60
relatedness, 2, 4, 9, 42, 146, 206
relationality, 4, 10, 17, 48, 152, 165
reproduction, 10, 117, 146
  assisted, 2, 146, 211
  of ethnic communities, 32
  of families, 7
  of political power, 173
residence (post-marital)
  Indian patterns of, 222
  matrilocal, 91n1, 106, 174
  with parents, 108, 166, 167
  separate from spouse, 155, 189
  with siblings, 106, 218
retrospection, 137, 205–6
rings, 185, 191, 196, 207

279

Index

rituals, 1, 4, 30–31, 152, 249
Rose, Phyllis, 19, 20, 208, 214, 228, 238
rupture, 2, 53, 132, 251

same-sex marriage, 3, 63, 89, 142
    prospects for, in Malaysia, 79, 227, 231
Seberang Perai, 43
security, 178–79, 212
Selangor, 70, 234
self-fashioning, 124, 128, 138, 143
sexuality, 89, 176, 231, 236
    non-normative, 240
    policing of, 87, 145, 233
    and power, 76
    public discourse around, 55, 57, 59
sharia. *See* Islamic law; syariah courts
siblings, 102–3, 111, 126, 137, 163, 186
    living with, 106, 218–19
siblingship, 35, 50, 150–51, 174
Singapore, 44, 70–73, 111, 114, 126
single women, 213, 216–17, 220, 223
Sisters in Islam, 75, 85, 87, 230n4
Siti Kasim, 60, 62
social mobility, 102, 105, 123, 141, 225
South Africa, 72, 75, 145
Sri Lanka, 120, 152
    marriage in, 13, 49, 94
    migration from, 44, 125
stability, 153, 179, 189
Star, 66
Stoler, Ann Laura, 74, 145
Straits Times, 72–73
Strathern, Marilyn, 10, 210–11
Stripes and Strokes exhibition, 56, 59–63, 67, 88
suffering, 14n4, 99–100, 117, 182
surveillance, 12, 42, 75, 145, 173, 180
syariah courts. *See also* Islamic law
    and age of marriage laws, 68–69
    and family disputes between Muslims and non-Muslims, 59n1, 64–67, 148, 157
    jurisdiction of, 33, 164
    outcomes for women in, 80–83, 131, 136, 136n5, 197–98
    trends in judgements of, 86–87

Taiwan, 46, 227
Tamil, 12, 50, 94, 148
Taoism, 170–71
tea ceremony, 98, 154, 169
technology, 2, 212, 221, 235, 236
temporality, 20, 27, 121, 182–83, 205, 206
Teochew, 32n4, 116, 147
Terengganu, 71, 74, 86–87, 89
theatre, 75–78, 88, 111–12, 113
time, 6, 25, 40, 134, 241–42, 252–54
trans women, 60, 227
transgression, 13, 25, 76, 139–41, 176–77
travel, 44, 113, 235–36
tudung (head covering, veil), 128. *See also* head covering; Hijab; veiling

uncertainty, 5, 26, 178–86, 202–7
unexpected, the, 179–80, 203–4, 207, 240, 242
United Malays National Organisation (UMNO), 51, 83n23
urbanisation, 33, 42–44, 148, 152, 175

values
    associations with significant objects, 121, 132
    changes in, 3, 96
    conservative, 108, 117
    of equality, 11, 108
    family, 183
    liberal, 74
    Malay, 199
    Muslim, 67, 116
    of mutual respect, 109
    patriarchal, 95, 182, 233
    of pluralism, 222

Index

pluralistic, 20
threats to, 7
traditional, 107–9, 111–12
veiling, 61, 67, 128, 215. *See also* head covering; Hijab; *tudung* (head covering, veil)
violence. *See also* domestic violence
   communal, 250
   gender/sexual orientation-based, 84
Virginia, 55–56, 63, 74, 89
vital conjuncture, 18, 152, 249

Walker, Kirsty, 45
weddings
   cancellation/postponement of, 183–86, 188, 205
   inter-ethnic, 154, 168–72
   Kerala, 125, 154
   lavish, 16, 116, 144, 245
   Muslim/Malay, 30–31, 107, 144, 186, 196, 199, 215

planning of, 169, 176
woman question, 9
Women's Aid Organisation, 85, 87
Women's Day march, 84–86, 88–89, 230, 235
women's rights
   activism, 23, 61, 72, 84
   future of, 231
   in legal system, 82
work of time, the, 15, 182, 202, 249–51
working-class, 8, 102, 189
Wu, Jialin Christina, 71–73

Yayasan Perpaduan Malaysia, 67
Yogyakarta, 229, 237n5
youth, 27, 176, 232, 240, 253

Zigon, Jarrett, 18
zones
   of engagement with the other, 17
   of intimacy, 4, 22, 49
   of possibility, 19

281

For EU product safety concerns, contact us at Calle de José Abascal, 56–1°, 28003 Madrid, Spain or eugpsr@cambridge.org.